W0345832

CONTENTS

BETRAYED BY THE MOTHERLAND

Confessions of a Russian fleeing the Ukraine war

Notes about Germany, Russia and Ukraine

Names of all the people in this book have been changed for privacy reasons.

I'm sending huge thanks to my friend Alice for her help with the first draft of the book, valuable comments, and a great deal of encouragement.

My immeasurable thanks to Tom and his family for all the help and support they gave us during our first months in Germany.

The photos in the book are my own.

AUTHOR'S FOREWORD. IMPORTANT TO READ

This book was not an easy one to write. I think it is understandable – the war, having to rush out of Ukraine with a minimum of belongings and an autistic child, settling in a completely new country, adapting there, etc.

Lots of stressful travelling, lots of stressful thoughts as you see days go by, as go to bed and wake up in the morning, such as: "Was it the right decision to leave or should we have stayed like many of our friends did?" "What would have happened if we had stayed in Ukraine?" or "What will happen to us in the future?" "How will we handle all the issues we are facing as asylum seekers?"

"How will we find a place to live?" "How will we earn money without knowing the local language?" The thought that visited me most often after all the others was: "F***ck!!"

Our forced trip to Germany was something I was completely unprepared for. I have studied English all my life – at school, at university, and then I worked as an English teacher, translator, I wrote articles for various online platforms in it. My English skills helped me make a fairly good living in Russia and later in Ukraine.

I watched British and American films, I read books written by British and American authors. I lived in Wales for a short while, when I was a student, I spent several years working with British native speakers in Russia at a language school. But having to move to Germany was a totally unexpected twist – if you want to make God laugh, tell him about your plans.

I was crushed by the fact of Russia attacking Ukraine – I am a Russian native, you see, who lived in Ukraine and made a family there; I was crushed even harder when Putin announced the "partial" mobilization and I drank a bottle of rum to suppress my grief about it (feeling awfully hungover the following day).

But I still felt like writing this book to tell if not the whole world then at least as many people as possible about the start of the war, about what me and my family went through as we first got to the safe West of the country and then left Ukraine (crossing the border on foot; that was so much "fun") to settle in Germany for the time being.

I wanted to get my message across that not all Russians support the war and why those who did not rush to leave Putin's Russia after it began can hardly do anything to stop this nightmare. I very much wanted to share how it feels to be a Russian fleeing this war, feeling squeezed between two fires.

I will tell you about the details of Prigozhin's mutiny that you will hardly find on the English-language media, about why Russia is using "Z" and "V" letters as the symbols of this war, and about the actual reasons that drove Putin to start the invasion. From this book you will learn who the "Babushka Z" is, what the "gravization" means for Russians and who "propacondoms" are.

I deliberately did not give the manuscript to a native English-language proofreader for the sake of maximal authenticity and realism: I wanted my readers to see that the book was indeed written by a Russian who witnessed it all and had his skin in the game. So you do not think that it was composed by a native English/American writer to hype on a hot topic and capitalize on it.

I have changed all the names in this book, including my own, so "Ivan Chelovekov" is my pen name here. I wanted to empty my memory of this into a file (a bit of self-therapy I guess) and now all I wish for is stay away as far as possible and not to have even my real name associated with this book, as well as all these memories.

"Chelovekov" in Russian is a possessive from "chelovek", which means a "human". This is to tell you that I'm just an average human being fleeing a zone of lethal danger, and that Russians now are pretty similar to Ukrainians in this sense.

Both nations belong to the human race, along with everyone else, and we are suffering from what Putin is doing. And all this nightmare is happening close to all of you – in the heart of Europe, not somewhere far away in the developing world. I hope I have made my point on this clear. Besides, "Ivan Chelovekov" is the name of a song by a popular rock band in Russia. If I get any Russian/Ukrainian readers, they will understand the reference.

While writing the book, I could not hold back from bashing the current regime in Russia, as you can imagine, nor did I spare Ukraine and Germany. They all got their fair share of criticism.

About twenty years ago, I loved reading Bill Bryson's books about his travels in Europe, the US, and his life in the UK. I thought that using a bit of his sarcastic and funny manner of talking about things he encountered on his travels would make the book a more interesting read. Therefore, there is a part about travelling: notes about modern Germany and how people live there.

The book also includes several episodes from the history of Russia, Poland, Germany, and the Soviet Union to explain a few things happening now.

This book contains my memories, my personal impressions of what I saw on our journey, my personal take on the events, and also how they were covered by the media, so you can get a view from different angles.

My narrative may look a bit messy since our move to Germany in it gets mixed with the war-related events in Russia and Ukraine. But that's the way we lived through this period in reality, and so it adds to the authenticity of my story.

Please take into account that it is not an investigation, not a research book on politics or history; it contains a bit of everything, plus facts from history and politics, and a minimum of statistics. Overall, reading this book is like having a conversation with me over a cup of tea (or a pint of beer, you choose) in your kitchen well into the night, when the whole house has gone quiet.

So, make yourselves comfortable, grab some tea, and let's start...

If you read my book from cover to cover and it gives you some food for thought as well as a bit of entertainment on an otherwise boring evening, my goal is achieved. Thank you.

Yours,
Ivan Chelovekov

P.S. This book was written between September 2022 and August 2023, so all the events from the news to do with the war I mentioned in it took place during either of those years, unless stated otherwise.

INTRODUCTION

If it had not been for this war, so many things would have happened and so many would have not.

Before I start telling you about the war and how my family and I made it out of Ukraine to settle in Europe, I reckon I should give you a brief story of who I am and how I ended up in Ukraine in the first place. And also, what political events between Russia and Ukraine preceded the current war.

My name is Ivan. I was born in Russia, and my parents are Russian too. However, my parental grandmother had come to live in the USSR from Ukraine after WW2 and stayed there until her death in the late 1990s.

In 2011, I met a Ukrainian girl on a Russian social media website. Back then, I lived in Moscow. We began chatting over Skype every day, often talking well into the night. After that, I went to visit her a couple of times in Ukraine.

In September of the same year, I packed my things and moved to Ukraine, giving up my job and a rented room in the glossy and noisy Russian capital. Moving to live to a nice quiet town in the East of Ukraine after my hurry-scurry life in Russia was a nice change from the big, restless Moscow (although I still sometimes miss living there). After a year passed, our daughter was born. Dasha proved to be slightly autistic, and she did not start talking until she was five. But we still loved that girl with pretty grey eyes and were happy to have her. We still are as she turned ten this year, in 2022, and celebrated her first birthday outside Ukraine.

During all those years, the relations between Russia and Ukraine remained fairly good; the countries collaborated; no visas or anything like that was required to travel from Russia to Ukraine and vice versa. A lot of Ukrainians constantly went to work in Russia to send money back home to their families. At that time, before 2013, Ukraine had a pro-Russian president Victor Yanukovych. He supported close integration and collaboration with Russia, being basically controlled and manipulated by Putin.

Then the second revolution took place in Kyiv (the first one occurred in 2003–2004 and it was called "The Orange Revolution"). It was in November 2013, and, like the first one, it was called "The Maidan". This time it was also referred to as the "Euro-Maidan" (or "The Revolution of Dignity") since Yanukovych broke up the negotiations about Ukraine entering the EU, so many Ukrainians rose against him that year. "Maidan" means "a (town) square" in Ukrainian, and The Maidan Nezalezhnosti ("The Independence Square") is a place in the very centre of Kyiv, an analogue of the Red Square in Moscow.

In late 2013, tens of thousands of people gathered on that central square in Kyiv (and stayed there in tents for several months) to insist that Yanukovych must give up his presidency. Yanukovych had been a gangster in the past, a convict with proven rape charges (a typical situation for politicians that emerged in the post-Soviet countries after the USSR collapsed).

His rule was pretty much similar to the regime in Russia, when state officials got away with crimes covered up for by government-controlled judges, they felt free to take huge bribes and steal money from the country's budget (we call that "budget sawing" in Russian when money is "sawn" like wood into "chunks", so it is easier to steal it). That is the scheme that still works very well in Russia; now even better than before.

To stay in power, Yanukovych did not bring out the police or troops to disperse the people. Instead, he brought gangsters from the East of Ukraine, whom average people called "titushki". They went around Kyiv in tracksuits, armed with baseball bats and pipe stubs, terrorizing people around the city.

I remember that time very well: people rushed to buy as much food in the supermarkets as they could carry away and withdraw all their money from cash machines, with lines of people standing there, each waiting for their turn to get their money. My colleagues and I had to work from home for a week, staying away from the office and the streets in the city centre, when it all was happening. There were no sane people who would go outside after dark for fear of bumping into those "titushki" yobs.

The Maidan ultimately won in 2014 – Yanukovych fled his gorgeous villa near Kyiv and got away to...Russia, of course. However, before the Maidan made him surrender, he managed to get a loan of $3 billion from Putin into the country's budget. In exchange for that, Yanukovych provided a guarantee that he would remain in control and break down the Maidan. But he failed to do that.

The next "ruler" of Ukraine was Alexander Turchinov – he was appointed to that position by the local parliament (Verkhovna Rada) after the revolution was over and the dethroned Yanukovych fled. After Turchinov, a chocolate magnate Petro Poroshenko was elected. He had a huge business both in

Ukraine and Russia, producing a popular brand of sweets called “Roshen”.

The Maidan gave a start to the process that eventually led to what people in Ukraine have to deal with now – the war against Putin’s Russia.

Seeing that his puppet-president was forced to escape and a lot of people in Ukraine did not want to stay under Russia and its imperial rule but were eager to become part of the European Union, Putin decided to act quickly.

Using the fact that during the Maidan some nationalistic sentiment among Ukrainians rose, and they began praising the name of Stepan Bandera (the nationalistic leader who defended Ukraine from the Soviet Union during WW2 and for this purpose he collaborated with German Nazis), Putin decided to use the fears of ethnic Russians who lived in Crimea. He spread the word that Ukraine planned to become a ‘Nazi state’ using it as a pretext for his next big move.

The worst ideological fear of those people was the imagined idea that Ukraine began praising Nazism and therefore, they thought, it would follow in the footsteps of Nazi Germany. That’s a sore point of Russians who had suffered in WW2 more than any other nation and lost millions of people fighting the Nazis.

Thanks to Putin’s political technologists, since the second Maidan, the victory in WW2 became the “national idea” of Russia, the basis of its national identity and pride. Putin annexed Crimea by means of a fake referendum, when the local Ukrainian troops were locked in their barracks watched over by armed Russian soldiers wearing uniforms without insignia. The official version is that the majority of people voted to join the Russian Federation.

Putin was afraid that since Ukraine had chosen a course

to integrate with the West, rather than stay under Russia's invisible reign, Crimea – where the Russian Black Sea fleet was headquartered – would allow NATO to set up a base there and the Russian fleet would be driven out. Russia would have lost its only strategic access to the Black Sea in that case.

Putin could not afford to give up that territory, which Russia had been renting from Ukraine since 1991 – when Ukraine declared independence once the USSR fell apart. Besides, he spread the idea around Russia that in that case the country would have NATO battleships with missiles ready to launch right near its borders. So he went for annexing Crimea, pretending that it was a "gesture of free will" from local citizens, many of whom were ethnic Russians.

The current president, Vladimir (Volodymyr in Ukrainian) Zelensky, beat Poroshenko during the elections in 2019. Zelensky used to run his own comedian show in Ukraine, a very popular one, and used to spearhead a producer company that created comic film series quite popular both in Russia and Ukraine (they were in Russian and mostly targeted at the Russian audience).

Besides, he was known in Russia as an actor thanks to several romantic comedies that collected large box-offices. Before he started running for president, his company made a comic film series called "Servant of the People" (broadcast on TV in 2015–2019) with Zelensky playing the main role in it. It was about a regular history teacher becoming the president of Ukraine, who started fighting the corruption in the government, opposed the local oligarchs and tried to change the lives of average Ukrainians for the better overall.

This series was popular both in Ukraine and Russia. As it turned out later, it was Zelenesky's election campaign, since he began acting like his movie character during the first three years of his presidency.

Anyway, that's a bit of pre-history to give you an idea of the historic and political context. I had lived in Ukraine for ten years until we had to get out of there. I did miss Moscow at first after Dasha was born. But with every passing year, I grew to understand that our decision not to go back to Russia was absolutely right – the country started to turn more and more authoritarian.

This thought became dead firm in 2020, when the Covid pandemic broke out – I just realised that I had lived too long in Ukraine and felt absolutely comfortable and at home there, including the linguistic aspect – I could speak Russian freely anywhere (opposite to what Putin and his government were telling on TV in Russia about the Russian language being gradually driven out from Ukraine and Russians being humiliated there).

And now that Russia attacked Ukraine, the shadow of the final doubt about moving back that remained somewhere very deep in my mind, dissolved, melted like snow in the sunshine. By that time, we had moved out of Kyiv to a small city of Olexandriia; it takes a four-hour train ride to the South-East to get there.

I was 40 when the war started and we came to Germany. By the time of publishing this book I turned 42. My wife Mary is ten years my junior. Our daughter Dasha is almost 12 now.

PART 1

FEBRUARY 24. WAR BEGINS

Ukrainians and those Russians who oppose this war often liken it to the Great Patriotic War that was initiated by the Nazi Reich against the Soviet Union on June 22, 1941, as an expansion of WW2 started by Hitler in 1939.

Back in 1941, the attack of German Nazis came unexpected and contrary to what Stalin expected and to what his scouts reported to him. Since the non-aggression pact between Molotov and Ribbentrop had been signed, the Soviet leader was certain that there would be no war under any circumstance. So he dismissed all officers and a lot of soldiers on the Western border, sending them on vacations if they had any coming up.

As 2022 started, and even at the end of 2021, the Western media kept writing that Russia had been drawing large amounts of troops to the Ukrainian border. Putin and his high-ranking officials stated that it was nothing but military drills. Nobody is going to attack Ukraine, they said, chuckling and adding that Russia has better things to do. Among those liars was the Russian Minister of foreign affairs Sergey Lavrov.

So, when on February 21, Putin officially recognized the

separatist Eastern areas of Ukraine in the Luhansk and Donetsk regions as independent states, everyone got alerted. A couple of my university friends from Russia texted me to ask how things were going in Ukraine, if there were any political decisions made after Putin's move and his demand that Ukraine must stop fighting separatists in Luhansk and Donetsk. Collectively, those regions are called the Donbas.

On the morning of February 24, I got up as usual at about 6. a.m. and went for a walk. I had to do these walks every morning and every evening after the awful Covid pneumonia I had a couple of months prior to that, with having to stay in hospital and breathe oxygen through a ventilator in the intensive care ward.

The night before that, Putin addressed the population of Russia on TV, announcing that he made a "difficult" decision to begin a *Special Military Operation* (*SVO* in Russian), as he officially called it, against the "Nazi regime" in Ukraine.

He had no other choice, he hypocritically claimed, but to start it in order to conduct the "denazification" and "demilitarization" of Ukraine to protect the Donbas area with ethnic Russians living in them on their official request, as well as, allegedly, all other Russian-speaking people in the country from "Nazis".

* * *

The first thing I saw on the morning of February 24 was lines of cars rushing along the streets and lengthy queues at petrol stations. Not far from our apartment block, cars waited in a line that lasted about 200 meters. There were long queues in the supermarkets too – I saw them as I slowly walked past.

First, I did not realise what was happening and what the whole rush in the streets was about. But having walked my regular 40 minutes and heard fractions of talks in the street and supermarket queues, I rushed home. Once I got in, I started to Google to check if the fears growing inside me were true.

This is when my family and I heard from YouTube that Ukraine had been attacked. This was no fake news, no just rumours or media speculations that "war would start soon", but only hard, painful truth.

Bloody hell. Can you believe it? My home country had started war against the country where I had lived for the past ten years with my wife and daughter. The country where my grandmother was born. The country that had been always friendly towards Russia after they had parted ways in 1991.

YouTube showed me that approximately at 4 a.m., the Russian army began shelling Kyiv, Kharkiv and other large cities in the east of Ukraine. Notably, Kharkiv in particular is very close to the Russian border, and it is a fully Russian-speaking city. The majority of cities and towns in the East of the country are full of people who speak Russian – those are people that Putin claimed he wanted to protect and rescue by starting the SVO.

Troops from Russia then crossed the border in several spots and headed for Kyiv. Besides, from the Donetsk and Luhansk areas, Russian troops also started moving towards Kyiv.

To make it clear, in the East of Ukraine, 80 to 90 percent of people speak Russian, preferring it in everyday conversations. The Russian government began war with a country, which had the closest and hardest ties with it.

Ties in terms of history, folklore, culture (literature, music, etc., even jokes and swear words), geographic location and mentality. It would have been the same if the US began war against any of its states or Canada, for instance.

While we lived in Kyiv for five years before that, and I had an office job as a translator, there were – attention! – just two-three people who spoke Ukrainian, with everyone else speaking Russian in my office. Everyone just did not care, believing Russian to be their preferable mother-tongue.

Anyway, the first thing I did after I found out that the war had started was wake up my wife Mary to break the news to her. Then I hurried to the cash machine, since the withdrawal amount from one bank card was cut down to 1,000 or 2,000 UAH (which was $30-$60 in late February 2022).

Queues near ATMs were very big, but mostly they were that big near the branches of the most popular local bank called Privat. Near smaller banks, queues were much smaller.

When I came to an ATM for the first time, I had to wait for about two hours in the queue. Then the machine ran out of cash, so I told the people in front of me I'd be back and went to check an ATM of a different bank close by. After waiting for half an hour, I drew all the cash I could from our cards and went back to the first ATM. The queue had not moved, and a bank staffer said that cash would now be brought there next morning.

I went there again the following day and it was the same story. Lots of people – young and elderly – waiting, hoping, cursing Russia for starting the war, cursing the bank for not being able to bring in enough cash, discussing the rumours and news regarding the war. The air was filled with shock, but still everyone seemed to feel like they had been expecting the war to happen after all. Everyone kept stating that Russia had now turned into an enemy.

Thank God, the temperature was high enough to stay long outside – plus 3–5 (we use the Centigrade system in Ukraine). Still, from standing on the same spot and hardly moving, I felt my feet somewhat freezing after about 30 minutes. Next time I come here for cash, I told myself, I'll have to wear thick woolly socks.

* * *

It must be said that during the first few days of the war, probably because I was Russian, I naively hoped that this whole thing would end very soon. I felt this to be a terrible mistake, a rushed decision of Putin, and it would all be over soon. Well, I thought, lying awake at nights nervous as hell about a high chance of myself and my family getting killed by the army of my home country. Putin cannot be such an idiot, I thought. It proved that I was wrong.

Until 2011, I was sure that he tried his best to build a prosperous country which would collaborate with its neighbours and integrate into the global society. Most of the 2000s, to be honest, I lived without paying much attention to politics, just enjoying life, but believing in the good future for Russia.

It was largely thanks to the new president, who, unlike Yeltsin, did not belong to the Communist Party during the USSR times. (The fact that he was a former KGB officer and head of the FSB did not bother me for some reason). These thoughts of mine got sort of shaky in 2014, when the Crimea was bluntly annexed, and now these idealistic thoughts about him finally came crashing down like a house of cards.

Since the annexation of Crimea in 2014 and the start of Russia supporting the separatists in the East of Ukraine (after also having brought Russian troops without insignia there to start the separatist mood in the first place pretending that it was "local people's movement"), constant discussions of a potential war against Ukraine filled talk-shows on state Russian TV.

All "thought leaders" of Putin's regime on TV, radio and on

social media as one declared that should this war ever start, it would not last longer than three days. This time would be enough to suppress the resistance (a weak one, if any at all) and take Kyiv by storm, they claimed.

I had this nasty and shameful thought that the things just might go this way and the war would be over within a week maximum, like it was in Georgia in August 2008, when Dmitry Medvedev who replaced Putin in the presidential chair briefly (but the country was still controlled by the latter) sent troops into Georgia. Back then, Russia also supported its Southern regions who wanted to become independent of Georgia. The war lasted for five days. But then, the West did not support Georgia against Russia.

Anyway, with Russia and Ukraine, I put my sincere hopes in negotiations. They indeed began soon in Belarus, near the border with Ukraine. The Belarusian dictator-president (Putin's ally) Alexander Lukashenko swore he would guarantee the safety of the Ukrainian delegation. However, the president of Ukraine Zelensky doubted that and insisted that a neutral territory should be used as a platform for peace talks. But he was finally persuaded to accept the Belarus option.

The Russian and Ukrainian delegations met several times. The talks indeed took place, but peace never happened. Russia's main demands were to get Ukraine to keep to neutrality, i.e. vow not to join NATO, not to create nuclear weapons, which it gave up in the early 90s. Russia also wanted Ukraine to officially admit the loss of Crimea and stop trying to reclaim control over it and the Donbas.

I kept checking news in Telegram channels every half hour, then checked it every hour. During the next several days, my hopes for a quick end of this war gradually faded out. I had to come to terms with the reality, get a grip on myself, keep doing the online job of writing texts that I had, overcoming constant fear of staying in a potential zone of an air strike, of getting killed just after I managed to beat the bloody Covid pneumonia when every day several people died in the hospital where I was staying. What the hell, I thought, I've gone from the frying pan and right into the fire.

As the US and Europe began supporting Ukraine, sending in weapons, on one of those days, Putin on TV ordered that the nuclear deterrent forces were brought to the state of high alert. When it happened, I first felt a sudden relief, thinking, perhaps a little hysterically, "the hell with that, it is going to be over soon".

One nuclear strike and whoosh – it is all over. But that did not last long either. No good emotions inside me, even if they were "perverse good" like a relief from a potential death coming soon, lasted long back then. Fear and panic – that was what kept coming back to me now and then. I did not feel fear about my own life, but I did have fear about my wife and daughter, their lives and well-being.

The overall state of fear and panic in Ukraine was common back then. In the Eastern cities that were being bombed and stormed by Russian troops, people felt a million times harder than I did.

Those who stayed in Ukraine in relatively peaceful regions and refused to go abroad gradually got used to this. But once Russia began hitting power stations in October 2022 that generate electricity and provide central heating with the cold season right ahead, many again began feeling panic, fear, getting even more angry with Russia, becoming frustrated and depressed.

AIR RAID ALERTS; IMPROVISED BOMB SHELTERS

Posters with warnings about air raid alerts and instructions on how to behave during them began to emerge on walls of buildings and lamp posts in Oleksandriia. They were made by the soldiers from the army base headquartered in our city. These posters said that when air raid alarms go off, depending on the number of signals and the length of intervals between them, it would be either a drill or an actual alert.

In the case of the latter, everyone was recommended to grab warm clothes, bottles with drinking water, some food and a first-aid kit and run for the nearest bomb shelter. All this had to be prepared in advance, like when you are expecting a baby and should have a bag ready to go to hospital with.

By shelter, a concrete basement under an apartment block was usually meant. However, not all basements were suited for that, some residential buildings were old and hiding in basements under them exposed you to a risk of being killed by debris or buried alive under them. Besides, some of them did not have proper basements.

In the case of me and my family, our block did not have a suitable one. We would have to dash to an apartment building almost a hundred meters away from our house, where our friends lived.

We did prepare two bags and left them standing in the hall by the door. There were air alerts a few times. However, those proved to be drills, God knows why they wanted to do them at all – you jumped from fear and shock every time sirens began to howl behind the window. They were high- pitched and they howled as loud as hell.

However, a change of plans came soon. Mary and I thought that residential blocks in the city centre may prove not safe enough. An actual bombproof shelter was located at least 15–20 minutes away on foot and by the time we would make it there with our autistic daughter Dasha (back then she was nine), it would have been packed with other panicking shelter-seekers.

Mary's brother Den is a soldier, in the past he several times signed a contract to serve in the East of Ukraine, fighting the separatists heavily supported by Russia. He insisted that we took his wife Julia and his one-year-old daughter and moved to his in-laws on the edge of the city. They lived in a private house with a proper basement, which would be much safer than hiding under an apartment block.
Pretty quickly we packed some clothes, medication, toys for my daughter. As we left, I locked the door of the flat on both locks, as I usually do when we leave for a long time, having made sure that I shut down water and gas.

Looking around the flat and recalling that Russian troops shelled living quarters in Kyiv and other cities, while they claimed they would only be targeting military objects and infrastructure, I wondered if we would ever see our flat intact again and would be able to live in it. The dark irony here was that we had just bought that flat in December 2019 and had managed to live there just a couple of years.

Den's in-laws' house was located in one of the districts with other private houses (they do not look like cottages in Europe, the UK or the US at all – most of them are old with multiple repairs visible outside on their roofs and walls, and just about 1-2 percent of them are brand new, tasteless, of kitch style).

* * *

Going to sleep at night back then was one of my toughest challenges. It was just three months since I had left hospital, so I was recommended to "stay calm", get "enough of sleep" and walk at least two hours every day to let my lungs recover after Covid. Besides, not only it was hard for me to go to sleep, but as this whole thing started I often woke up at night from the sound of air raid alerts howling loud as hell.

I had to take sedative pills as I had done when I was in hospital. As the war kept intensifying, I began to take more of them, sometimes during the day too.

Working at my laptop and writing articles partly helped me to get distracted from the nightmare that was unfolding around me. I went deep into the world of sports, travel, cryptocurrencies and other topics – this took my mind away from the war around us for a while, took it off the constant risk of being hit by a rocket or a bomb from one of the Russian airplanes.

Recalling that time now, I can't even say for sure if our city was bombed at all. Air raid alerts were frequent, but rockets and bombs mostly hit military objects around Oleksandriia, not within it.

Still, it was either down to the great work of Ukrainian air defence forces or no rockets were sent to specifically our city yet. Being in the middle of Ukraine and a little on its eastern part, away from the borders with Russia and from Crimea, Oleksandriia is hardly of any strategic importance. Even taking into account the fact that there is a military base there.

* * *

In the house where we moved, we stayed with Julia's father and her close friend Kate, who taught biology at a local primary school. They both were in their early 20s. Julia's Mum was in the Arab Emirates on holiday when the war began. As it started, she wanted to come back, but her husband told her not to be stupid and stay in the UAE.

It was good to stay together with other people in that period, when air alerts started going off pretty often, like several times a day. It was easier to get distracted and get myself busy when there are other people around who share your fears.

One bad thing for me there, for the first time in my ten-year stay in Ukraine, was my Russian nationality and my pure accent. As I said before, the doctors told me to take mandatory walks every single day in order to help my lungs recover. And I did follow their recommendations daily until the war broke out.

When we moved to the cottage area, Mary told me I must not walk around by myself from that point on. The reason was my pure Russian accent. Despite the years I'd lived in Ukraine, from time to time my accent would give me away and somebody would ask me in a shop or in the food market: "You're from Russia, aren't you?"

I would admit this obvious fact, and in the times of peace.

Even after the war in the Donbas began, Ukrainians around me were okay with that – we lived in Kyiv back then. The same thing with my Russian accent happened after we moved to Oleksandriia – if people figured out by the way I talked that I was a native Russian, they did not mind it at all and were quite friendly, especially elderly people who remember the USSR times.

However, now, there were Russian spies sent in, sometimes there were local collaborators though who wanted to help Russian invaders voluntarily (since they believed in the "Russian world"). Those defectors were leaving special signs for the attacking Russian army.

Those were "Z" or "V" letters drawn on walls of buildings. Locals all over Ukraine where there was not an immediate land attack organized themselves into squads of terrestrial defence and patrolled cities, towns and villages during the day and sometimes at night. They were empowered to stop anyone in the street and check their ID. Often, these spies were caught red-handed.

Those letters "Z" and "V", by the way, were not only used as landmarks for rocket strikes or used for marking objects of military importance. These were marks of distinction for the invading Russian army in Ukraine. One of these two letters or both of them was drawn on tanks, trucks or on soldiers' uniforms. Usually, "Z" or "V" was painted in white for best visibility. Later I will tell you why these particular Latin letters were chosen for this and how their usage expanded.

* * *

During the first weeks of the war, many of those spies were arrested, therefore chances were high that terrestrial defence squads could hear me replying in pure Russian to them and consider me an enemy spy too. It would be a pity to get suspected of that and arrested, let alone getting smacked, which was likely, after living for ten years in Ukraine.

I stayed in most of the time in the evening after I finished work. When I felt it was difficult to breathe and I could not get a lungful of air, I would go outside into the courtyard. It was not visible from the main street, so I stayed there, inhaling fresh air, like a fish that returned into a lake from the shore. However, breathing in motion is best in this condition and important for a successful recovery.

Also, at 20.00 sharp, every house was obliged to switch off lights or if they left a small lamp on, they had to close the shades or shutters really tight. Blackouts were a must, so that Russian planes, if they were flying to drop bombs, could not use your house or residential block as a target.

* * *

Air raid alerts started happening more often. I kept reading news on Telegram and signed up to a local channel that spread the word about attacks from the air, telling people in certain regions of Ukraine when they should head for shelters.

For this purpose, an "emergency bag" with warm sweaters, first-aid kit and some food that is easy to carry around (like biscuits or something similar) waited ready by the door. Drinking water was already down in the concrete basement of Julia's parents' house. To descend there, you had to carefully walk down a pretty steep and narrow ladder, so Julia's dad, Sergey, would usually go down first and then help the others to get over the last few steps without falling down and breaking their necks.

Sitting down there with a torch switched on, Julia would play with her nearly one-year-old daughter Sophia. Mary and I would talk to Dasha, telling her that this is a game, and we are playing hide- and-seek, a special adult version of it. When this game is over, we kept telling her, she will get a prize.

Dasha asked for a big-sized chocolate "Kinder-surprise" egg, so we promised she would get it afterwards.

But even a hint at the end of the war was nowhere to be seen. I kept scrolling down news channels, hoping for peace talks to resume, but there were no signs of that. Air alerts began howling every morning, then often during the day. Often they went off from two to three or four times in the evening for all the region around Oleksandriia.

Hell, I thought frequently, the enemy is now my own countrymen who have been sent to bomb peaceful cities in Ukraine, killing military and non-military, killing Russian-speaking people Putin claimed to protect in this war from "Nazis" and any Russian who happened to have moved to Ukraine a long time before that or just several years ago, like me.

These gloomy thoughts kept buzzing in my mind over and over. I felt deeply offended and betrayed by my home country. I felt sorry for Ukrainians, and thankfully nobody around me told me a single word of rebuke for being Russian.

Once when we were down in the basement hiding from an air alert, my brother-in-law Den climbed the ladder to the outside to take a pee.

I followed him with my torch on, but he told me to switch it off even before I came out of the basement. Russians military have night vision devices, he explained. They allow spotting you in the dark a long way off, even if you are holding a lit cigarette. This why in the army, when smoking, soldiers cover their cigarettes by rolling fingers around them, putting it basically inside a fist.

I heard a noise in the sky. Looking up, I saw a silhouette of a plane flying high above amidst the clouds. Searchlights of our air defence were flashing across the sky, so I thought I had seen a Russian plane. But who knows if that was really what I saw.

After the alert died out, again, we were notified about the end of it in the Telegram channel, which I kept checking, and we climbed out.

As we went back into the house, Den told us that it was pointless to rush down into the basement every time an air alarm went off. You will ruin your nervous system, he said, get all wrought up, which will play against you in the long run as long as the war lasts. He strongly advised that it is worth going into an underground shelter when you already hear an explosion somewhere in the city. Or near the house.

Another drawback of hiding from air alerts in that basement was that it was deep underground, Den said. If a rocket or a bomb hits it, the risk was high to be buried alive under the debris. Days would pass before anyone would notice you are there, he told us, and help get you out of there. And while staying there you might be wounded, have a heavy bleeding or bones broken. Den gave us these recommendations as he was expected to be summoned on one of the coming days, so when he is gone we would have to manage on our own.

Taking Den's advice to go down to the basement only if there was an actual threat to our lives, we began doing what many people did back then in the same situation.

When an air alert went off, all of us would gather in the corridor in the middle of the house, shutting the doors to all the rooms tightly. The outside walls would in theory be strong enough to take the hit of an explosion of a bomb, but then the shock wave would be weaker and would be stopped by the inner walls. Those, behind which we were sitting in the corridor.

We also secured the windows by putting cello-tape on them crossways. If the house got hit, the cello-tape would reduce the damage and the glass would not fly around in splinters so much.

Pretty quickly, these air alerts became a sort of habitual thing, and at night I sometimes woke up from a howling siren but then would go on sleeping and did not move, not giving a damn.

Sometimes I would wake up in the morning, check Telegram for bomb notifications and see that during the night there had been one or 2-3 air raid alerts, but I slept right through them. Indeed, as they say, human is an animal that gets used to everything quickly.

RUSSIAN SOLDIERS RAPING WOMEN AND CHILDREN

I kept reading various news reports and often bumped into one horrible thing - Russian soldiers raping Ukrainian women, teenage school girls and even children under ten years old. It mostly happened in the towns and villages where Russian troops entered and stayed.

Some women were raped because the soldiers knew that their husbands were in the front line at that moment - so it was a sort of revenge. Sometimes, they shot men to death and then raped their wives or threatened the women that it would be either them or their daughters/little sons.

In the majority of cases, those soldiers were not punished. However, in April 2022, a young soldier born in 1997 was arrested after he posted several videos, where he raped toddlers with a tea spoon, on social media. Mary and I were afraid for Dasha in case Olexandriia became occupied. She was afraid for our daughter. I was afraid for them both.

Usually, it takes quite a lot to give me a shock. But here I was shocked immediately by the sudden awareness that my countrymen were able to do that. Regular Russian army, bloody hell, does what the Taliban or the ISIS would likely do during a war. What kind of monsters and psychos do those men have to be to rape teenagers and children? Until then, I had been under an illusion that such things were long in the past or were made only by thugs these days. It was a real eye-opener to see how many seemingly normal people turned into thugs and psychos once they were ordered to attack Ukraine.

Not everyone in the Russian army did that or would do that, I'm sure. Still, the fact of those rapings happening gave me the creeps and sobered me up about how strong the animal part remains in some people even though back at home they are probably good family men: somebody's husbands, fathers, brothers.

So we began thinking about leaving Ukraine. But we did not know how to go about this, where to go, etc. And it was also a scary thought about leaving your house and your city.

Even though you felt that staying there may become dangerous sooner or later, still, your house, your friends and relatives around made you feel sort of secure. But the anxiety that Mary and I felt kept growing. It was increasing every day. Besides, Russian troops kept shelling the airport and the military base in a city near Olexandriia. Every time it happened, we had an air raid alert. Mary was worried that unless we left soon, in the end they would surround our city, and then it would be impossible to get out.

NEGOTIATIONS KEEP FAILING

There were a couple of times when I had to get back to our flat to pick some of our stuff. I had to bring in some toys for Dasha and my desktop PC, so I could work properly – writing articles on my laptop I bought three years prior to that was not too convenient – I had got used to a better keyboard which can be moved around, to my big monitor where I could open several windows, while working, etc. Besides, the laptop for some reason failed to catch a good Wi-Fi connection.

I would call a taxi and again tried not to get much attention for the risk of getting confused for a Russian spy. The flat now looked lonely and empty. Still, I got a feeling that I came home when I went over to pick up our things.

On my way back to the cottage district, once I asked the driver to stop as we went past a shopping mall with two cash machines – one inside and one outside, right at the entrance. Looking around, just in case, I quickly got out and popped into the mall to see if I could withdraw some of the cash that remained in Mary's account (I did not have one, using hers was pretty fine with me).

Both ATMs were empty, though. Not a big problem, because I had already got enough cash last time, but there were still hryvnas (UAH) on my wife's bank card, and we were expecting shops to stop taking card payments at some point in the future. A war is a war, you know. When a country gets attacked with its cities bombed, banks in the end stop functioning and then, like in some kind of post-apocalyptic Hollywood film, cash would be the only way to buy food and medication. Even Bitcoin and any other crypto would be useless due to a potential lack of electricity and the Internet connection cut off.

Therefore, while I was unable to withdraw cash, I tried to pay with the card every time I went to the supermarket or to the chemist's. I had to get enough medicine for my post-Covid recovery – the doctor told me I had to keep taking blood thinners and some sort of hormones for my lungs for a couple of months on a daily basis. And I was to take them at more or less the same time every day.

Five minutes earlier or five minutes later would not make much difference, but still I had to worry about remembering this on top of what was going on already. Bloody awesome, isn't it.

* * *

I kept checking Telegram to see what was going on in the flines of fire in Ukraine and if there were any signs of the war ending soon. At that time, to be honest, I did not care on what terms for Ukraine this war would end – whether Russians would storm and seize Kyiv or Ukrainians and Russians would reach any sort of peace agreement.

Still, neither of those took place. Each round of negotiations would end, and a new one announced to be coming soon after.

Each time, the chief of the Russian delegation, the minister of culture of Russia Vladimir Medinsky, would say that significant progress had been reached and that the Ukrainian negotiating party now took time to consult with president Zelensky. It never went any further than that, though.

What Russia wanted from Ukraine officially was to give up plans of restoring nuclear weapons, eliminate plans to join NATO and publicly admit that Crimea remains Russian. Besides, Russia wanted Zelensky to stop fighting separatists from the Donbas region and admit them as independent republics.

What Ukraine demanded from Russia is that Crimea went back to Ukraine and that Russia withdrew its army from the Donbas. They also demanded that Russia would stop military offence and withdraw the army from all of Ukraine. At least within the borders before the assault on February 24.

Following Putin's orders, the Russian delegation refused to accept that. The army continued attacking. Ukrainians kept fighting back as hard as they could.

I have already told you that Russia and Ukraine used to be (and remain) closer to each other than Russia and any other post-Soviet country, but it is worth emphasizing once again. Cultural links, family relations, language, jokes, even swear words were nearly the same. Ukrainians even swear mostly in Russian.

Let me tell you about a curious and a funny thing that happened between Russian soldiers and a local Ukrainian guy during the first week of the war – I watched it on YouTube, it was shared by somebody on Twitter (now "X app") as well. This case just confirms the high idiocy of this war and that it started to worsen things between the two countries that had already gone bad in 2014, when Crimea was annexed, the separatist mood in the Donbas was quickly raised by Putin's people and that military conflict began.

Anyway, this video showed a column of Russian tanks standing on a road on their way to the Kyiv region. The tanks were standing still, apparently, out of fuel. A middle-aged Ukrainian was driving past them, going in an opposite direction. So he stopped, wound down his window, and they began a careful but a friendly chat. The dialogue sounded like this.

- So boys, out of fuel, huh?
- Yeah, man.
- Where are you going?
- In the Kyiv direction.
- Do you even know why they sent you there? Are you aware of what is happening there?
- Nah, man. We only know there's fighting going on now.
- How come you don't even know where you're being sent and what's going on there?
- Well, they just told us to cross the border and move here. That's all. In the army, you don't ask for orders to be explained, you know.

That part seems to be true – Russian media outlets which opposed to the war and which later received an official status of a "foreign agent" (read "traitor of the state") and were forbidden to operate as their licences were withdrawn, wrote that when the war started, many Russian troops were just sent to Ukraine with no explanation or clarification. The soldiers had their phones and passports taken away. They were told they were heading there for military drills.

So, those guys in the tanks possibly were sent to Ukraine blindly, without knowing what they were going to do. Still, they could have refused, as some other soldiers did and were fired from the army.

Coming back to that conversation, that middle-aged Ukrainian told them that his country's army was beating the shit out of

Russians near Kyiv. The soldier then asked if he could have a cigarette. The Ukrainian gave him one and jokingly suggested pulling their tanks back to Russia with his car.

The Russians laughed, appreciating the joke, and told him to bugger off.

In no war between two other countries in the world, this would have been possible, I guess. That began indeed as a war between two fraternal nations.

They say that when people who used to be really close to each other begin fighting, that fight gets to be much more severe and cruel than if strangers went to fight each other. Now, with Russia and Ukraine, this is a solemn truth on a large scale.

RUSSIAN "Z" AND "V" SYMBOLS OF THIS WAR

"Z" and "V". These two Latin characters initially were used for marking Russian vehicles on which soldiers crossed the Ukrainian borders during the invasion. Soldiers had "Z" letters on their uniforms and helmets.

Later, when it became clear that Kyiv will not be taken in just three days, as Putin planned initially, and the war will take much longer than expected, these letters were turned into the symbols of this war that the government began to use.

There are several possible explanations as to why these particular letters were chosen. The first one is that "Z" and "V" are the initials of the Ukrainian president – Vladimir Zelensky. This theory has it that the initial plan was to remove him and set up fake elections to make people vote for Putin's puppet president.

Later, a theory emerged that "Z" stood for the Western military district of Russia ("Zapad" means West), "V" for the Eastern one ("Vostok" is East), "O" stands for the Central military district. Later on, Putin also began using these letters for spreading propaganda across Russia. All the TV anchors who emphasized the absolute necessity of invading Ukraine, all war correspondents started putting a "Z" on lids of their laptops, Telegram channel logos, etc.

First, "Z" became an informal symbol of supporting the war, later on this letter turned into an official one. Especially, a "Z" drawn in a deliberate course style with the top and bottom lines unstraight, looking a little like elements of arches, like this letter was daubed.

Often it is drawn in the colours of the Russian flag, just white colour or using the Ribbon of St. George (another symbol of the USSR's victory in WW2). The hashtag in the picture below says "We do not leave our own people in trouble" and as you can see it has a "Z" on it.

Ordinary people, who began to support the war, started putting a Z on their social media profile pictures.
"Za Президента" ("For the President"), "Za Россию" ("For Russia"), "Za Победу" ("For the Victory"), "Za Мир" ("For peace", what an irony) became official slogans written on big posters which hang above stages during concerts on the Red Square and then during the pro-war music tours when many local rock bands (mostly half forgotten but popular in the past or not very famous ones) went around Russia (receiving huge honorariums for that) and sang with those posters hanging above the stages.
Many rock groups and artists, however, refused to do that, and they were forced to leave Russia or got deprived of concerts as defectors and/or fined.

Ukrainians then began spelling Russia as "Ruzzia" and Russians as "Ruzzki". The irony here is that a "Z" letter was widely used in the Nazi Germany. Plan Z was the re-equipment and expansion of the Kriegsmarine (German navy) which

Adolf Hitler ordered to make in early 1939.

A "Z" with a stroke stands for "Wolfsangel", a symbol of Wehrmacht troops inspired by medieval European wolf traps that consisted of a metal hook shaped like "Z". This symbol was used completely or partly by a dozen of Wehrmacht military divisions, including the 4th SS Polizei Panzergrenadier Division. "Z" is also half of the well-known Nazi swastika symbol (initially a pagan symbol of the sun).

Now, opponents and critics of the war in Russia and outside it refer to these "Z" symbols as swastikas.

Funny that there is an old Soviet cartoon, where children dive into a sea and find an old Nazi German submarine which sank during WW2. The vessel has a "Z" with a stroke drawn on its side. After the war with Ukraine began, search results for this cartoon were banned on the Russian search engine giant Yandex, but it can still be found on YouTube.

LEAVING FOR WESTERN UKRAINE

As days went by, we saw that refugees from the East and the South of Ukraine kept coming into our city. Now, the streets were full of cars of those fleeing the war from the attacked regions as they were trying to get to more peaceful areas. Oleksandriia proved to be one of such places. There were a lot more folks in the streets now, and news came that people who kept flowing in had rented all the spare flats and rooms in the city they could find.

At the same time, friends kept telling Mary that lots of local people were grabbing their most necessary stuff and also fleeing. They were going to the Western part of the country where things had been quiet so far, cities were not bombed and no air raid alerts howling.

One afternoon, my wife came back from the city centre and started frantically packing our stuff. "Masha with her husband and the children are going to a place near the Carpathians" (that's the Carpathian Mountains in the West of Ukraine), she told me. "We decided to go together, let's pack quickly!"

As Mary told me, it was virtually impossible to find someone who would agree to drive us to Chernivtsi (a city in the West, near the border with Moldova and Romania). My wife and her friend Masha had tried their best, calling all their friends or friends of their friends to get someone to drive us to the other end of the country.

Finally, my wife succeeded – an acquaintance of our daughter's paediatrician had just returned from Kharkiv in his minivan. He had delivered food products and medication to the military stationed there, who were defending the city from constant and harsh attacks. He had not slept the previous night, while driving to Kharkiv and back. About 400 kilometres in one direction.

This guy's name was Vladimir. He said he would pick us up in the evening and until then he needed a few-hours' nap. A prospect of riding a van at night was a little scary to Mary, but the driver told us that it was the only option.

After that, he would have to be back in Oleksandriia and drive somewhere else – to deliver something again to help the military. Here's why our choice was the best option under the current circumstances: now that lots of people were fleeing to the Western part, the majority of them drove during the day.

That meant huge traffic jams, taking into account lots of block posts on the roads who are checking your IDs and sometimes demand that you open your car's boot for inspection. So driving at night, at least in theory, would let us reach the destination quicker.

The estimated time of the trip, according to Vladimir, was about three days because of the awful traffic. Two days if we were lucky. But, fortunately, we managed to reach Chernivtsi much quicker.

* * *

There were nine of us, not counting the driver, with suitcases and bags and, somehow, we all were able to fit in the minivan. We were crammed in, Dasha sitting on my lap, bags almost hanging around us and threatening to fall onto our heads if the minivan hit a bump on the road. Mary sat ahead of me. Masha and her family were in the back, crammed in and surrounded by bags, just like us.

They also brought a pet carrier with their cat. All the way, he kept mewing, so Masha's daughter had to take him out of the carrier and hold him for a while or let it lie on her lap, so it stopped mewing so loudly.

It was the first week of March, so the weather was cold, but, luckily, the heater inside the minivan worked fine. The drive was pretty hard and promised to be remembered for the rest of our lifetimes, just like everything that had been happening since February 24. Sounds like I will have something to tell Dasha when she's older. Being autistic, she probably would hardly remember all these details now.

We managed to get out of Oleksandriia without going through thick traffic and somehow avoided all the checkpoints. The driver used a small, quiet road that the majority of others who were leaving the city, apparently, did not know about.

After that, as we went on, we several times had to wait in long lines of traffic. Looking ahead to see if there was a big traffic jam, every time I saw that a long line of cars, buses and trucks that looked like a long fiery serpent going into the distance. Sometimes it was climbing a hill ahead of us, sometimes it simply froze on the road that lead to the night horizon.

The idea that this trip could indeed take from two to three days, along with the prospect of spending them cramped in the minivan with the cat and lots of bags was a bit discouraging.

However, the thought that we left the city which may soon be surrounded by Russian troops and were heading for a town that was safe, at least for the time being, was a good incentive not to complain and left no room for doubts or regrets.

Vladimir was driving stoically without even stopping for a break, despite his previous sleepless night behind the wheel. Now and then, Mary kept asking him if we should pull up, so he could get a nap. He thanked her, but still said no.

Mary hardly slept at all as she watched him driving – his manner of steering sometimes got a bit reckless as he began overtaking cars and heavy trucks going ahead of us. He had to do it quickly enough to manage to fit back in the lane out of the way of the oncoming cars. He was slightly under 60, so Mary feared that after a sleepless night he might have a heart attack or something like that. In that case, we all might also get killed on that trip.

Several times we were stopped at checkpoints. Regular military and terrestrial defence soldiers demanded to see our IDs. We would pass out biometric cards to them without having to get out of the van. At a few block posts, they gave the IDs just a quick look, asking where we were headed.

Then they saw that the van was full of children and waved us to move on. Obviously, they had seen hundreds of cars with similar families that night. And the night before, and I'm sure they saw plenty of similar cars many nights after. So, if there was nothing suspicious about you or your vehicle, they would just let you drive on.

When showing my ID, Mary would always cover the bit of it stating "citizen of the Russian Federation" in the corner with her thumb. During most of the checks, the military looked at the documents in her hands. Only once, a fussy guy in a bullet-proof vest and a Kalashnikov gun (AK- 47) asked to pass the documents over and examined them under the light of a torch. But then he gave them back and told us to move on. At a couple of block posts they did not stop us at all, just waving at us to drive on.

As we approached the end of the journey, we got stopped at another checkpoint. A soldier there took our IDs, examined them carefully. Then he asked additionally for an official paper that confirmed that I had lived in Ukraine at the exact address in Oleksandriia. After seeing that and looking at me attentively, he, somewhat reluctantly, allowed us to continue with our journey.

As Vladimir slowly started off after a check at each of the block posts we passed, I looked outside through the window and saw tired, freezing soldiers. Some of them were warmly dressed, but still were stepping from one foot to the other or breathing into their fists to keep warm.

Sometimes there were fires in metallic barrels, helping them to warm up. Some soldiers, especially from the terrestrial defence, looked really young, like under twenty or in their early twenties. Tall and skinny, wearing khaki winter uniforms, holding Kalashnikov assault rifles and breathing out steam into the cold March night, they looked like tousy freezing sparrows to me.

CHURCH REFUGEE CAMP

By midday, we already arrived in Chernivtsi. Driving overnight and then part of the following day, we covered roughly 664 kilometres, plus-minus a few. Vladimir never stopped for a nap even once, moving on tenaciously and just pulling up just one time around 4 a.m. so everybody could use a smelly wooden box of a public toilet outside a petrol station closed for the night.

While we were doing our "business" there, Vladimir chewed on a sandwich with cheese and ham Mary made for him. We had a snack after we got back too – dry sandwiches, biscuits. We washed them down with water from the bottles we had brought along. Once our "snack stop" was over, we drove on.

In the morning, I already saw mountains in the distance. Covered in the morning fog, they were hardly visible and therefore seemed to look more like hills, rather than mountains.

We drove through a bit of a land that already belonged to Moldavia, where the borders of two countries slightly overlap, but nobody seems to care. All we saw from the windows were small old and shabby looking private houses made of wood and bricks with paint coming off and cracks looking like frozen snakes on the walls.

Old people, middle-aged men and women, teenagers, all poorly dressed. Some men were drinking vodka from plastic glasses and smoking outside a shabby café near the road. The area looked gloomy and depressing, like many villages in deep Russia, as if they had been cursed to forever stay in the early 1990s. Compared to that, every Ukrainian town and village produced an impression close enough to Abu Dhabi.

We then went through two more checkpoints, both well-fortified – the control of vehicles was rigid there, because this was the Dniester Hydroelectric Station, not far from Chernivtsi where we were going.

One military checkpoint rose on our way as we entered the territory around the station. There was a long line of cars before it, slowly moving as the soldiers carefully checked the IDs of the drivers and passengers, scrutinizing them as they walked past the waiting vehicles, holding their Kalashnikovs hanging around their necks on belts.

We passed through that pretty easily, without having to get out, just showed them our passports and told them we were heading to Chernivtsi from the middle of the country. We seemed to be lucky, but overall the check-up there was rigorous as cars kept coming. Vladimir told us that the soldiers at the checkpoint did not rule out an attack or an act of terrorism from Russians on this strategic object, hence they were tight and very attentive to the passing cars.

The block post on our way out of the station's territory was easier to go through than the one via which we had entered.

More than a year after that – in early June 2023, Russians blew up a similar station in Kherson region. The Kakhovka Hydroelectric Power Plant. They dynamited the dam on it, making all the towns and villages around flooded – 80 towns in total. Around 30 people died, a lot of local people lost their homes and were evacuated. Russia accused Ukraine of this explosion. Ukraine did vice versa.

A little historic digression here – in 1941, during the Great Patriotic War, Soviet high-ranking commanders feared that Nazis would try to go across the Dnipro river, and so they ordered the same dam to be exploded. Thousands of Russians and Ukrainians died over that back then.

* * *

Eventually, we parted ways with Masha and her family as they headed for a village in the mountains where the mother of a friend of theirs lived. They had never seen that woman before. This Ukrainian guy worked at that time in London, but he had arranged with his mother for them to stay in their guest house.

Mary was a bit offended since Masha, who she believed was a good friend, did not even invite us to come over to stay in that village together with them, though they did know we had nowhere to stay in Chernivtsi.

I told Mary that probably they were afraid that in that case they would not be allowed to stay either.

But that is true – Masha at least could have said something like: "Guys, sorry, we can't offer you to come with us – we are going to be guests ourselves. Good luck and let us know how you will settle there". Masha did not say even that as she and her husband waved goodbye and Vladimir drove his minivan off.

* * *

Fearing that we would be left to ourselves without any accommodation in a completely unknown city, Mary opened Google on her phone and began searching for somewhere to stay. Then she made a few phone calls.

Finally, she arranged for us to stay in a camp for refugees based in a local Evangelist church. Vladimir let us off near it with our two suitcases and a couple of bags, we chipped in with Masha to pay him, and then they drove off.

For some reason, I did not feel worried at all. This began to seem like a sort of adventure for me. As long as we were out of the dangerous territory, I relaxed. But this is how I often react to difficulties – I do not start solving them until the very last moment. Mary, on the other hand, prefers to find a solution immediately, she will not be able to relax until she has done it. So she took over to solve this issue.

The city of Chernivtsi seemed welcoming. There were also plenty of cars and noise from them, as many people then were passed through the city or had come there from regions that were under attack. Still, it seemed to be sort of wrapped in a cocoon of calmness compared to Oleksandriia, where panic and fear filled the air.

Two young women in their early twenties met us and showed us into the church. Mary carried the light-weight bags. I pulled the suitcases, following my wife and daughter, thankful that we had finally made it to a safe place and happy that our heavy as hell suitcases had wheels attached to them.

Those wheels also saved us when we were crossing the border with Poland on foot, running along with several hundreds of other people, who were chilled to the bone, frustrated and tired. With children, babies and pets. But I will get to that a bit later.

* * *

The Sinai church, where we ended up, looked modern and cozy both from outside and inside. A spacious three-story house right in the city centre. The guy who Mary had spoken to on the phone was the pastor of this church, also called Vladimir. He met us as we came in, kindly saying with a smile that we could stay for as long as we needed. He warmly encouraged us to feel at home.

Pastor Vladimir was a thin young man in his early thirties. His hair slightly shaved on the sides of his head, his face edged with a thin trimmed beard. He often smiled and got on easily even with strangers, with his polite and appealing manners.

He did not look like a strict pastor, but rather like an elder brother to everyone in the church every time I watched him. He did not give any orders, he just asked the volunteers in the church to do something, and they did it gladly without feeling any pressure. Everybody in the church seemed to like him. As I found out later on the Instagram account of the church, he is also the father of three good-looking children – two boys and a girl, the oldest is not even ten yet.

Anyway, a girl of about twenty took us to the second floor into the spacious room. Air mattresses and regular ones with blankets and pillows on them lay along the walls and in the middle of the room. It was shaped like a letter "r" and had a door in each of the two wings.

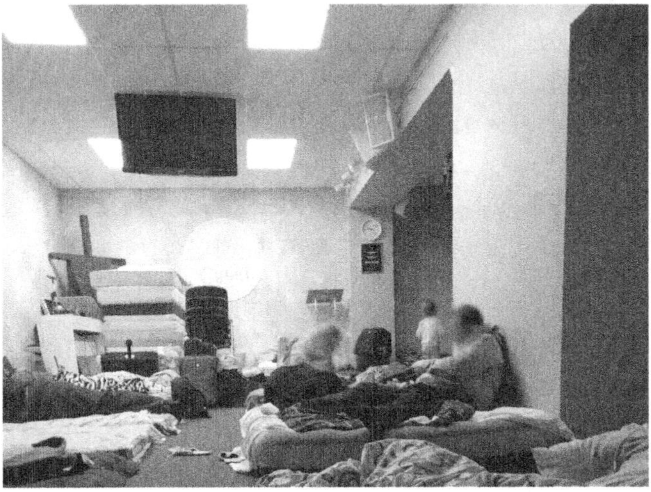

A small platform with a big wooden cross towered above the floor by the wall. The cross was put against the corner, and on the platform where Vladimir had previously preached to the audience now lay a heap of mattresses. Lots of chairs had been piled on top of each other at the farthest wall – apparently, this room was usually used for services but had been cleared to provide space for the improvised beds.

As soon as we had chosen two mattresses by the wall near the door with a socket right at that spot and put down our belongings, one of the local volunteers took us into the kitchen upstairs. That was a roomy attic. In the centre of the room under the triangle roof stood a long table, where a few people sat drinking coffee and tea. The kitchen also looked cosy and stylish, with wooden panels covering the walls and big windows right in the roof above your head, through which you could see the grey March sky.

Mary and I, even though relaxed a little, still felt a bit uneasy being in someone else's place and now dependent on the people and pastor of this church. Still, the attendants, who apparently helped to deal with refugees that kept coming, did their best to make us feel at home, smiling and treating us in a welcoming manner.

Behind a big wooden counter with a coffee machine, plastic cups and other kitchenware stood an elderly lady. She poured soup into plates, some teenage girls brought them to the table, and they said we were welcome to have breakfast. We were pleasantly surprised and thankful as it was clear that breakfast had already finished, and they warmed it up now specially for us.

A hot meal topped with a cup of coffee after chewing on biscuits, cold sandwiches and hard-boiled eggs in the crammed minivan during our overnight ride seemed like a king's meal now.

Besides, unlike the basement of Julia's house back in Oleksandriia, this church somehow felt protected and secure.

In the past, churches were used as shelters when an enemy attacked cities and people locked themselves inside a local church or a cathedral. Back in the Medieval times, they ran a risk of getting burned alive there. Now, you can get instantly killed if a rocket hits your flat or a car in which you are trying to escape from an attacked city, like it happened to many people in Ukraine.

Many got killed by rockets when they got out of their shelters to get some water or bread from a nearby shop. I realized that basically the same could happen to us in that Sinai church. Still, Russians did not target their rockets at the Western part of Ukraine so far, except maybe the city of Lviv, one of the largest ones in the Western Ukraine, close to the Polish border.

We decided that we could finally relax, at least for now, as we did not have to take care of accommodation and food. We went back downstairs and lay down on our mattresses. Dasha fell asleep quickly, even though it was only about noon. The half-sleepless night took its toll.

* * *

For me, there is a certain dark irony about the fact that weapons are the first thing improved by technical progress. As for important things like medicine and education, it comes second. This is particularly true for authoritarian countries, such as China, North Korea, Iran. Now, Russia has joined the club.

First, there were ten years of anarchy and poor life for Russian people in the 1990s under Yeltsin's rule (topped by the wars with Chechnya). During the ten years that followed, the first decade under Putin, life in my country seemed to begin to improve in terms of economy, security and there even seemed to be a resemblance of democracy.

There's an old Russian joke to be told here. An American meets a Russian and says: "We have democracy and you, idiots, do not". "Bugger off, we have it too", says the Russian. "Well, you see", says the American guy, "any of us can stand in front of the White House and shout that our president is a moron! And nobody would arrest them. That's real freedom and true democracy". "Big deal", says the Russian guy sarcastically, "I, too, can stand in the Red Square, in front of the Kremlin, and shout that your president is a moron! And I won't get arrested or even fined for that".

This was true about the first ten years of Putin's reign between 2000 and 2010, more or less. After that, "unauthorized meetings" in public places emerged, people began to protest against Putin, and they were arrested and sent to jail.

The Federal Security Service (KGB-turned-FSB) gradually began to regain the authority and influence it had lost over the previous 20 years as the Russian president (a former FSB director too) felt the taste of power (and all the privileges plus billions of roubles and dollars that come as part of the package) and decided to stay for the third term.

But first, in order to follow the constitution's rules, Putin put Dmitry Medvedev on his throne (2008 – 2012), while he formally worked as a Prime Minister, in fact still holding the power over Russia in his hands. In 2012, Vladimir Putin was elected again.

* * *

After breakfast, one of the young women-attendants, a volunteer called Elona, took the three of us over to her flat for a shower. Another guy, also the attendant at the Sinai church, drove us all to Elona's flat. It was pretty far from away the church.

Elona lived in a quite simply decorated flat with two rooms, a kitchen. There was an electronic piano in the living room. As we had walked from the car to the apartment building, she told us that she rented this place with her friends, and they were all musicians who played and sang anthems and songs in church.

It was her day off on that day, that is why she was able to help us and overall could be in church to assist with all the refugees. Gosh, Mary told me later, shocked with surprise, this girl just like that gave up spending her day off relaxing with her boyfriend or doing something pleasant to take us all for a shower at her place.

It was amazing to see ordinary people who worked simple jobs earning 4,000-5,000 UAH (that's about $135) per month go to church-turned-refugee camps during weekends and/or their days off to help those who had fled from shelled cities in other regions.

They spent their time in the church cooking, cleaning, arranging sleeping places, buying food, plastic dishes and cups, and other necessary things for the refugees (money was provided by the church, but sometimes they paid with their own cash). They took complete strangers to their flats, letting them shower, use their hairdryers and washing machines. Then other volunteers would change them, and they would go back to their low-paid jobs and daily lives until it was their turn to come back to help with the refugees.

* * *

During our short stay in Sinai, we met people from various regions of Ukraine, talking to them over breakfast, lunch and then dinner. Well, it was Mary who did the talking, women are more talkative than men, that's a medical fact, but I also tried not to trigger negative reaction from all these people who have been attacked by my home country. So I sat next to my wife at the table, busy eating or talking to Dasha.

After the war started, many Ukrainians remained untroubled, seeing a Russian among them. Still, sometimes something seemed to change in their facial expressions that clearly said that they were not too happy to see a Russian guy dining with them.

Occasionally, I would answer friendly questions, like where we came from and how the situation was in our city that made us leave. But otherwise I just sat next to Mary, nodding when I thought it was necessary, and that was about my "generous" contribution to the talk.

Most people we met during meals had come from Kharkiv, Donetsk area or Odesa. Those were families with one, often two or three children aged from six to sixteen.

It is important to note that by that time, Ukraine had issued a bill that forbade men between sixteen and sixty to leave the country. So those men with families – husbands, sons, brothers

– were either heading with their women and children to stay in the so far peaceful Western Ukraine, or they were planning to see their wives off at the border to a neighbouring country and then stay in the Western Ukraine or go back to where they had come from.

I have already told you about Kharkiv – it is located really close to the border with Russia, and the majority of people there speak Russian.

The idea of Russians shelling cities where the majority of the population speaks Russian was also wildly ridiculous to me. You see, one of the many pretexts for starting the war in the first place was "rescuing the Russian-speaking population of Ukraine from the local Nazis".

The idea of bombs and rockets hitting any city full of civilians, including women, children and the elderly, is horrible. But also when it comes to rocket attacks on a Russian-speaking city, while Putin claimed that he wanted to protect the Russian-speaking population of Ukraine, you just feel sick from these outright lies that cover all those murders and destruction.

Odesa is another big city, a port at the Black Sea, where almost everyone speaks Russian and has a peculiar accent along with a specific sense of humour of the local Jewish community. Odesa jokes used to be well-known during the Soviet Union times in Russia.

Here are a few examples. Albert Einstein is travelling to Zurich to participate in a big scientific conference. In the train compartment, his travel mate is a guy from Odesa. The Ukrainian asks Einstein what his report at the conference is going to be about.

"You see, I have discovered a relativity theory, and I am going to present it to the scientific society", says Einstein.

"What the heck is that about?" the

guy from Odesa asks.

"Well, in layman's terms – two hairs on your head is too little and two hairs in your soup is too much. Something like that."

The Odesa guy grunts out a laugh.

"Gosh, professor. You are taking this crap of a joke to a scientific conference!"

Another one is about the well-famous KGB, back from the USSR times and about the USSR.

Two guys are having a conversation on a train, travelling from Moscow to Kyiv. One of them is from Odesa, he says: "You know, my friend, the first part of my surname hints at what the Bolsheviks promised to give everyone when they pulled off the Revolution in 1917. The second part of my surname hints at what they actually left us with."

The second man stands up, takes a gun out, points it at the Odesa guy.

"You're under arrest, Mr Raikher", he says. "I'm from KGB."

"Rai" in Russian means Heaven. "Kher" (pronounced as German "Herr" but with a rolling "r" sound) means "dick".

This what is happening in Russia pretty much at the moment – Putin talking on TV about major achievements in the sphere of economy, agriculture, etc., about opposing the "rotten West" (typical speeches of a general secretary of the USSR and news reports on TV from the Soviet past), despite the sanctions, successful import phaseout, and so on.

In the meantime, average Russian people, especially in the provinces, who are not engaged in oil business or in the IT sphere, are getting a "kher" rather than a life in heaven at the moment.

* * *

In Sinai, there were people from other regions of Ukraine as well. They mostly spoke the Ukrainian mova (Ukrainian for "language"). There were also those who would rather use "surzhick" (a mixture of Russian and Ukrainian). Mary and I tried to speak Ukrainian with them, just out of respect for their great efforts to help us. It was easier for her than for me, as you can imagine.

During our short stay, we went to one of the local open air markets to buy suitcases, as the one we had with us was practically falling apart from an extremely old age. So we bought those suitcases and two pairs of jeans for me. Two women who sold clothes on stalls heard us, first speaking Russian and then Mary switching to Ukrainian and my feeble efforts to speak it as well. Hearing my Russian accent, they told us we can feel free to speak Russian.

Mary was really impressed, since this was the West of Ukraine, where before the war they preferred to use Ukrainian. This is regarding the issue constantly mentioned by Russian propagandists on TV: "In Ukraine they are suppressing the great and mighty Russian language, forcing everyone to speak Ukrainian mova". That's bollocks, my dear readers. However, as the war continues, even many of those who preferred to speak Russian before now start talking Ukrainian on principle.

Those two ladies also kindly gave us some of the clothes they had for sale for Dasha without charging us anything. I was impressed by that gesture – when I only moved to live in Ukraine ten years ago, Mary told me that in the West, people prefer to speak only their dialect of Ukrainian and did not like those who spoke Russian.

So we never went to travel in the West. But now, these two

women showed us that it did not matter what language you speak as long as you support Ukraine in this war and especially if you live there anyway.

* * *

Mary kept talking to new people, she made some friends with refugee women in the camp. We tried to decide on what would be our next move. We could try and rent a flat or a house in Chernivtsi or somewhere in its vicinity, otherwise we could move closer to the mountains and try to find a house to rent there.

However, pastor Vladimir and other people in church told us that renting a flat in the city was hardly possible now because of the massive refugee inflow. Everything what could be rented had been occupied already. Odds to find something decent (or anything at all) were close to zero.

We then switched to thinking about crossing a border with Romania or Poland – the closest countries to Ukraine here. Lots of Ukrainians were heading to Poland at that moment, we heard stories of thousands of people having to wait on the border at the crossing points for many hours, often having to wait for a few days there, sleeping in the field.

Mary had a younger sister living with her boyfriend in Poland, who had immigrated there several years before – they invited us to stay with them. She also had a half-sister in Germany, and there was also an elder one in Canada. Sometimes, it is wonderful to have lots of relatives, isn't it.

We could only choose between Poland and Germany – these countries were welcoming refugees, offering accommodation and financial support during the first period of stay. Canada at that moment did not offer any program of asylum seekers.

There were also Moldova and Slovakia – the closest countries to Ukraine. But we had no friends or relatives there. And travelling to places like the UK, the US, etc, would be a difficult undertaking now financially.

It would basically be okay with Mary and I to stay in the Sinai refugee camp for a week or longer, but it would not be good for Dasha. She was not nervous yet as she had so far been making friends with the children here.

But living like this for a longer period would certainly be harmful for her emotional state. Being autistic, she would start feeling insecure, start asking that we go home, eventually would become depressed and then tears would begin to flow. This is how she responds to what she feels is strong stress for her.

Eventually, we decided to head for Poland and then on to Germany.

HELL AT POLISH BORDER

After staying about two days in the camp in Sinai, pastor Vladimir told us that there were vans taking refugees to the Polish border from Chernivtsi.

He gave us a lift to the petrol station in his car, where one of these small vans with about eleven or so seats inside picked up passengers. To get to the border you had to drive North to Lviv – a large city in the West close to Poland and famous for its exceptionally tasty coffee and chocolate. On our way there, the van went through a few other cities, where Russian rockets did not reach yet back then.

As we were approaching our destination – a crossing point on the border – I asked the driver, just in case, how much he would charge us. His first answer was that the ride is supposed to be free. But after that, he stated that to be honest, he would accept a "donation" because the petrol had become quite expensive, you cannot find it easily now and overall life has become difficult, so he said that he would charge 300 bucks for the three of us.

A little taken aback by that cheekiness, I told him we did not have that much and just gave him a hundred USD in hryvnas.

We did have more, but what the hell – we had a long journey to Germany to undertake.

Besides, we were not sure Ukrainian border guards would let me out (I am Russian, and I am younger than 60), we might have to try and pay them to let me out. You never know what may happen under these circumstances.

I had read about an Israeli guy getting shot dead on the border when he was trying to leave Ukraine because he was mistaken for a Chechen. And Chechen platoons sent in by their president Kadyrov were at that time near Kyiv, helping storm it. But as the Ukrainian media wrote, mostly they were making video clips of themselves for TikTok, where they threatened to kill Zelensky and everyone who will resist their "glorious entry" into the Ukrainian capital.

Looking at that driver, I could not help but think that some people are offering free help from their hearts, like those in the Sinai church, in their free time, while they could just have used that time for themselves. Light shines brightest in the dark.

And meanwhile, people, like this guy, are trying to cash in on those trying to get out of Ukraine, often having hardly any money at all, having managed to escape from cities and villages occupied or surrounded by Russian troops. The latter were storming those cities, hitting them with missiles, levelling residential blocks and private houses on the outskirts, killing civilians.

There is a Russian saying which goes, "While for some people it is war, for others it is their loving mother". It clearly explains why some people love wars, and not only in the 20th and early 21st century.

It is necessary to mention here that the Russian "blitzkrieg" included a plan to seize Kyiv within three days. This was a popular opinion even before 2022 – Russian propagandists eagerly began discussing an option of a war with Ukraine on their lavishly paid for by the government TV shows (or rather, a war against the "collective West led by America" that sees wet dreams of conquering Russia to get hold of its oil and natural gas deposits, killing 90 percent of the Russian population and turning the rest into slaves so they could work as oil and gas miners).

These talks started all over Russian TV after Putin annexed Crimea. As they boasted the perfect shape the Russian army was in ("the second-strongest army in the world"), they stated that three days would be more than enough to suppress firing points around Kyiv and enter the capital.

Ukraine is small and weak, they would say. It would hardly offer any resistance. They would all surrender immediately. Three days would be even too much. Easy-peasy lemon squeezy. Yeah, right, guys. After that "blitzkrieg" failed, a sarcastic term "blyatskrieg" emerged in Ukraine and began to be used when talking about the first wave of Russian attacks on Ukraine. "Blyat'" means "fuck!" as in when you want to express frustration or anger.

Two heavy suitcases on wheels, two small rucksacks and a bag with laptops proved to be a little too much to cross the border on foot with. Aside from having to roll those suitcases on the tarmac, there was Dasha holding on to my hand and the three of us doing our best to keep up with the running crowd in the evening, when everyone was already knackered.

After long hours in the cold March day and then after the sunset at the border we managed to get across in quite an unusual way, which in those conditions seemed a pure miracle. All of a sudden, help came out of the blue. But, wait, we are getting a little ahead here.
Click the "rewind" button, dear readers. We have now arrived at the border with Poland.

* * *

When we got off the minivan, we saw hordes of people waiting to get from Ukraine to the neighbouring Poland, mostly on foot with plenty of luggage on them.

Thick lines of people filled the wide motorway that was going towards the horizon. People stood on the left side, next to them waited a line of buses. Some of them were letting more people off, some were moving ahead slowly, careful not to run anybody over from the crowd.

I saw that someone raised their phone to take a video, but then a border service worker in a toxic-green vest rushed up to them, shouting that filming or taking pictures here was forbidden.

All those people here were women (often with babies), children and old men over 60 mostly.

Since there was no way we could let ourselves wait for hours in all these horrific queues with Dasha Mary went off to find out if there was a way to get through for a family with a mentally disabled child, before Dasha's resource of patience, morale and strength to wait in the cold in an unfamiliar place outside was over. She went around asking if there were other people with disabled children and found several other mothers with disabled kids.

Together they approached a volunteer who also was wearing one of those bright green vests that made your eyes bleed, and they told Mary and the others to get out of the main queue. They showed us where to walk forward and around it and then wait basically closer to the crossing point itself.

We did so, feeling a little relief. More families with little

children were coming up to stand there with us.
About ten minutes later, the volunteers told us there were too many people wishing to cross the border here and that all of us with the children were to be taken to another crossing point not far from here, where chances of crossing today until dark were potentially higher.

Mary, holding Dasha by hand (and wearing the bags) and me holding the two bloody heavy suitcases, managed to squeeze ourselves into one of those buses. All the people around us also carried heavy luggage, some also had pet-carriers with cats or tiny dogs.

I remember having to stand on only one foot on the crowded bus, the other one was jammed by our suitcases, my body half bent as I was also reaching out to hold on to a rail. I held those suitcases tight so as not to let them fall on people standing next to me in a similar position. It seemed almost like one you'd expect to see in the Kama Sutra. And all that happened in the aisle of the bus.

* * *

When we arrived and got off the transport, this second place turned out to be not much better. In was about 4 pm already. This checkpoint was called Grushev. We saw one enormous line of refugees waiting to get across. The air was filled with voices, sounds of cars and buses slowly driving past.

The people were just talking, laughing, arguing, walking around, walking along the huge queue to keep themselves warm. Eating sandwiches, drinking hot tea from their thermos flasks. Children's voices were to be heard from everywhere around. It all mixed in a flow of pleasant noise that made the cold day feel lively.

Right ahead of us, in about fifty meters, there was a big white tent with generators and blankets, where people could stay for a while to get warm and have hot tea. However, these fifty meters were packed with people so tightly that you would have to actually push your way towards it. I had never seen crowds so big in my life. But then again, I had never tried to cross a border on foot with hundreds of other people seeking asylum. Everyone faces their firsts one day.

Just to remind you that I originally come from a more or less wealthy country (and once free and peaceful one), meaning Russia, had a job in Ukraine with a higher salary than a great deal of people earned in our city, without leaving my flat. A lot of people in Oleksandriia (and in Ukraine overall, unless they lived in big cities) had to regularly go to Kyiv, Russia or Poland to work at factories or do other hard manual low-qualified jobs, away from their families at least for half a year. This allowed a lot of Ukrainians also to have a high enough income to live more or less comfortable lives.

Do you see what I mean? There were no Taliban around, no

ISIS or anybody else with assault rifles taking Islamic laws to extremes in their population, no oil deposits – the main factors that usually spark wars in the developing world.

This gives me another reason to be bloody shocked by the war that broke out and the scale it had taken by that time. It began only because Putin did not want to let go of what had been one of the Russian (Soviet) colony states. I now understand what people in Chechnya felt like back in the 1990s when Yeltsin began war against them and then Putin took over from him.

* * *

Dasha soon began crying – she got tired, cold from standing on the same spot for more than an hour, and most of all she was stressed out from the pretty much eventful day.

Overloaded emotionally from an inflow of new impressions, most of which she felt as negative. Mary began explaining to people around that we had a child with a mental diagnosis. Some women around us said we should walk around the crowd and go right to the front of this massive queue. We did not have to be told twice.

You really had to be dressed warmly to stand there on the motorway for hours and hours. Many people stood there by the big white tent, as we passed it by, wrapped in blankets and holding plastic cups of steaming hot tea. We really hoped we would be able to make it across the border before the nightfall. Otherwise, it would be a hell of trouble with Dasha.

After we got to the front of the line, we had to wait there for another hour or so. There were guards standing next to a closed lifting gate right before us. People in the queue kept asking each other what was happening and how come nobody was allowed to move on. But the guards, who were wearing those vests of toxic green colour (some of them were also dressed in military uniform), just told us to keep waiting.

Cars and buses were slowly driving past towards Poland. Some of those buses let more people off, and they joined the queue, which was already enormous.

Mary and I cursed ourselves for not finding out about these buses which headed from Lviv directly to a Polish city, taking their passengers across the border without them having to get out and wait in this crowd. The biggest trouble for these people riding the buses would have been their bums and legs numb from sitting after a long journey.

A train from Lviv to Poland could have been another option – that's what a woman told Mary while we stood there waiting. But then it was a big problem to get tickets on a train like that as they get sold out instantly.

* * *

After nearly another hour passed, the guards said we should now quickly get to the next checkpoint.
People dashed forward, trying to be the first to get there and then the first to cross. We followed suit.

Good thing there was tarmac under our feet, so I could roll one of our suitcases as I ran. Dasha was running at my side, holding me firm by the hand. As we ran with other people moving fast ahead of us and keeping up on both sides, I turned back from time to time briefly, without stopping, to find Mary behind us running and rolling the second suitcase, holding her bag over her shoulder.

Dasha again began crying, getting exhausted from running and from having to keep up with me. I began to console her, trying to catch my breath at the same time. Talking while running with a suitcase, bags and a stressed child by your side does not dispose one to talking, though.

I was sweating as hell, despite the chilly March evening, and felt my already wet shirt getting stuck to my back. Pretty soon, this run to the next checkpoint began to seem endless even for me, I felt my legs growing heavy and stiff. I kept turning over my shoulder to make sure Mary was keeping up. I saw her blond head with a red scarf and tired face among the crowd running behind us.

It all ended abruptly as we finally made it to the checkpoint. I could already see flags now – Ukrainian and Polish one on a building right ahead just behind the crossroads and a little to the left within about three hundred metres – that was already Polish territory.

Now, there was also a massive queue here. Luckily, this time we stood right at the front with just a few people ahead of us. However, those who had been running behind started getting ahead of us from both sides, getting smart-arsed, hoping they would get through earlier this way. Among them were, surprisingly, a lot of young men who were not allowed to leave the country.

Thus, very soon there was again a giant crowd standing between us and the checkpoint – a big yellow tent, three times bigger than the tent with generators behind us. More than a hundred heads around you, a sea of people, sending ripples in all directions.

I could hear bursts of nervous laughter, someone complaining, women talking, children crying, their young mothers consoling them. Elderly mothers of those young mothers, consoling both them and the crying kids.

It's not like people were going to fight to get through to the yellow tent or anything like that. But anyway, it seemed that it was every man and every family for themselves now.

* * *

It began to get dark quickly. We did spend a long time there, and I will not be describing here all of what happened and how we felt as we waited. It was only our horrible experience and emotions that were overflowing us from standing there in the cold March evening that was quickly fading into night, there's no point describing it all here.

There were none of those plastic transportable toilets, so if anyone needed to "get their things done", they had to push their way out of the crowd to the field and then move back in the same manner. There was one girl under fifteen who was trying to make way back to her mother that stood near us. The girl began crying as she was unable to even push her way back through the crowd, and began calling her mother. The woman had to start shouting so that people would let her daughter squeeze back to her.

From not moving at all, Dasha began to feel cold, even wearing a winter coat. So I opened one of our suitcases, making people standing tight around us move aside a little. Rummaging through our packed stuff, I grabbed my jumper and put it on my daughter right o top of her coat. She looked a bit funny in that and under different circumstances Mary and I would have turned that into a loving joke, but not now.

At least Dasha was warm, but she was desperate to go to bed. By all means, not somewhere in the field.
Time went on and the enormous crowd around us did not move an inch. Those frontier guard officials did not even start

letting anyone through. Very soon, people started shouting and then chanting: "Let us through!" "Let us through!".

Their voices merged together, getting louder, like at "unauthorized meeting" somewhere in Moscow against Putin in the early 2010s. People were around me as far as my eyes could see in the thickening darkness, and all of them (or the majority) were chanting in an attempt to make those officials in the big, warm tent get their asses off the chairs and get down to work. It had no effect whatsoever, though.

I lost count of time but when it started getting closer to midnight, I realized we had spent there on that very spot more than four hours, but it seemed like a lot longer to me. Some sort of movement seemed to have started by the entrance of the tent. But then, the word was spread from the people in the front of the queue that the border guard officials had just finished their "four-hour break". Some were also saying that the computer system on the Polish side was down since there had been too many people getting through.

But knowing the mentality of Eastern Slavic people, I found the version with the long break more convincing. Drinking tea and resting while thousands of people were waiting outside in the cold was a typical Russian-Ukrainian, etc, behaviour of officials and bureaucrats. And it does not matter whether it is a government deputy or an official who accepts documents in a passport bureau.

At university dorms, a concierge or even a janitor often feel they have the same power as the dean and exercise it on students by not letting them back into the dorms after midnight or shouting at them for walking accidentally on the freshly washed floor.

By that time I had enough of all that. Looking at Dasha, who again was cold and knackered so much that she was falling off her feet, I told Mary we should get the hell out of this crowd. I told her we must bloody head back to the tent with a generator and blankets to spend the night there.

In the morning, I thought, we would go back to Lviv. No more crossing-border-on-foot idiocy – we should get on a direct train or bus that would take us to Poland. Believe me, waiting for two-three hours during the day at a railway station and then hopping on a train is much less inconvenient than waiting for four or twenty-four hours in the field (like many people did) ending up having to spend the night there without even a bloody sleeping bag or a blanket.

* * *

We began to elbow our way out of the crowd. That was not an easy task, considering that people standing tight next to each other were growing exhausted and angry pretty quickly now. I finally got out with the suitcases first and crossed the road to the opposite side where we could now walk back.

Ambulance carriages drove past pretty often from the side of Poland. They were striped yellow- greenish, like jackets of those volunteers at the checkpoints that we saw today.

Mary and Dasha emerged from the crowd a few minutes later, let a couple of cars slowly pass, and then joined me on the other side of the road. Parked automobiles stood next to us with nobody inside, looking dark and deserted as if they had stood there for years, dumped by their owners.

It was a great relief to have got out of that huge body of people. However, the idea of walking back even to the tent with the generator seemed crazy now – we'd rather stay here and sleep on our suitcases. If it were not for Dasha, perhaps we would have done that. We would have even stayed in the crowd, waiting for however long it would take to get through. Still I was growing very tired and indifferent to everything that was happening around me, but my knackered child did not let my mind drown in that to-hell-with-that attitude completely.

I was already going to take Dasha by the hand and start a long walk back when Mary asked me to wait and began making some phone calls. She finally managed to get an acquaintance of the pastor from Chernivtsi to drive over, pick us up and accommodate us for the night in his house not too far from where we were. The guy was already on his way to collect us.

I was again amazed at the willingness of complete strangers to be that much helpful under the circumstances. This man had dumped all he was enjoying or busy with at the moment, perhaps even a family dinner, and went off to bring people he had never seen before over to his house to put them up for the night.

However, in the end, that plan did not play out. As we waited for this guy to come over, I was walking around the car park to get warmer. Suddenly, Mary began waving at me, beckoning to come over. While I had been walking, an ambulance van stopped by and my wife and daughter were now talking to a guy wearing a volunteer's green vest – its driver.

When I approached her, she was finishing a plastic cup of hot tea and Dasha was holding a chocolate bar.
"Get in", the volunteer said in Russian. "Get in with your suitcases, quickly, come on!"

I had no clue what was going on. Mary said we would stay in their van to get warm, but then the second guy who was also wearing a volunteer's waistcoat told us, also in Russian but with a slight accent: "We will drive you across the border".

Two minutes later, we already were inside the van, warm and not quite believing that this was happening for real.
Both guys were tall, in their late forties, and only now I heard that they both spoke Russian with a specific accent.
"They must be Polish", Mary whispered to me.
They introduced themselves to us in a friendly manner. We gave them our names in return as well.
"We will drive you over to Poland", told us, the guy called Piotr (a Polish version of the name Peter).

"Do not worry now, relax", said the other one who was driving the van, called Jacek. "This difficult time of waiting is over for you". He wore glasses, the winter pull-on hat on his head was a little awry, but he gave us a friendly smile.
We were in the dimly lit rear part of the ambulance. Mary and Dasha were sitting almost in the dark, and I could hardly see my daughter's face. But she looked tired and serious, with a grown-up wise look which many autistic children often have.

Jacek started the engine and the ambulance slowly drove towards the checkpoint for cars. I did not know what they meant exactly by offering to drive us through the border, and asked if that was legal. The last thing we now wanted was to get in trouble with the border guards.

Piotr again assured us that everything would be fine. "Trust Jesus", he told us.

Jasek and Piotr exchanged a few phrases in Polish, I was only able to distinguish a couple of words that sort of sounded similar to Russian. The rest seemed like double Chinese to me, and the language sounded a little funny too.

They asked us if our passports were okay. When I told them I was Russian and then looked at each other as if they were confused for a moment and again exchanges a few phrases in Polish.

"You know, we are volunteers from a church not far from here in Poland", Piotr said finally, turning to us from his front passenger seat. "We have been driving between Poland and Ukraine over the past few days here, doing our best to help Ukrainians who are waiting to get through. We have driven some of them over the border, like you guys. But you are the first Russian we have met among them." "And this is a sign from the Lord", Jacek added, also turning to look at us for a moment, "that we must not judge those we are helping, since even a Russian living in Ukraine is fleeing this horrible war".

A few minutes later, as we approached the checkpoint with an armed guard, Piotr told us to prepare our IDs.

I gave him our passports, my Ukrainian residence permit and documents that prove Dasha is on the autistic spectrum. In theory, I was allowed to get out of Ukraine since I was a foreigner and a father of a disabled child. We were not sure, though, if it would work. Mostly, our doubts were about the part of me being Russian.

The Ukrainian guard checked our IDs carefully, took a few minutes longer to study my residence permit. Then he returned the documents to Piotr with no further questions.

"Go ahead", he said. "Move". The barrier gate slowly lifted.
"Spasibo!" Piotr thanked him in Russian, and Jacek slowly drove forward. The Polish checkpoint was about fifty meters ahead. Seeing it, I felt my heart beat faster. Okay, I thought, the Ukrainians have let me out. What if the Polish guards won't let me in? My Russian passport might be a red flag for them.

"So far, so good," Mary whispered, leaning against my shoulder. Dasha sat quietly, as if fearing that it was not going to work out, and we would have to be outside again soon, taking a long hard walk or running along with a few hundred people in the night.

The Polish officer was polite and did not look strained, like the Ukrainian one who had checked my ID, with a look that suggested he was considering whether to let me out or shoot right there.

However, after getting our IDs checked, I was invited out of the van. Piotr told me I had to go to what seemed like a kiosk illuminated inside. In the front, it looked like a desk in a bank with a clerk behind a bulletproof glass barrier. Through a small communication window, the lady officer in her late twenties took my passport and began looking at it thoroughly, as if checking every single letter in every single word there. She did the same with my Ukrainian residence permit.

She then asked me in broken English about our destination. When I told her we had no intention to stay in Poland and were only going through it to Germany, where my sister-in-law expected us, I thought I saw a hidden relief on her face. The lady-officer then remained silent for a minute or two, making notes in her laptop, the keys producing soft knocks under her fingertips. Then she finally clanged a stamp in my passport and returned it. Her wave made it clear I could get back to the van.

* * *

With the border left behind us, the van took us deeper into Poland in the dark and only the highway in front of us was visible in the thick rays of the headlights, viced in darkness on both sides. Cottages and small buildings sometimes sailed by, glancing at us with the eyes of lit windows from the dark.

I felt damn exhausted, so did Mary, and she was also holding Dasha – the girl was fast asleep, sitting next to my wife and embracing her.

This seemed like a totally miraculous rescue to me. If it had not been for it, tomorrow we would have had to go through this nightmare again, attempting to get a place on a train or bus. Plus, we would have to get to Lviv first. The city, which had also been hit my Russian missiles a few times since the war started. My wife took my hand and squeezed it softly, giving me a weary smile, happy we had finally made it.

Right after crossing the checkpoint, Jacek picked up a few other refugees on the other side of it – three old Ukrainian women. One of them in a wheelchair, so the ambulance van now was full.

For a moment, I felt like in a Hollywood film, in which illegal immigrants were being driven from Mexico to the US, a closed truck full of them, wearing ponchos and wide-brimmed hats, attempting to deceive border guards at a checkpoint somehow. And I was truly grateful to these two guys, who got us out of that nightmare.

As we drove on, Piotr and Jacek told us it was finally over, we were now safe, and they would drive us to a place where we could stay for the night.

They had a pile of Bibles with them in the back of the van and gave all of us a copy. Mary and I were still very much impressed by the quick happy ending, so the least we could do to thank these guys was to accept their Bibles.

One of the old ladies carefully but confidently began a theological dispute with Piotr, when he offered her a Bible as a present. Half joking, half serious, she started praising the Christian Orthodox church as opposed to Western versions of Christianity and its followers – Catholics, Baptists, Evangelists, etc. But Piotr just gave her a big, hearty smile as if it did not matter to him at all.

MEN LEAVING UKRAINE LEGALLY AND ILLEGALLY

Before we move on, I need to tell you that even though men are not allowed to leave Ukraine now that the country is engaged in war, there are still ways – legal and not quite – that let them do that.

I will briefly tell you about these "white" and "grey" schemes because this adds another shade to the whole picture I'm trying to paint for you in this book.

The first category of men who can legally get out of Ukraine during the war now are fathers. These are the cases when parenthood can literally save your life, so to say. Especially if you have three or more children.

So, you can leave Ukraine as a father of a child with a (mental) disability, children with hard or rare diseases, as well as with children with delays in mental development.

A man can cross the border if he alone is bringing up a child under eighteen. They must have the relevant paperwork to prove that. Men can leave Ukraine if they are providing for three or more underage children, even kids from different marriages. But then again – they need documentary proofs, like birth certificates, etc.

A husband can also leave Ukraine with his family if he and his wife have two children, and she is pregnant with the third one, but it only works if she is due in one or two months. The term of pregnancy should be proved by a paper from the doctor. Well, certainly it needs to be obvious by the size of the belly too.

The next category are "non-effective", i.e. those men who have proved they are not in condition for actual military service due to their age, illness or for other reasons. Those who are non-effective temporarily (up to a period of six months) can also use this method.

Men who accompany a disabled relative abroad, men who have disabilities themselves – mental or physical ones – are also permitted to leave Ukraine as long as they can prove their diagnosis with proper medical paperwork. Wounded soldiers may legally go abroad to receive medical treatment.

There is also a category of workers who can cross the border if they are hired by an international vessel, drivers who are delivering humanitarian aid, etc.

Now, here's the most interesting part. Many young men are using fake documentation to fit into one of the categories I mentioned above to escape from the country. Mostly these are people who have not served in the army before, who are not psychologically ready to take part in the war and basically would be quickly killed during the very first attack. I know one guy in person who had done that – left Ukraine on a false pretext. A friend of my wife's was the second guy who managed to get out of the war-struck country using fake documents that I know of.

The first guy, Arthur, is my former colleague. We shared an office in a small IT company seven years ago. He is fluent in several languages – German, English and Arabic. He managed to flee to Romania with fake documentation which stated he was accompanying a sick relative abroad. The "relative" came with him. This cost Arthur several thousand dollars. When I asked him, he said that he had to leave Ukraine to keep his job with the American company where he works as a technical writer.

The company now does not allow anyone to access its servers from inside Ukraine, so he and many of his colleagues had to find a way to leave for a EU country. He was not afraid of getting hit by a Russian rocket in his flat, since the probability of that is too low, he reckoned.

And he was able to get himself an exemption from military service to avoid being thrown into a hot spot somewhere in the South-East of the country. If it had not been for a risk of losing his job, he would have stayed in Kyiv.

SHORT STAY IN POLAND

Jacek and Piotr told us first they would drive us to their church, which had been converted into a refugee camp. However, after making a phone call, they told us with a regret that the place had been full by now.

I watched and listened to all of that, half dozing, still unable to grasp that the hell with crossing the border had all of a sudden ended so easily. Piotr again began dialling a number on his mobile, spoke to somebody in Polish. A minute later, he told us all in the van that another refugee camp would happily admit us right now.

As we drove along a quiet road for a while, I watched an unknown town outside the window. It was wrapped in darkness, with a lit window or a street lamp-post sometimes emerging and then dissolving in the night again.

Then the ambulance took a turn and soon pulled up. As we all got out, and I took our stuff out of the van, Piotr showed us the school building. "Our church is over there," he said, pointing at a building just across the road. "Very nice", that was all I managed to say to that then.

Piotr and Jacek led the way. It was a spacious school with several floors, nice looking from inside.

Two women met us, they seemed to be local teachers to me, greeting us with warm and welcoming smiles. They spoke Polish to us and I could not understand anything, but just occasionally a word or two that sounded a little familiar slipped in their speech. The language sounded as a strange version of Russian, recognizable as a Slavic language to me but otherwise totally incomprehensible.

The young teacher took us to the second floor along half-dim corridors and showed us into the huge school gym. It was brightly lit with big lights under the high ceiling. And there were quite a lot of people already in it – mattresses lay by the walls on all the four sides, mattresses lay in the middle of the gym in lines too. I saw young and elderly women with children, mostly very young, toddlers, but some were in their early teens.

The children were quietly playing, despite the fact that it was nearly midnight already, their mothers just resting or chattering. It seemed they did not mix at this late time – everyone was sitting on their mattresses, only some of the kids playing together. I saw a couple of big plastic boxes full of what I thought was donated toys. Those were good for the children, keeping them happy and busy and letting their mothers get some rest.

The teacher kindly showed us several free mattresses lying next to each other, telling us we could choose where to sleep. They had pillows, bedding and blankets on them.
I picked two at the far wall, right inside the football gate. Partly because there were two sockets here, and also this way we could be a little on our own – there was no space for other mattresses on either side near us.

Also, from here the whole gym could be observed easily. This football gate made me feel like we had scored a hard goal by making it here after all, while other refugees at the border

checkpoint tonight were not so lucky, unfortunately. I felt sympathy for them, and so I hoped they would finally make it to Poland in the morning and would be able to rest before moving on or stay here if they wished so.
It was warm here, the place much roomier than in the Chernivtsi church.

After we left our stuff by the beds, we followed the teacher back into the long corridor and then into the school canteen on the same floor. There were two lines of tables made of desks pulled together. By the walls stood desks with piles of plastic plates and cups, bottles of water, packets of coffee, tea, milk, spoons, knives and forks on them.

The room was mostly empty, except for just a few people at the table eating in a slow, relaxed manner, and those who had just finished their meals – probably also refugees who had just arrived. Some of them were quietly talking, some were staring blankly into the wall, sipping tea or juice from plastic cups.

A lady in the kitchen poured us some soup from a big, half-empty casserole. It looked like a big metallic cylinder with handles on both sides. We made a sandwich for Dasha, as she is not keen on soups. Autistic people can be very choosy with food, refusing to even try anything they had never eaten before.

The soup was dark red. As I stirred it with a tablespoon, I saw olives, vegetables and bits of small sausages emerge onto the surface. The soup tasted nice, albeit a little fatty and spicy. I had never eaten anything like this before, but then I had never been much interested in Polish cuisine. I wish I had taken some photos there, but it did not seem appropriate at that moment. Besides, back then, I did not plan to write this book.

* * *

That night we slept well, feeling completely relaxed and secure. The feeling that we were finally out of the dangerous ground swept over me. Back in Ukraine, even its safest Western part, where we had briefly stayed, could stop being safe at any time. This is basically what indeed happened half a year later.

In the morning, I went out of the gym to explore the vicinities, so to speak. There were two school shower rooms on our floor – one for men and one for women, each room containing several shower booths with doors that locked from inside. In the corridor, stood tables with plenty of stuff for washing and keeping self-hygiene – bottles of shampoo, shower gel, various sorts of creams, liquid soap, soap in bars, liners, toothpaste, tooth brushes, plastic packets of toilet paper, etc.

Mary spent the day talking to the other refugees, listening to their stories and sharing ours. Dasha made friends with a Ukrainian girl two years her junior, and they were playing together picking some toys from a big plastic box in the gym.

At breakfast, we saw our rescuers – apparently, they had slept right there in the school as well, and now they were drinking coffee. The asked us if we did not mind having a photo taken together with them. I thought it would be a great idea. Then Piotr sent me that photo via Messenger.

I found out the name of the town we were in – Lubaczow. Later on, I checked out the map in Google – the place was really close to the border with Ukraine – the checkpoint in Grushev, where Piotr and Jacek picked us up.

One of the volunteers in the kitchen was a French guy named Jean. His English was perfect, so we were able to chat easily.

Jean was in his early thirties. He told me he lived in Krakow or some other big city in Poland, the name slips my memory now, but when the war started and refugees began flowing through the border, he immediately came over to offer his help as a volunteer.

This guy looked like a classic hippy to me – a longish trimmed beard, plain (even worn out a bit) tee-shirt, shorts, and sandals on his feet. He had an old model of an iPhone. I noticed that all volunteers at that refugee camp-turned school were dressed simply and did not wear posh, expensive looking clothes.

I did not pay attention to it back then, thinking that this is common in the Western countries. In Russia, Ukraine, Belarus and other post Soviet places the mentality in this respect is different. People try to dress as best as they can to show that they can afford it. And if it is an iPhone, it has to be of the latest model. Even if they spend the last of their money on it or take a bank loan to buy one to show off to colleagues in the office. Those with old ones are considered close to being big losers.

But then I read a book written by a refugee who came as a ten year-old with her mother and younger brother from Iran back in the late 1980s. She wrote that after she and her family had passed through various refugee camps, staying there sometimes for months, getting pushed from one country to another, she learned English and finally settled in the USA.

Years later, she began volunteering in refugee camps too, giving away food and clothes to her former countrymen who fled the regime in Iran, she wanted to make the whole process as less stressful for those refugees as she could.

When helping refugees, that author of the book put on plain and even old clothes deliberately, like creased or stained tee-shirts and jeans, in order to look as close to the refugees as she could. They were already under huge stress, fleeing their country, often with no spare clothes, almost or no money at all, many of them with children and with foggy prospects of the future in the new place.

Having to accept basic things like food and clothes was a big blow to their dignity, especially for those who used to live a great life back in Iran and had a rich house, lots of money, social status, etc. I did not feel this way, but still I was grateful to all the volunteers we met in Ukraine, Poland and later in Germany for treating us and other refugees with respect.

I guess this whole situation has made me change my attitude towards refugees. You know, in Russia people are quite harsh to them or at least they are indifferent.

When I read posts of bloggers with big audiences and famous writers on Russian social media in the past when they shared their take on refugees fleeing from Syria, Africa, Iran, etc, to Europe, their posts were pretty cruel. They wrote that those people are extra mouths to feed, while the EU is not having its best times, economies of many countries are degrading, etc.

The message from those thought leaders was that those refugees should stay where they are, since if they keep flowing into Europe, the whole EU will go bankrupt soon.

What is more, Russia would never accept any, they fiercely claimed. To be honest, I did not care much about those poor people seeking asylum back then either. It was about 7–8 years ago. But now, that I myself got into these shoes, I feel sympathy for them. I think that thousands of Russians who are on the run from the war, leaving Russia for whatever destination they can find, now feel the same. I guess, some things, especially in one's mind, can be changed only in the hard way.

Here's the last thing I'd like to mention here. The day when we stood in that huge crowd of refugees waiting to cross the border was March 8. The International Women's Day in the post-Soviet space. Well, for sure it is in Russia, Ukraine and Belarus. Women get flowers and presents on that day from their husbands, fathers and sons.

They are also relieved of all the housework they usually do, since on that day the men take it over from them. This was the worst ever March 8 my wife has ever had in her life, she told me later. And the one she will remember too well for the rest of it.

BRIEF HISTORICAL JOURNEY ON RUSSIAN-POLISH RELATIONS

Now prepare for a short historical journey. It sheds some light on the true reason why Russia started the war against Ukraine, on its current revival of the "Iron Curtain" and Putin longing for the "Great Russia of the Past".

Russia and Poland have a long history of a "hard relationship". Did you know that there was a short period in the not so distant past, when Polish troops entered Moscow and occupied it for two years? That was during the Russian-Polish war that began in 1609 and ended in 1618.

That was a period known as The Time of Troubles in the Russian history, when an impostor (the second one already), (known as Lzhe-Dmitry 2 – False Dmitry 2) pretending to be the son of the passed away tsar Ivan The Terrible, Dmitry wanted to seize the throne in Russia with his army. The actual Dmitry was killed as a result of a conspiracy at the age of 8, almost 20 years before False-Dmitry 2 emerged. I will not bore you with his story, nor with the fact that there were also False-Dmitry 1 and False- Dmitry-3. It is not relevant to this story.

Anyway, in order to protect Moscow and the government that consisted of high-ranking noblemen in power (the boyars), they invited Polish-Lithuanian troops to enter Moscow in 1610. Polish prince Władysław IV Vasa was elevated to the Russian throne temporarily to keep it safe until the new head of the state would take over from him. The Polish-Lithuanian military station in Moscow consisted of approximately 6,000 armoured and cavalry soldiers and about 1,200 infantrymen. Apparently, Władysław was happy to sit on the Russian throne and unwilling to let it go. The Polish soldiers behaved in Moscow as if they were the bosses in the captured city. As a result, fights between the Polish and Muscovites took place often, in which many of the latter were killed.

In 1611, The First People's Militia (folk self-organized troops) made up of Moscow dwellers attacked the Polish military. The invaders set Moscow on fire, which lasted for about three days. The fires and the Poles killed slightly under ten thousand Muscovites back then. That was the first time Moscow was ever set on fire. The second one was during the war of Russia against Napoleon, when the warlord Kutuzov (he had a recognizable feature – only one eye and a patch on the other one) ordered to set Moscow on fire as Russians retreated from it, so as not to leave anything to the tired and battered French army.

Finally, in November 1612, the Militia spearheaded by a respectable merchant Minin and prince Pozharsky freed Moscow. There is a famous monument to these two guys in the Red Square near St. Basil's Cathedral. The day when Moscow was freed from the Poles was presumably November 4, it is now celebrated in Russia as "The Day of National Unity".

However, there used to be another national holiday in the first week of November that existed during the Soviet Union times and was eliminated after the USSR collapse. It was November 7, the day of the October Revolution of 1917. It was October 25 or November 7 (new style). The "birthday" of the USSR.

The "October Revolution Day" was renamed "The Day of Accord and Reconciliation" in 1996, and it carried that title until 2004. Then the name of this habitual holiday was changed into "The Day of National Unity", which was sort of commemorating the victory of the Militia over the Poles in 1612.

"The Day of Accord and Reconciliation" name instead of "Day of the Great October Socialist Revolution" was taken rather sceptically by the older generation who had celebrated the 1917 Revolution Day all their lives and by many middle-aged people who had grown up with it too.

Back in the late 1990s, with less than a decade away from the crash of the Soviet Empire, the spirit of communism was still rather strong in Russia with the Communist Party holding one of the few leading positions in the government.

Long after the victory over the Poles, Napoleon conquered Poland and added its army to his own huge army in an attempt to invade the Russian Empire. He lost that war and since then part of Poland belonged to Russia until after WW1. In 1918, when Poland regained independence, it managed to recover its lands from Russia.

SOVIET INVASION OF EASTERN POLAND

In 1939, the USSR and the Nazi Reich signed a treaty known as the Molotov-Ribbentrop Pact. The official title of it was "Treaty of Non-Aggression between Germany and the Union of Soviet Socialist Republics". Unofficially it was called the Stalin-Hitler Pact, Nazi-Soviet Alliance, etc. Based on this document, the USSR and Hitler's Reich vowed they would not attack each other and would not support each other's enemies should the Reich or the USSR become involved in war with "a third party country". A secret additional agreement to this document stated that Nazis and the USSR would share Poland and the Baltic States between each other – the Eastern Europe, basically. Lithuania, Eastern Poland, Estonia, Finland and Bessarabia (now parts of Bessarabia belong to West and South-West Ukraine and Moldova) were included in the sphere of interests of Stalin and the USSR.

On September 1, 1939, Hitler's army invaded the Western Poland, thus starting WW2.

Soviet troops did the same on September 17, entering Poland from the East. The concerns about ethnic Ukrainians and Belorussians were used by the USSR as an official reason for invading the Polish lands. This is pretty similar to the major official pretext of "defending ethnic Russians" in the East of Ukraine in the current war, as you can see. In 1945, after the war was won by the USSR and its allies, the territories in the Western Poland which had been annexed by Hitler, were returned to Poland by Stalin.

There's no need to recall all the historic details here, I'm not writing a book on history, so I'm giving you only basic facts necessary for understanding what is happening now.

Thus, the chain of historical events looks ironically curious – first Poland invaded Moscow and Russia, then the USSR invaded Poland. And now Poland, well remembering the latter fact, is helping Ukraine in the war by providing weapons to its army and accepting thousands of refugees. Besides, Poland is spreading anti-Putin rhetoric.

In return, Russian propagandists (anti-Putin people in Russia call them "propagandons" – a blend of the words "propaganda" and "condoms" – "propacondoms" in English, if you wish) are threatening that the first thing Russia will do after defeating Ukraine is taking the Eastern part of Poland back, as well as continue to return its former Baltic territories. In particular, those include Transnistria – now it is part of Moldova that wants to separate and join Russia.

Many Z-bloggers are talking about that on social media as well, already making predictions of how Russia will move on to recapture the Czech Republic, Lithuania, Estonia, and other lands that belonged to it during the Soviet times. Minister of Foreign Affairs Lavrov or Putin's press-secretary Peskov are not giving any comments on that.

As another option, less realistic one hopefully, Russian "propagandons" are just threatening Poland with nuclear strikes during their highly rated TV shows.

GOODBYE, POLAND. "RUSSIAN WARSHIP" MEME

We did not stay in the Polish camp for long. During the day after the night when we had arrived, we just relaxed, lying on our mattresses inside the football gate in the gym, reading news on Telegram or texting to friends in Ukraine to ask how they were doing and tell them that we were okay, where we were now, etc. Mary kept telling her friends about crossing the border – women are more emotional, so she felt an urge to get this out of herself and share with other women to get an emotional response from them. Dasha made friends with a Ukrainian girl who was a couple of years younger. They played together, riding toy cars, taking turns to run ahead and pull each other's tiny car by a rope to get it going.

One of the teachers of the school walked around gathering information from the refugees, such as if they had any particular destination in Poland, if they wanted to stay in the country but had no friends or relatives and needed help with accommodation. When she came up to us, we told her we wanted to move on to Germany, Munich.

This teacher smiled at everybody when talking to them, but when she heard that we were not planning to stay in Poland, her smile just for a moment seemed a little happier. You can easily understand these people – lots of refugees had already come to Poland. A lot of them wanted to stay, not knowing if they would be able to live in Germany or other countries of Western Europe, non- Slavic ones. For us, people from the former USSR, it is a lot easier to adapt in Poland or the Baltic States, mostly because there is not such a big difference in mentality as there is with Germans. Besides, nearly in all these countries, people speak and understand Russian.

Back to Poland. There had been quite a lot of Ukrainians there before the war, as many simply came over to work at factories and in shops, doing manual or low-qualified jobs. Many also decided to emigrate there.

Anyway, later that day Jean came up to me, saying that their driver would take us to the train station in the nearby city. From there, he said, we would be able to get a train straight to Germany. We do not even have to pay for train tickets, he told us, just need to show our Ukrainian IDs at the ticket office, and they would give us a free ride.

That was good to know since we did not have any local currency (Zloty). Earlier that day, I tried to get Mary and Dasha out for a walk just to see what this town of Lubaczow looked like. To see what Poland looks like in general. But Mary convinced me that walking around a town as a tourist (rather than an asylum seeker) on a cold day in March without having money even to buy a coffee in a café when you feel like resting was not the best idea. So, when the evening came, we got into the van with about five other women. Some of them were travelling with children about three to five years old. Luckily, the little Ukrainians were quiet – probably still shocked from spending long hours on the border before finally crossing it.

Unlike Russian and Ukrainian roads, in Poland they are built well, and the tarmac does not get changed once a year to steal the money from the city budget (as it is usually done in Russia). This means there are no or almost no pits, so none of the children felt sick.

The ride to the nearby city took less than an hour. The driver spoke poor English. Besides, I was naive to think that someone from the school would come along to help us get a train to Germany. Explain things in Polish to the ticket sellers for us, etc. That expectation did not come true.

Well, they had already done more than enough: provided us with sleeping places and meals in their camp, which even had a weak Wi-Fi signal. After all, I thought that with my knowledge of English (the only person among us in the van who had it, though) we would manage somehow.

Back in 2000, when I was nineteen and enjoyed my third year at university, I went to Bangor in North Wales for a month for a summer English course. That was the first time I had left Russia ever.

My plane landed in Manchester. From there I managed to get to Bangor, asking local people for directions (happy I was able to understand the local accent) from the airport to the train station, took all the changes on all trains without accidentally heading off to the North Pole or some other wrong destination. So, I thought getting train tickets from Poland to Germany should be easy, as long as people in the station spoke at least a bit of English.

These days, English is like Latin in the days of the Roman Empire. Nature absorbs vacuum – once culturally, educationally and military superior Romans turned into a friendly harmless nation that lives off tourism, ancient ruins and pizza.

Barbarians, whom Roman legions used to fight in the woods and swamps of the British Islands, have spread their language modified after centuries and full of Latinisms around nearly the whole planet, replacing lingua latina. Later on, the USA took over with its military, strong economy (a lot stronger than now, though) and Hollywood, spreading English even wider and deeper. That was a scale of cultural dominance Caesars could not see in their wet dreams.

Unlike inflected Latin, English is analytic, it is much easier to learn and speak (I don't want to exhaust you with linguistic details), which, aside from other factors, ensured its place as the global language.

Wherever you go, educated and forward-minded people, especially young ones, speak fluent English, you can ask them for directions in the street when you feel you got lost in the labyrinth chased by the Minotaur. You can buy clothes or breakfast in a café from them. English works like Ariadne's thread.

Otherwise, you have to run down to a mixture of local and English vocabulary, gestures, mime and Russian idioms rich in f*** words. By the way, in the former USSR countries, Russian works almost in the same way. Except it is now hated in Ukraine.

* * *

During the ride, Mary and the other women began chatting, asking each other where they were going, how long they had been in the camp, and stuff like that. So now, we all headed towards the station as a group, feeling that sticking together for now was reasonable in all aspects.

For some reason, this feeling of national unity fails to work in

Germany, though – when Ukrainians (or any Russian-speaking people) hear each other in the street, they make stone-like faces and pretend not to notice each other unless their lives are in danger.

The driver let us off at the small train station, brightly lit inside, helped us take our suitcases from the back of the van. Then he said goodbye in Polish and drove off.

In the station, we saw volunteers in the same toxic green waistcoats as before. Speaking Russian with an accent, they told us that the next train to Dresden (that's already Germany) would be at about 1 a.m. This would mean about four hours of waiting.

In the meantime, they took us to the second floor into a big hall. By the walls there were mattresses with blankets on the floor. We were welcome to sleep there and then get on that night train or wait until the morning – there would be more trains and buses heading for Germany too.

Mary talked to the others, and we told the volunteers that we'd rather get on the night train. They then went off downstairs, leaving us in that empty hall. It looked like they were building something in it, a restaurant was my guess – the walls, the floor and the ceiling were bare concrete. The decoration unfinished (or not even started properly, I'd say), the big pipes in the corners wrapped in tinfoil. The lights under the ceiling were too bright for sleeping under them, so we switched them off, and lay down on the mattresses. Dasha fell asleep at once, Mary and some of the other women continued to chat in whisper. Light was now just coming down from under the entrance door.

I went down to the first floor of the station and found my way to the restroom. The first thing that got my attention inside a toilet cabin was a "Putin, fuck off" graffiti written in black marker on the door. It was in Polish, but since the language is related to mine, I was able to understand that one easily.

This reminded me of a now famous case that occurred during the early days of the war.

A Ukrainian military base was located on the Serpent Island in the Black Sea. In April 2022, a Russian battleship approached it and a Russian sailor said in the megaphone: "Serpent Island! This is a Russian warship! I suggest you lay down your weapons and surrender your position. Nobody will get hurt! Do you copy."

There was a short silence. Then a response came from the base on the island, also loudly, as a soldier spoke through a megaphone: "Russian warship! Go fuck yourself!"

The Russians attacked. Some of the Ukrainian soldiers were killed, the others were taken captive. Later on, Russians withdrew from that island and the Ukrainian army got their soldiers back through a captives' exchange. However, that phrase "Russian warship, go fuck yourself" became a meme in Ukraine used when talking about the Russian invaders and later turned into a meme.

People started calling them "Ruscists" (pronounced as "rushists") – a made-up word from "Russian" and "fascist". Before that, this word for the first time was used in Georgia, when the Russian army attacked it in August 2008. This was the time when Putin "took a break" after his second presidential term and Dmitry Medvedev became his puppet president.

Currently, Medvedev is Deputy Chairman of the Security

Council of Russia. On his Telegram channel, he keeps saying that Russia is "fighting demons from the West", draws parallels to the Soviet Union fighting in WW2 and is threatening the West with nukes for supporting the "Nazi regime" in Ukraine, while Russia is fighting its "holy patriotic war" against it.

In Chernivtsi, we saw this slogan about the Russian warship printed on billboards with a ship drawn there too. I mean specially created billboards, not graffiti written on top of old ones.

Ukrainian creatives took it a little further and made billboards that said "Russian tank/soldier/plane, etc – go fuck yourself". Later on, an official stamp was issued by the Post of Ukraine with the same picture and slogan. In this war, I expect, every Ukrainian began collecting those stamps even if they had never done it before.

* * *

Eventually, we never spent the night on the mattresses on the concrete floor of that construction site.

As I began to doze off at about midnight and so did my family and the women around us, the volunteers walked in with a young woman that we had not seen with them when we first arrived.

She told us in natural Russian that there is a bus waiting outside to pick us up and transport us and other refugees over to Germany. A discussion on whether we should keep waiting for the train until the morning or to get up now (sacrificing a few hours of more or less comfortable sleep here) and ride that bus during the night took about three minutes.

Pulling our suitcases along, we walked downstairs to get on that bus. The joyful feeling that we would soon reach our destination and then have no more fugitive travelling to do swept over me.

PART 2

GERMAN LANGUAGE, LONG TIME NO HEAR

Compared to all the travels we had undertaken since the war began, this bus ride was the easiest and the most comfortable of all. Lots of space, and comfortable seats, which could be pushed back so you can take a nap. This was a proper bus for long-distance travel, which means it even had a toilet.

But above all, there was no threat that a rocket would hit us or the bus would be shot at by Russian soldiers.

The driver looked like a good-natured guy, in his fifties, named Klaus. He did not speak English or Russian because he was German. So I had to brush up on my German a little earlier than I planned to. I really felt like calling him "Opa Klaus". "Opa" is the German for "granddad".

Klaus kindly showed us a mini-fridge in the front end of the bus, to the right of the steering wheel, right near the glove box, also built into the dashboard. It was actually like a glove box but went deep to the bottom. There were small plastic bags of sliced ham and cheese in them. On a couple of the front seats the driver showed us a few packs of sliced toast bread, next to it I found packs of bottled water, lemonade, and biscuits.

The last time I tried to speak German was during my exams at university about twenty years ago. Actually, I did not even pretend to speak it, I recited a topic in German that I had had to learn off by heart. Among these topics were "My Family", "My Hobby", "My favourite German writer", "Berlin – the capital of Germany", etc. Typical old-school method in Russia of making students learn at least this tiny bit of a language.

Unlike English, I had trouble with my German and I thought I would need it only to pass my exams and get my teacher's diploma. That's funny but my diploma indeed says that I am a school teacher of English and *German*.

I did spend about ten years teaching English on language courses in Moscow and Kyiv but I always said that German was my second language at uni and everybody understood that I did not succeed in it. In Russia, the second language is most often a burden and a pain in the neck when you major in a different one, like English. With rare exceptions, of course, but that was the case for me or my classmates.
We did our best to focus on English and subjects like Methodology of Teaching, so we had to do at least satisfactorily in our German exams, to avoid getting our diplomas ruined with C marks.

I did not even like German back then. Otherwise, perhaps I would have done better at it. But I loved English and was motivated to learn it. Besides, learning a language with noun cases (four of them) where all parts of a sentence, even pronouns, and articles, must agree with each other after learning English, which was easy-peasy compared to that, was pretty hard and totally discouraging.

Now, riding that bus with my wife, daughter, and a few other Ukrainian women, I was trying hard to recall all my German I could use in the current situation. When it comes to English, everyone who did it at school in Russia/Ukraine (the majority of people), can still tell you that "London iz ze capitel ov Greit Brittan" with a heavy accent. But I did not even know how to say that Berlin is the capital of Germany, whoops.

There are a few German words and phrases that many Russians know and use jokingly or sarcastically – they have to do with WW2, contemporary music, and..oh...
German adult films.

Among them are these: "Ja-ja! Das ist fantastisch!", "Jawohl, mein Führer", "Gut!", etc. Also, music fans love the German band Rammstein ("Du hast mich"). Richard Wagner's "Ride of the Valkyries" is well-known thanks to the "Apocalypse Now" movie and Russians have also borrowed the German "Fest" word to add to the titles of multiple local festivals that may involve drinking beer but are not limited to that.

Now, I had to look up a few words, like ham and cheese ("Wurst" and "Käse"), on the Internet – thank God for the Google Translator app. When I worked in Kyiv, translating documents, I sometimes used it and laughed out loud abou the way it translated English into Russian. But eight or nine years have passed since then, so maybe Google used that time to make some radical improvements.

Thus, using German grammar whose bits I managed to summon in my memory and the translator's app I managed to ask the driver if it was okay for us to make sandwiches and where the toilet was – these two fundamental needs were covered, hurray. The toilet was built into the lower part of the bus and you walked past it as you got on through the door in the middle of the vehicle.

There was also a portable dispenser with hot water, packets of coffee and small portions of cream, plastic cups, and spoons – yahoo! Coffee was something I really felt like but I wanted to have it a bit later – after a few hours passed and we drove into the dawn of the next day. I don't usually drink instant coffee for medical reasons but this time I made an exception.

I really felt like a big adventure was beginning. Mary had never left Ukraine before, or rather, she had never been outside the territory of the former Soviet Union – she visited me in Moscow when she was pregnant and then a few years later she went to Belarus with a friend when her family attempted to move there in search of a better life. They came back pretty quickly, though.

As for me, not only did I have vast experience dealing with foreigners, mainly students in their twenties from the UK (elderly people too) who came over to Russia to study Russian, but also lived in North Wales for a month with a host family. For me, our current trip seemed like fun, I was anticipating a lot of interesting and exciting stuff to happen in the near future as we would arrive in Germany and settle there somehow.

Mary seemed a little nervous but later on, she told me she was VERY bloody nervous, because of this new experience, because she did not speak or understand English, let alone German, and overall she was really worried about the future.

Dasha slept for a few hours in her seat next to her but then as the morning arrived, she woke up and gladly ate a sandwich I made for her. She spent the rest of the trip looking out of the window with curiosity in her pretty grey eyes.

I looked at my wife and said jokingly with a proud smile: "See, what a universal husband you have? When we need German, I can actually speak a bit of it. Go on, tell me it's great to have me around".

Mary gave me an ironic and half-sarcastic look and said: "I'll say you should have studied it better at uni".

* * *

As Klaus drove on, the sun kept shining in the sky, making our first day out of the refugee camp feel welcoming as we looked forward to reaching our destination. I normally get adapted quickly and so I felt fine sleeping on mattresses in the gym in that Polish school. However, now that the prospect of sleeping on a proper bed appeared ahead of us, I was also looking forward to finally rolling into Germany.

We were headed for my wife's half-sister Kate's place. Mary made an audio call with her via Instagram and then gave the phone to the driver. Klaus had a few words with her in German and then she told me that he would drop us off at Dresden.

From there, we were to catch a train to Munich – this is where Kate would pick us up and take us to her flat in the suburbs of the city. In short, we would end up in Bavaria – land in the South of Germany famous for the German Alps, same-name football club, and a great variety of beer.

On the phone, Kate told us we would get free train tickets to our destination. This is what all those who flee from Ukraine get as they enter the country. Kate has been living in Germany for about 7-8 years now, she speaks fluent German, has graduated here, and is working in the IT sphere now.

When we arrived, during the first year she helped us a lot with finding out about the local rules and laws, such as whether we have to wear masks on public transport; she made all the phone calls and wrote emails to the authorities on our behalf. But the most important thing is that she used local chats in Telegram and found a volunteer who agreed to accommodate us for a while.

I spent another couple of hours on the bus drowsing, while, as if through a thick layer of cotton, I could distantly hear Mary playing with Dasha and talking to the other Ukrainian women in the bus. Then Mary woke me up as Klaus pulled off at the Dresden central railway station - "Hauptbahnhof" in German.

That was one of the first words that all three of us picked up soon on arrival.

We got off, heartily thanking the driver and waving goodbye to the Ukrainians who were headed for the final destination of the bus – a city further in the centre of Germany, I can't remember the name, where they would be admitted to a refugee camp.

There they would wait for their temporary residence permit to be made and then would be transferred to a proper accommodation – either with a volunteer host family or the one which would be paid for by the state. As I found out later, that can take weeks or even months as back then there was an inflow of Ukrainians to Bavaria.

Imagine weeks or months having to sleep on a camp bed or a mattress on the floor in a room or gym with another twenty or thirty people. Many are staying there with little children, elderly (grand) parents, and often with their pets.

Unlike refugees from other troubled countries (with all due respect to them), who fled from political and religious regimes, Ukrainians were not prepared for that war psychologically. Ukraine is a country on the territory of Europe and the last war it fought was WW2.

People there had all lived if not easy, then at least more or less happy lives. They are fleeing not because of the religious fanaticism of the government. They are not fleeing from a war that has been going on for dozens of years just with short breaks for peace talks.

They are fleeing from a war initiated by a neighbour state together with whom they had won WW2 and who have always been friendly to each other, with mutual strong ties of all kinds on both sides. This war came like a bolt out of the blue. Something that no one in Ukraine could believe or take rumours of it coming up soon seriously before it actually happened.

They will remember February 24 from now on as the day when Russian missiles struck their country at 4 a.m., hitting the capital and major cities in the East. This is similar to what Nazi Germany did to the Soviet Union on June 22, 1941.

In this regard, Ukrainians are now likening Putin to Hitler, calling him "Putler". Many of them have been calling him that since 2014 actually, when Crimea was annexed on the pretext of a referendum and the separatist war in the Donbas followed.

TRAIN RIDE TO MUNICH

In the ticket office at the station in Dresden, they gave us a paper saying that the three of us could ride a train free of charge. Our itinerary included a stopover in Leipzig to change for another train that would take us to Munich.

The cashier spoke English, so we showed her our Ukrainian passports and my residence permit.

Whenever I showed the plastic card of my Ukrainian ID in Germany, they never even looked askance at me after reading "Russian Federation" in the space with my citizenship. There is a Ukrainian flag at the top of the card and that seems enough here for everybody. Or maybe they just do not bother to look a little lower to read about my native country.

Just so you understand, it is not that I want to give up my Russian citizenship. I am strongly against this war, but there are plenty of other Russians who are against it too: public figures, celebrities, and average citizens. Some of them fled, especially celebrities, and kept voicing their anti-Putin position from abroad out load. Others, those who cannot afford to leave or have sick elderly relatives to look after, stay in Russia and just keep silent to stay out of prison and avoid a baton penetrating their back passage at the police station.

But I hate explaining to everyone that I am Russian who has lived for ten years in Ukraine, have a family there, and a ten-year residence permit. So whenever I meet any Ukrainians here when I'm with my wife or daughter, I just tell them "We are from Ukraine too", should they ask. If I hear somebody speaking Russian with a Ukrainian accent on public transport and I'm alone at that moment, I simply keep reading my book or watching the scenery behind the window.

I have noticed, by the way, that many Ukrainians are doing the same thing. Especially in a supermarket when standing in a queue at the checkout. They hear people behind them speaking Russian or Ukrainian but never even say a word, not even just to let you know they come from the same place and are fleeing from the same bloody war.

* * *

Anyway, in Dresden, we got on a big double-decker train, I think it was white colour and had ICE written on it. "ICE" on trains stands for "InterCity Express". These trains connect all major cities in Germany and they are pretty fast ones. I will tell you more about our experience with German trains and especially the Munich underground later. I promise it will be "fun", so stay tuned.

The conductor checked our paper from the ticket office, and looked at our IDs, it was all neat. No questions came from her, so we sat back in the comfortable seats, watching the scenery flash past outside the window.

About fifteen minutes later, a train attendant offered us a menu. After a night spent on the bus, it was nice to have a cup of hot coffee and a sandwich.

To my surprise, they did not charge us anything, although we had a bit of money on us, so we were prepared to pay. That was a nice way to welcome refugees from Ukraine. Many were coming with no cash at all, or having only hryvnyas (UAH) on them, so these free rides to refugee camps and free meals on trains were very much appreciated.

Unlike Russia or Ukraine, here all staff on trains are friendly, and they smile at you. At least that was our first impression.

* * *

Mary sent a message to Kate to let her know that we were on our way and would be at Munich Central Station in several hours. We were actually very lucky to have someone in Germany who would let us stay in their spare room at least for a few days – a little nervous after leaving the war- struck country, a little bloody nervous about how you would be able to settle in the new place, deal with all the bureaucracy when your knowledge of German hardly surpasses zero and you can use only your English. On the other hand, the majority of other refugees cannot even speak English, so I was lucky. In the land of the blind, the one-eyed man is king, as the saying goes.

Having my wife's close relative here and the social payouts offered were the two main reasons why we decided to make this long, hard journey. Another option we had thought of was Poland but without any friends or relatives there it would have been very difficult (Mary's other sister from there planned to move to Canada).

I'm not talking about myself or my wife now, but mainly about Dasha – autistic people have a hard time adapting to everything new. If you have never heard of autism or do not believe it exists, I recommend you watch "The Rain Man" movie. That's a great illustration of the subject.

The majority of refugees just wait in camps for weeks and months, waiting to begin receiving social payments and to be provided with accommodation. Many begin taking language integration courses while still living in those camps. The majority are coming with little children, which makes it even more difficult for these people.

A WORD ABOUT MY AUTISTIC DAUGHTER

As we waited for our next train on a platform at Leipzig main station, we saw another Ukrainian family. Two women with two children under ten. Since men were not allowed to leave Ukraine legally during the war, mostly all Ukrainian refugees that we met on our journey were women, teenage boys under eighteen; and sometimes elderly men and women.

This family looked lost, frustrated, and a little angry. My wife engaged in a conversation with the woman, and Dasha was listening. She and the children were looking at each other with shy curiosity. Then my daughter approached them and they began to chat.

In the meantime, I saw a McDonald's sign further down at the station and decided to go and taste the local coffee and have a chicken roll – something that I often ate there in Ukraine. McDonald's coffee in Ukraine and Russia was pretty good, so I was hoping to get a cup of nice coffee here too.

Alas, my expectations were not met. The cappuccino had plenty of what looked like some sort of white chemical foam, unfortunately (let's be polite). It filled almost half of the paper cup and the coffee was to be found under a thick layer of it. After taking a few sips I put the full cup into the nearest rubbish bin. And they had no chicken rolls.

After I got back to Dasha and Mary, I saw a group of teenagers a few meters away from us with a guy who looked like a teacher. But he was just a few years older than them. The boys and girls were having a heated discussion in German. I came over to ask the teacher in English about the train times because it seemed to be late. In return, he asked me where I was from and so I told him.

He immediately began asking questions about the war, about what the situation was like at the moment, and how we managed to make it out of Ukraine to Germany. He seemed very friendly, his young face expressed sympathy. When he heard my answers, his eyes began slightly glittering with tears. However, since he produced this emotional reaction very quickly, I first suspected him of being dishonest. I am the type of person who prefers to stay away from sympathy and handle my own problems. But here I thought, maybe, it would be impolite to do so. After all, we are "asylum seekers" in this country, so it would be rude to just abruptly end this conversation, turn my back on them and walk away. Besides, we were on the same platform waiting for the same train. Fortunately, this company was headed not for Munich and they planned to get off earlier.

As we talked, the boys and girls aged about twelve to fifteen were casting curious glances at me and Dasha, who was enthusiastically posing for photos on the platform while Mary was taking pictures of her.

You see, our daughter had dreamed of travelling somewhere abroad – she grew up watching kids' video blogs on YouTube, where they travelled to various sites around the world and kept unboxing expensive toys in front of the camera.

Watching these videos with Russian-speaking children and their parents, Dasha basically learned to speak. Because of her diagnosis, she speaks Russian like a foreigner, making mistakes in case endings, confusing declension, getting grammar genders wrong, etc. It is useless trying to explain the language rules to her, even in a playful form, she shows no interest and changes the subject immediately.

The only way is to correct every single phrase she says, hoping that she will remember and get it right next time. It's like being a foreign language teacher to your own child. It is often fun because seeing her progress makes me happy. But frequently also you feel frustration about it.

A year ago, when we took Dasha to expensive Tomatis therapy sessions (that's when your brain gets gently stimulated with various classical music through headphones) in Ukraine, the therapist told us that for autistic children Russian and Ukrainian languages are very difficult to master. English is much easier. Many of his former clients eventually left for the US or Canada. There those kids began communicating in English much better and easier than they spoke their native languages in Ukraine.

Anyway, back to YouTube bloggers. Watching tonnes of these travel and unpacking videos made Dasha want to travel herself. As soon as she learned to express her thoughts verbally, she began talking about travelling.

For two years now, she has been telling us nearly every day that she wants to visit China, Spain, the UAE, the US, Kazakhstan (I've often wondered about that particular choice of hers) and now, since we are here, she keeps chattering about how she would love to visit various cities in Germany, especially those with huge toy shops and Legoland theme parks in them.

Now her dreams have begun to turn real. You never know the ways that your wishes may start coming true one day. She does not yet fully realize the circumstances that made us leave our cozy and comfortable life behind and head for Germany.

She just knows that war is a very bad thing and people are dying as Russia is "offending" Ukraine. But the way she perceives the reality, and this bit of it in particular, is very different from mine or yours. Anyway, this brings us dangerously close to slipping into phildickian talks about the nature of reality, lol, so let's move on.

GERMANY THROUGH EYES OF "MADE IN USSR" GUY

As we finally got on the train to continue our journey, we watched the world new for us flash by behind the window. Dasha first kept asking whether we would arrive soon, like every fifteen minutes but then Mary and I persuaded her to take her pencils and some paper out of the bag and this got her busy drawing. (Now, almost two years after our move to Germany, she can spend hours drawing and she also attends classes on it).
The company of teenagers and their "scoutmaster" sat in the same carriage in another part of it, so we were now left to ourselves. Mary sat back in her chair and began dozing off, and I just sat there looking out of the window.

Now, to make it clear, I prefer writing about our travels here, avoiding negative historical moments and politics. However, these departures from the main subject of the book are sometimes necessary to clarify and better explain what I'm talking about. So, here we go.

As we passed stations on the rest of the way to Munich, I kind of felt surprised as to the part of Germany we happened to be in. As a person who was born in the Soviet Union, I strongly associated Germany as an enemy defeated almost eighty years ago in WW2.

Over the past ten years, this feeling has been intensified in Russians artificially, especially after Putin annexed Crimea. Luckily, I had left the country by then and did not have to listen to all that immense flow of propaganda.

It seems that until that time, the Russian government was unable to think of what is called a "national idea" for the country. As a gangster character said in an iconic Russian novel "Babylon" by Victor Pelevin about the 1990s and early 2000s – "first we had Communism, now it is over and there is no bloody national idea. This is why they hate us abroad, thinking that all Russians can do is steal bags of money and then hide with it in a flat behind an iron door. And we need an idea to unite us all so that these bastards can feel such spirituality coming from us as Nazis felt during the battle at Stalingrad". This quote is not an exact one but it certainly shows the idea.

It seems that Putin has finally won the jackpot with the national idea and it is based on the big role of Russia winning WW2. In Russia, it was known as the Great Patriotic War, which started in 1941 and finished in 1945. Every year under Putin recently, this role has been growing and becoming more significant with constant reminders being made to average Russians about it regularly as if trying hard to beat this as deep into their heads as possible.

Crimea initially belonged to the Russian Empire, then it was part of the Soviet Union until Nikita Khrushchev (who ruled the USSR from 1953 to 1964) decided to give it to Ukraine (USSR – the Ukrainian Soviet Socialistic Republic back then) in February of 1954.

After the peninsular was forcefully taken back by Russia

(pretending there was a referendum, same as in the several regions in the South of Ukraine during the current war to vote for "entering the Russian Federation"), Putin began intensifying the revival of the importance of the USSR's victory over the Nazis in WW2.

During the celebration of Victory Day on May 9, a lot of people now get together in the centres of big cities and slowly walk along the major streets empty of transport, carrying the portraits of their grandfathers and grandmothers who perished during the war.

Over the last ten years, this movement "The Immortal Regiment" became close to iconic for Russian patriots, and nearly everyone tries to join these May 9 marches. Many Russians also put stickers on their cars which say "We thank our granddad for the victory", "1941-1945, we can easily repeat that", etc. They are proud of having these war-related slogans on their cars not only on May 9, if you see what I mean.

So, back to where I started – my basic associations of Germany are about the war, Hitler, concentration death camps, the Soviet flag put on top of the Reichstag, etc. That's subconscious stuff I guess. Only after that comes associations with Mercedes Benz cars, beer and sausages, Wagner music, and Goethe's Faust.

So as the train carried us towards Munich and made brief stops in other big cities, my brain had nothing better to offer me but those historical associations. So when I saw we were going past Düsseldorf, I felt creeps going down my spine – there used to be a concentration camp near this city. Nurnberg – the famous trials of high-ranking Nazi officers after the war, and I got the same feeling as if I'm touching the long-broken skeleton of a monster that lived ages ago.

For good or bad, I was not very good at WW2 history at school, otherwise perhaps I would have had a stronger flow of associations coming. Later on, I found out that Hitler began his political career in Munich but this knowledge did not prevent me from enjoying walks around the city.

Still, the overall WW2 associations are still strong for every Russian and Ukrainian. For the latter, it used to be strong enough until February last year. But after February 24, 2022, Ukraine vividly experienced that feeling again as Russian troops in Ukrainian perception turned into German Nazi soldiers.

Even symbols chosen by Russia for this war are Latin letters "V" and "Z", they are drawn on military vehicles and on soldiers' uniforms – signs that originate in Hitler's Germany and his invasions in Europe. Perhaps it is not more than a coincidence but you never know...I wonder why Putin did not think about that. He should have perhaps used Russian letters to avoid this idiocy.

Speaking of history lessons, the children in Russian schools now, are going to have their brains washed about the cult of Russia's victory in WW2. Of course, the role is important, no doubt here.

But if you ask me then using this to justify Russia's current aggression against Ukraine and for turning the population of Russia hostile towards the rest of the world – that's discernible, it puts a big stain of disgrace on those USSR veterans who fought the war and did their part to win it, and those who died fighting for the victory.

It also looks pretty miserable. Putin wants the country to live in the past, and to be proud of its long- gone achievements. Having nothing to show for now over the 23 years of his presidency but corruption, poor economy, and poverty, Putin is making Russian people think they are saving the world from Nazis once again.

A substitute for economic prosperity and personal freedoms

Western countries have. And, most importantly for Putin, he is playing the "great leader" for the Russian people here, as Stalin did during WW2, for those poor-minded and broken by the propaganda who believe him. The only difference is that back then the threat was real and now it has been made up deliberately.

BRAINFART WITH MUNICH TRAINS

Munich's system of city and regional trains is rather peculiar and it needs time to get used to. I assume the same system works all over Germany. My first reaction to it was that I had a brainfart.

It has U-Bahn (underground city trains), and S-Bahn (they run on the ground and can take you not only around a city but to the suburbs as well). Other regional trains are called RB, RE; they run faster than U-Bahn and S-Bahn and they also go further. Then there is ICE, which I have mentioned before, and it takes you on long-distance trips.

There can be several floors on some stations in Munich and from the same platform trains can go in totally different directions. During the first few months of our stay, this simply drove me crazy. But then some guys in the street (when I asked them for directions) told me I should use a Deutsche Bahn (DB) mobile app – it can show you an exact itinerary from the place where you are to start for your destination with all the changes you need to make.

But before they advised me and Mary to install "DB", we used Google Maps, which often shows you the wrong stuff. Besides, it cannot tell you which platform you need to take a train from, for example. You also need to carefully look at electronic boards on the platforms that show where the train is headed and how long you need to wait for its arrival before you get on it.

The train map in Munich looks like a knot of a few dozen snakes, where you have to find the right direction (which is the line of the right colour), then find the station where you are now and the one you need to get to. It all takes patience (tons of it!), time, and a great deal of swear words at first.

In Russia and Ukraine, you get one train, one platform, one destination. Sadly, all these "A-B-C-D- E-S-Bahns" give you a lot of hassle and you get lost in them and their routes as you look at a train map on a platform at the main station.

Such a complex system of city trains and platforms could be easy to understand if this were a megapolis with hundreds of millions of people. But hey, according to Google, at the end of 2021, there were 1,561,094 people living in Munich. At the same time, Moscow had almost ten times as many – 13,015,126 people. Twice more people than in Munich lived in Kyiv before the war started – 2,950,702.

Something tells me, Kyiv and Moscow still get on pretty fine without all the confusion and brainfarts that the Munich city train system makes newcomers (tourists and now refugees) go through during their first encounter.

This train system covers the whole country. But after getting used to it in just one city, you get a devil-may-care attitude, even to the fact that trains are constantly late (as I have seen plenty of times later on), tracks get repaired all the time or somebody jumps on them to commit suicide, sadly. As I was told, you can even produce this as a reason for being late for work or an important meeting/appointment in Germany – yes, "it's not my fault, it's the bloody train delay for the fifth time this week".

Often, strikes also take place when train and bus drivers do not go to work expecting a pay rise. This makes the whole public transport freeze in the middle of the week or at a weekend.

And nobody gives a damn how you manage to get to a destination which is beyond any reasonable walking distance. I guess, this is one of the reasons that a lot of people here own a car or have a bicycle – how else can you get by when a train is delayed for the millionth time and you are in a rush to get somewhere?

Besides, you often plan your itinerary in the DB app, and so you have two/three or more changes along the way. So, once one train/bus is late, you automatically miss the one you were to catch after it and then you wait, sometimes for 20-30 minutes for the next one.

Too bad if it's raining or it's below zero outside. Luckily, local media always warns people about these strikes in advance. By the way, a lot more strikes are expected in 2024.

MUNICH CENTRAL STATION. STREET FOOD AND COVID TRAVEL RULES

We finally got off at the Munich Central Station. All announcements on the train were made in both German and English, which made it easy for me to understand them.

Kate (her actual Ukrainian name is Katya) met us heartily, gave us tight hugs, and took us to the underground platform to catch a train to her place. That was the second time I had met my sister-in- law. The first one was in about 2013 when she was a teenager and went from Germany to her hometown of Odesa with a stopover in Kyiv, where we lived back then. No communication between us since then, except for Mary saying hello from me during their Skype chats.

Neufahrn is a suburban town northeast of Munich, where Kate and her boyfriend Andrey rented a flat. Dasha was especially glad to meet her aunt. Since our daughter has an issue with communicating and building up social connections with other children, she gladly makes friends with my wife's relatives and friends, who are much older.

Munich central station had a similar architectural design as the one in Leipzig, similar to train stations in Moscow as well – long train tracks pulling and then ending under a roof with an immensely high ceiling (in Munich it is partly made of glass to let light come through in the day time) with announcements made loud somewhere above your head.

If you did not know exactly in which of these German cities you were now and were there for the first time, perhaps you would easily get confused. What surprised me was to see volunteers in their acid green waistcoats near a stand with a Ukrainian yellow-blue flag.

I spotted some of them on the platform too as Mary was explaining to the refugees, who had arrived on the same train as we did, which way to go and pointed at the stand with the Ukrainian flag. Besides, I heard an announcement in pure Ukrainian, welcoming refugees and telling them to come to the stand where they would be met by volunteers or advising them to go to thc information desk.

Looking around, as I was pulling the suitcases and walking behind Mary, Dasha and Kate, I saw quite a lot of people here and there who were speaking to each other in Ukrainian or Russian with a slight accent. The majority of them spoke Russian, after all, as they were probably coming from the East of the country. Poorly dressed, they had children with them and were carrying a lot of luggage.

Most of them were carrying not even suitcases but shabby old sports bags. Even more often they were carrying their stuff in regular plastic shopping bags that you get in a supermarket (they would be torn from heavy and bulky purchases pretty soon) or strong plastic bags sold in open-air markets.

You can carry several kilos of shopping in those without

getting them torn or their handles coming off. Some young women were dressed pretty well and smartly too but those cases were rare.

Right there at "Hauptbahnhof" I saw lots of kiosks and stands with food – mostly sandwiches or salads, coffee and pastries of various kinds. There were queues everywhere as if people had not had a chance to eat at home and suddenly all of them had a collective urge to eat right here at the central train station.

As I found out later, buying and eating sandwiches, burgers or doners was not a very good deal. In Ukraine and Russia, such a street food kiosk (even the shabbiest one) always has a microwave and they heat up cold meat rolls, burgers and other fast food for you. Often, they would make it so hot that you have to wait for a few minutes otherwise risking to burn your mouth.

Here, in Germany, or at least in Bavaria, the only time when you are lucky to get hot food in the street is if you buy it soon after they have cooked it – that is, in the morning or midday. Come starving later than that and you will end up choking on cold stuff. All my requests to heat up rolls or sandwiches were met with surprised and slightly annoyed glances as if I had asked for free food.

None of these kiosks had microwaves. Everybody seems to enjoy cold stuff without realising that microwaves were invented not only for private use at home. Maybe they do not realise that eating cold sandwiches, meat, etc., is bad for your stomach and warm food is a lot healthier.

Anyway, we walked downstairs, found the right platform (out of around twenty) and soon got on a train, which pretty quickly got to an open-air track. My impression of Munich from that very first train ride was a bit disappointing – I mostly saw old shabby buildings of industrial style that looked like ones from the Soviet Union times or from Russia in the 1990s to me. There was also quite a lot of graffiti on the walls of the buildings as we went past. I got a bit of a shock as I expected Europe to be "pretty and clean", and did not think I would see graffiti in the centre of bloody Munich.

So much about cold street food, though. Moving on. Back then, there were still strict rules about wearing masks on public transport. Since we did not have any, Kate took three FFP2 masks out of her rucksack and handed them to us. She warned us that Germans love following rules and want everyone to do likewise in their country. Besides, if you were not wearing a mask, you could easily get a fine.

Another thing she told us was that in order to travel, we needed to have either vaccination certificates on us or results of Covid tests not older than 24 hours.

We had neither of those. Kate is also a very much law-abiding person (maybe after living for eight years in Germany), but even she thought that hassling with express tests would be too much at the moment. After all, you get this Covid stuff checked seldom on public transport, Kate told us, it is much more important to wear a mask and have a (valid) ticket on you. As for the latter, once again, we did not have to buy any. At least upon arrival in Germany, anyway.

CHALLENGE TO FIND MY SISTER-IN-LAW'S HOUSE

Neufahrn-bei-Freising is a town with approximately 20,000 inhabitants located northwest of Munich, about thirty minutes of a nice and easy train ride. The scenery we could see after Munich was left behind was green with fields and dotted with nice-looking cottages, their windows and sun panels on the roofs shining as they reflected the afternoon sun. But, as it turned out, epithets "nice" and "easy" could not be applied to our further journey to Kate's house.

We got off at the main station in Neufahrn and here Kate told us that we would have to catch a bus to get to her place. Explaining that she would be unable to go together with us, she asked if we would be okay getting to the place without her since she had to pick up her bicycle from the train station – to meet us in Munich she cycled to the Neufahrn railway station and left her bicycle here. Now she had to go back the same way, so as not to leave her "steel horse" there for the night. I told her that it was no problem and we would meet her outside her place.

She gave us the address, which I immediately typed into Google Maps, and told us to take a bus. The only unfortunate thing about this is that Kate forgot to tell us which bus to take exactly but she probably thought that I could find that out in English from the drivers. Luckily, there was only one bus stop, so nothing could go wrong, especially with Google Maps, could it? Off she pedalled then.

It was my own brave decision, but there we were now, standing in an unknown town, with heavy suitcases and people around us speaking an unknown language. Well, I thought naively, my English should help me here.

We got on the bus, which the blessed Google Maps told us to take. After we passed two or three stops, I felt a little worried and went to ask the driver if we were going in the right direction. The elderly guy behind the wheel did not speak English, so I had to use my poor and broken German and gesticulate to explain we needed to get to the Alte Kirche Strasse stop.

He thought for a second as if trying to digest what I just said. When he finally latched onto what I was doing my best to say, he told me we had got on the wrong bus. He began explaining in German which way we should go, sometimes using gestures to make himself clear. The fact was we had to get back to the train station first and get on a different bus – he told us the exact number.

Okay. We got off near what seemed to be a local entertainment multi-complex with a cinema. There were a couple of other similar long grey buildings surrounding the place and the bus stop where we found ourselves. But beyond that – corn fields were running away to the horizon. Bloody hell, I thought. Great stuff. Still, I reminded myself that it was my own decision and my own fault. Probably, my man's pride but I guess I should have asked Kate at least for the right bus number.

By the way, this was not my first encounter with Google Maps, but from that point on in Germany, I used only the "DB" app and opened the Maps only for directions when I was within walking distance from my destination.

After waiting for about twenty minutes in the cold March wind, we saw a bus. As it pulled over, we got on and the first thing I did was ask the driver if this was the right one to get to the train station. We showed him our Ukrainian IDs. He nodded and waved us to move on into the salon. What a relief...

We were back outside the train station pretty soon. I saw the bus that we supposedly needed at the stop there and I went to ask if it would take us to the Alte Kirche Strasse stop. The driver first nodded, then he began telling me something in German. A guy standing next to us overheard his speech and then told me in English that this was actually the wrong bus, and we needed a different one.

I was hungry, tired, and growing irritated after this failed bus ride. I began feeling anger rising. So I decided it was time for radical, foolproof measures. I told Mary and Dasha to wait for me there and marched off to get a taxi. There were a few beige-coloured cars with checked taxi signs on their roofs.

I was prepared to pay from the tiny amount of cash we had but a young Turkish cab driver, hearing we had come from Ukraine, did not charge us a penny. He drove us to Kate's doorstep.

GERMAN LIFEHACK WITH WINDOWS

Kate had done us another great favour, aside from meeting us and putting us up in her spare room. As I mentioned before, she had arranged long-term accommodation for us.

Andrey and her, when Mary spoke to Kate as we moved to Chernivtsi, were happy to have us stay with them for a couple of weeks until we found another place to live. However, her landlady, who was, apparently, a difficult person, allowed us to stay only for three days. Kate told us this woman was a pain in the neck to deal with, she could easily make a scandal, tell them to move out if she did not like something, or could even sue them.

Thus, Kate found accommodation for us with a young German guy for longer than a just week. She said it was a house not far from a lake in the Bavarian Alps, in a small resort village called Seeshaupt.

But before moving there, we stayed for four days with Kate, even despite her landlady's permission only for three.

As I wrote somewhere above, this was not my first time in Europe, so I was far from being in a completely new environment – I had seen all these similar cottages before in North Wales. But it still felt good to dive back into this, streets in European towns look in a way that makes you feel cozy and – for me as a Russian person – to recall Stephen King novels and old Hollywood movies since these were the main source of an idea what the little quiet town of Castle Rock may look like.

However, I did find something new for myself here immediately after I entered Kate's rental flat – windows in the roof. The flat was based in a long two-storey cottage with maybe fifteen or twenty apartments in it and an Indian restaurant on the ground floor. Many flats were in the attic and for adding more light during the day to save up electricity, here windows were built right into the roof or in the walls but right under the ceiling. This was actually a simple and elegant solution that caught me by surprise.

Well, you learn something new every day but you die being an idiot anyway, as the Russian saying goes. Now, I had some new neural connections in my brain – well, great stuff, I guess.

The apartment looked more like a greenhouse, though, thanks to green plans everywhere, a glass wall between rooms and the door that separated their room from the living room, and plenty of daylight.

The sunlight poured lavishly through a narrow window in the high ceiling of the living room. The same thing was in the bathroom – you did not even have to switch on the light during the day there.
Curiously, Andrey is also Russian, coming from Kaliningrad – the former German city of Königsberg, which has belonged to the USSR and then to Russia since 1946.

Andrey was a nice slim guy, a little reserved, rational, clever, and obedient to rules, just like Kate.

They are both programmers, coding to make software at home as part of big teams, sitting in different rooms so as not to

disturb each other and meeting during their working hours like in an office – only to have lunch together. But they spend evenings and weekends together, at least.
Funny that both Kate and Mary, Ukrainian sisters, had men from Russia, staying together for many years now.

THREE DAYS IN NEUFAHRN

Neufahrn was a small quiet town and over the next three days, we explored its central part during our walks. The house was surrounded by corn fields. A few lines of smaller cottages stood right on the edge of those fields – a sea of green and yellow fields then ran away towards a forest on one side and a motorway on the other.

The city centre had a church (the Alten Kirche) that was being redecorated and partly surrounded by scaffolding. There were also small pretty squares with benches on the way to the train station.

During our walks, we went through them and passed the local town council (Rathouse); we went past a lot of small cafes that made the place look cozy. But stepping just less than a hundred meters away led you to streets that looked typically like ones in my hometown in Russia – with plain concrete buildings, similarly looking apartment blocks, and large deserted spaces of land covered in grass with nothing built there.

On the "border" between cottages and the fields within a five-minutes' walk from Kate's flat there was a playground. We took Dasha there a few times during our short stay. There was a very simple cable car on which both children and teenagers liked to ride. You sat on a small wooden seat on a vertical pipe that was attached to a long wire (thick like a rope), held on tight, and pushed away with your legs.

Off you then went fast towards the other end of the wire rope. This looked like fun for Dasha and other kids on the playground. I envied them a little because, despite the simplicity of this mechanism, there was no such thing in my Soviet Union childhood.

Back then, I spent lots of time hanging around my neighbourhood with friends, kicking a football, playing "hide-and-seek", etc, or looking for interesting trash to play with that the neighbours in our block threw out of their windows (bolts, empty cigarette lighters, bullet cases (!), razors, etc).

We even smoked cigarette butts and then chewed on flowers to get rid of the smell on our breath, since chewing gums were rare and kids seldom got pocket money (very little if they did, just enough to buy lemonade or an ice cream).

I wonder what prevented people from "the great country" (I mean the USSR) from building those simple things when it was proud of its high-quality engineers, leisure time clubs for children where they learned to build models of planes, ships, learned to draw, etc. Besides, eastern Slavic people (like Russians and Ukrainians) are famous for their ability to build or make complex things using a limited set of very simple but universal tools.

In Russia, we call it creating great things "using shit and sticks" or doing a really hard job using just "a crowbar and "fucking hell"". This means that plumbers, carpenters, and other people "with the hands growing from the right part of the body", as we say, who could fix anything, often used a lot of swear words when repairing hard breakages.

And they usually drank a lot after working hours (sometimes, they got wasted during them too). Maybe it was this particular aspect of talented people (not only technically talented) that created a saying: "You can't lose your talent through drinking. Regular attempts keep proving that".

But as for that cable car near Kate's house on the playground, that's probably the case when the plumber's house leaks and the carpenter's house creaks.

Anyway, we arrived in Munich and then got to Kate's flat on Thursday. After a three-day breather, we continued our journey on Monday morning. Kate's landlady was getting nervous and kept phoning them to make sure they did not rent out the spare room to immigrants.

That paranoid lady in her fifties once even came in, using a spare key, without notice, when I was alone at home. In English, she apologised and told me she had come to pick up some of her stuff. But it was clear that it was a mere pretext – she was there to see if her precious apartment was still there, intact, not burned or destroyed completely by her tenant's relatives.

* * *

The other side of this love of windows is that in a lot of German private houses in the countryside windows are so big (sometimes taking a big part of a wall and starting right on the level of the floor) and have no curtains on them that you can see everything inside even if you do not particularly want to see that. Especially when evening comes and lights get turned on.

You then see people sitting at tables, walking across their rooms, reading, playing the piano, etc. Once I asked a German lady, what if somebody decides to walk naked around their house, will they also leave the windows uncovered? The response was – it is the problem of passers-by outside, rather than of the people inside. If they want to peek in and see house dwellers having sex (I'm exaggerating a bit here but you get my point), they are free to do so.

However, every German house also has huge shades outside their windows, which they put down (by pressing a button on a remote control inside) during storms or sometimes in the evening.

These shades can be literally huge. They look like those that are used for covering the doors of shops and offices in Ukraine after you lock them. I still have not figured out when Germans prefer to leave their windows transparent for the public eye, so to speak, and when they decide to modestly pull down those outer shades that seem big enough to absorb a torpedo.

PART 3

NEXT STATION – SEESHAUPT

The name of the young guy who was willing to accommodate us in Seeshaupt was Tom. Kate had arranged that through a Telegram chat at work and had never met him in person but just communicated online about us and our upcoming arrival. She then told us that he asked for our names.

Off we went with our suitcases and bags to our new accommodation after spending the weekend with Kate and Andrey. I thought maybe we could rent a van with a driver or a taxi to get there with our luggage. But Kate shocked me by telling me how much that would cost, so we had no choice but to take a train (with a change). It was useful anyway – we had to gradually get used to living in Germany and using the local public transport.

Besides, in a few days, we had an appointment ("Termin" in German, another important word that Mary and I picked up quickly and have been using since then even when talking Russian between each other – this borrowed word is much shorter than the Russian equivalent) with the immigration service. We would have to travel there on our own (Kate had to get back to work and was unable to accompany us on that day), so getting to know how to use local trains was a must as soon as possible anyway.

At least using trains outside Munich was easier than catching a U-Bahn train. It was S-Bahn we took as we went to the first destination – Munich Hauptbahnhof. S-Bahn is the German for "Stadtschnellbahn", literally meaning "urban rapid train" (that's a combination of urban and suburban trains). In Munich, we changed to RB (R-Bahn or RegionalBahn – regional train) as we went directly to Seeshaupt. In Russian, we call it simply an "electric train" – “electrichka”.

But our “electrichkas” feel and look awful inside compared to pretty decent S-Bahn and luxurious R-Bahn trains. In Russian trains, often you can travel for long hours, pressing your butt against hard wooden seats, especially if you live in the suburbs of Moscow, for instance, and have to commute every day to work and then back home in an overcrowded train carriage. But before you finally get on that train, you often have to wait in a queue that can run for fifty meters or longer in the morning, evening, and during rush hours.

When it hits minus twenty in winter, those train journeys become particularly "pleasant" and character-strengthening.

R-Bahn (RB) trains proved to be much more comfortable and cozy than even S-Bahn. They had a couple of tables in each carriage, a toilet, and comfortable seats which is great if your journey lasts an hour or longer. Besides, these trains have a little futuristic look from the outside.

Overall, a lot of things – transport, buildings – in Western countries, China, the UAE, and Malaysia have a futuristic look compared to Ukraine, Russia (and especially Belarus). There are a lot of good and pretty-looking modern things there too, but their design is clearly copied from the West and East.

In Russia, a lot of buildings remain from the old Soviet times with panel pictures depicting a man and a woman holding a hammer and a scythe (the USSR emblem) look more like something from an ancient culture which somehow still has a big impact on the minds of people there.

RB trains even have "quiet sections" in the head of a carriage where you are not allowed to talk, so people can read a book, work on their laptops or just sit in silence looking at the scenery outside.

They sit there in total silence with glass doors separating them from the rest of the carriage where you can pass the time of a long journey chatting to other passengers or by listening to other people talk. Sometimes, it can get pretty loud there, like when teenagers or men coming back from a football game get on, drinking beer, laughing. Then you wish you had chosen the "quiet section" in the first place.

PERFECT PLACE FOR RECOVERY

As we got further away from the Munich area, the landscape behind the train window became more rural. I saw single-standing cottages float by, open sheds with hay and symmetric piles of chopped wood, green pastures with cows and horses grazing in them.

Dasha had taken out her notebook and colour pencils and started drawing on a table we were sitting at. There was also a map of the train route with all the stations from Munich Bahnhof to Kochel am See (a mountain village at the end of this line) drawn. This map looked like a picture from a children's book about travels, so Dasha began looking at the stations, counting how many were left until the one we headed for. One of the stations we passed was called Starnberg.

As we reached it, the train took us past a lane along the beach, I saw a pretty grey lake spread to the horizon and to the sides. Seagulls flew above it, some of them walking on the rocky shore. The lake was a pretty site. Kate then told me that it was Starnberger See ("See" means "lake", pronounced as [zeyeh] and not going far from the English word "sea" in spelling, as you can see) and that the village where would arrive soon was also located by this lake. This was a nice thing to look forward to. To be honest, I had never seen a lake in my life, not even in Russia. Yes, you have a weirdo for a story-teller here.

Being a homestayer, I preferred to stay in during the summer with a book or watch a movie rather than go somewhere to travel. Even my trips to the countryside took place rarely. This is how life makes us change, I thought – a homestayer in the past, I have been forced to become a traveller now. I certainly did not mind, I just wished the circumstances were different.

Finally, a recorded man's voice from under the ceiling announced that the next station was Seeshaupt – first in German, then it repeated the same in English.

We got off at a quiet station, which indeed looked not like that of a town but of a tiny village. Since it was the first time for Kate there too, we mistakenly took a longer path to get off the platform, pulling our suitcases along. Later on, as we began travelling to Munich often and to the immigration service in the nearby town of Weilheim, we found a shortcut – an underground pass leading right to the trains. But not on the day of arrival, of course, as you can imagine.

There was something that looked like a road going around Seeshaupt and past the railway station. There were several smaller streets, with fewer of them than you have fingers on your palm, going into the village itself.

Using Google Maps, Kate led our way along one of them. In about ten minutes, we reached a white old-looking house surrounded by a small fence. In the summer it turned into a hedge thanks to the tall bushes that grew right near it inside, so the house got almost completely hidden behind the green hedge with pretty roses.

This was one of the things that struck my eye here. In Ukraine, if you lived in a cottage surrounded by other cottages, you would build a fence that would be tall enough at least to cover a person from the feet to the neck, since nobody wants other people to see what is happening in their yard. Totally opposite to German windows with no curtains. Also, you often have dogs that begin barking madly as you walk past. Usually, they keep thieves away.

However, often enough, a whole "dog concert" begins because dogs along the whole street, in every yard, start barking even before you approach their house – one single dog begins woofing and then the others just join in eagerly.

They bark in different voices, depending on the dog's size, and so it indeed sounds like a concert of various instruments playing loud high and low notes. Crazy and very annoying stuff to listen to, especially when you are dozing off in your house on a summer night (with the windows wide open because of the heat) and all those dogs, including yours, start "going off".

They sound like grenades exploding right in your yard – that's your own bloody dog barking sometimes louder, sometimes quieter.

Tom came out to meet us on the doorstep, holding a big carton with our names and "Wilkommen" ("Welcome") written on it. He was in his early twenties, smiling and he obviously was glad to see us. He gave each of us a fist bump.

We did not expect such a warm welcome. To be honest, not only we had never been refugees ourselves, but we had never dealt with or even seen them in Ukraine when life was still good and stable. I suppose it was also tricky for Tom – he smiled all the time and was very friendly to us throughout our stay. He did his best to welcome us.

Still, I bet he did not know what to expect from us, what sort of people we were. According to what I heard, not all refugee families got on well with the families that volunteered to accommodate them.

Sometimes there were even conflicts with both sides to blame, and so the Ukrainians had to go back to the refugee camps soon after moving in. In particular, we heard a story about Mary's relative, who also fled the war with four physically disabled children she had adopted in Ukraine. They did not get a warm welcome in the Netherlands, even though they behaved with respect and politeness to their hosts.

When you flee a war and head for another country, seeking support and understanding, you try to keep your dignity, and the person who accommodates you should certainly understand this. We were lucky to find Tom since he did his best in this situation because he is just a friendly, sympathetic, and good-natured guy. And a generous one too as it turned out later.

TOM'S VINTAGE HOUSE

The house Tom lived in was painted white on the outside. It had two floors and two "wings". In the right "wing", there was a room on the second floor, which was given to Dasha, the bathroom, and the kitchen on the first floor.

The left wing on the second floor contained two rooms – a bigger and a smaller one – right under the roof in the attic, next to Dasha's. Mary and I stayed in the bigger one. Tom's big room (converted from the living room), small dining room, and a tiny toilet were located on the first floor in the left "wing" as well. A spacious basement ran, branching out, under the whole house.

The house looked very cozy, it was pretty old – built in the 1950s, as Tom's dad Robert told us later – and as we entered the house, pulling our suitcases to the second floor up the creaky staircase, Tom kept apologizing that this whole place was old. I thought the house was cool as if you went back to the age of seven to visit your grandma who lived in the country. I was born in 1981 but still, I had that feeling of coming to my grandparent's dacha – the Russian word for a Soviet times country house where people mainly came in the summer and at weekends to grow vegetables and fruit, then they would put them in glass jars with hermetic lids to eat during the winter.

But most importantly, this house looked as if I went to the golden 1960s and 1970s, when rock-n- roll emerged in the US, when "flower children" appeared. Man, that house really looked like history coming back to life – it stood here as the Vietnam war took place and finished, as Kennedy was assassinated, the Woodstock festival gathered thousands of people in the audience along with the brightest musicians; in a way, it witnessed the appearance of Bob Dylan, Deep Purple, the Beatles, the Rolling Stones, and other rock bands/singers that shaped the global pop culture.

It definitely looked like it was part of that long-gone world. Everything in Seeshaupt still seemed to carry that magic spirit – I saw this later as we explored that small village. Every corner of it, especially the quietest ones.

* * *

First thing we did after unpacking our suitcases was explore the new place as far as the local supermarket. The idea was to combine a foray into the "downtown" with a trip to buy some food for dinner.

There was only one supermarket in Seeshaupt – Edeka. A chain shop popular in Germany and, as it turned out later, with prices higher than in other supermarkets. Kate told me about the prices, but later on, to be honest, when I began visiting other chain stores, I saw that the difference in prices was tiny. Locals in Seeshaupt pronounce this word as [Idika], while in Munich, for example, they say [Edeka], so we tried to pick up the local manner of calling it.

Tom gave us an approximate direction but we still had to use Google Maps (this app keeps chasing me) so as not to get lost in the village that was going deeper into the dark as we left the house. Kate had told us that Seeshaupt is a resort place where lots of people go in the summer for a long stay or at least for a short weekend visit.

The street Tom's house stands on is one of the few ones that lead from the edge of Seeshaupt towards its centre where Starnberger See is located. It awaits all tourists longing to sit on the beach and have a cold draught beer. The street had old houses, some were big mansions with huge hilly lawns around them and with automated gates.

Old houses and very tall trees that were mostly fir-trees or seemed to be that. We walked past a playground and a long two-storey house of the local kindergarten.

We saw people riding bicycles, children riding bicycles, all of them wearing protection helmets. Some of those children were four or five years old, already pedalling away on tiny bicycles. Germans teach their kids to cycle from an early age as if to prepare them to go on a bicycle tour around the world or to conquer the North Pole. Bicycles seem to be one of the obsessions in Germany.

Later on, when we moved out of Seeshaupt and I still saw people riding bicycles everywhere even when it rained, I recalled ancient Scythians – this title described all ancient nomads. The most famous tribe described by Herodotus lived to the North of the Black Sea on the lands near the Danube and the Don rivers where the Slavic tribes later emerged.

Scythians were excellent horse riders. They rode horses all the time, often even shooting arrows or fighting holding swords with both hands while controlling their horses with knees, which had to be really strong for that.

Scythians were such skilled horse riders that they could allegedly urinate and defecate as they rode without stopping, sometimes at a high speed, by merely shifting their bums to the side. There is also a semi-scientific theory that the figure of centaurs in ancient Greek mythology appeared after Greeks saw Scythians riding their horses masterfully, without saddles, so they really looked like men above the waist and horses below it.

Here's why I mentioned those masterful ancient horse-riders: people in Germany cycle at all ages, it seems, that no matter where you go, you can see men, women, and children riding bicycles, even when it rains or snows. Like Scythians but on bicycles. Teenagers often ride without holding to the handlebar, adults often manage to steer and text on their phones at the same time.

The problem with cyclists in Germany is that they ride literally everywhere, even where they are not supposed to. When we later moved to another town, I every time nearly jumped out of my skin, when walking to the supermarket and then ALL OF A SUDDEN hearing a bicycle bell ringing right behind me. I quickly had to take to a side of the path to make way for those cyclists. Otherwise I felt I would be run over. And this was a path, which started from a sign showing that it was for pedestrians only.

Also, as you enter a train station tunnel in that town you see a sign that prohibits riding a bicycle inside. Cyclists could not care less and there you are hurrying to catch a train during rush hour in the sea of people who are moving both in the same and the opposite directions from yours and – guess what – you have somebody riding their bikes in this crowd, slowly but surely.

* * *

When we finally reached Edeka, we saw that it was a small but pretty place. The shop assistants spoke English, which was helpful, although I honestly did my best to summon all

German words about food that I could remember – like three or five, lol. This is the time when you start appreciating the fact that German is of the same language family as English–Germanic, so grammar and vocabulary often sound similar. But best of all is...forget the fact that both languages are Germanic.

English is the global language that is spoken even in Africa and many words are not just recognizable by Germans as familiar, they are simply borrowed from English and are used without any particular changes. So, basically, all the years spent studying English with passion in the past were now paying off lavishly. If I had studied, say, Chinese, Arabic, or Spanish, I would feel numb now and be unable to make even basic communication.

LIVING NEAR STARNBERGER SEE

Kate had told us that we would be staying in a resort place near a lake and mountains. I imagined Seeshaupt to be a green valley with rare trees and hills and cottages standing on the bank of a lake with mountains towering right around that lake like giant pillars holding the sky. That kind of picture I later on saw in Kochel.

The reality with Seeshaupt was a little different but also nice. This seemed to be the realization of a universal principle life follows – it gives you what you want, although in a little different manner from what you expected and in a way you were unable to imagine.

We found ourselves in a small but pretty cozy village. Tom's house was about a ten-minute walk from the Starnberger See. When I looked up this place on Wikipedia, Seeshaupt was described as a municipality in the Weilheim-Schongau district in Bavaria. The name can be translated into English as "head of the lake": "Haupt" is the German for "main" (as in "Hauptbahnhof", "main train station"), and "See" means "lake".

First, I thought it would sound good in Russian as a "king of the sea" and already imagined an elderly beefy bloke with stylish grey hair descending to his broad shoulders, with a bare muscly waist and a huge fishtail under it and a trident in his hand. Women can forget about marrying this rich underwater guy, though, because his fishtail excludes the existence of the necessary man's part that is a must to fulfill one of the important aspects of a good marriage.

Anyway, if you think of the Triton King from Disney's Mermaid cartoon, that would be close enough to my idea. But then this fairy-tale image turned into something more prosaic and simple like merely a stone head (the German word for the head is "Kopf" by the way. Somehow here it replaced "haupt" for me) of a giant statue lying somewhere at the bottom of the lake.

Or perhaps it is a head of an ancient dinosaur, who never made it to become a local legend and a specialty for tourists (unlike "the Lock Ness monster"). Maybe ancient dinosaurs prefer to feed on haggis rather than eat Curry Wurst and drink German beer.

Seeshaupt had lots of tall trees, small streets, stretching from the train station to the lake, cozy- looking restaurants and cafes where people sat outside (it was warm enough already in mid-March there). It had a school, shops where Mary and I had never seen any buyers, the supermarket I mentioned above, and what we in Russia call – an "alco-market".

This means a huge shop, which looks like a warehouse, where you can buy various drinks, mostly alcohol (lots of beer brands, whisky, gin, rum, etc) but also coke and other less harmful drinkable stuff. A convenient place, because if you buy some strong booze here, you don't have to ride your bicycle to another shop to buy a chaser. Germans seem to be very well-thought-out here.

This particular "alco-market" also contained the local post office. The logic of this was lost on me, but perhaps that has no other explanation but space-saving since they say it is very hard to build new houses in Seeshaupt because it is quite a closed place.

The reason for this is because you can only live in this village if you were born there with your parents living there since childhood and their parents too and so on. Since the land in this area is very expensive, some people prefer just to rent out their houses or rooms for the summer to welcome young or retired tourists.

You cannot buy a house in Seeshaupt even if you inherited billions from your wealthy grandpa, Tom told me once. But you buy your way into Starnberg, he said. That is also a pretty village, (also considered to be a "village of billionaires, like Seeshaupt) with a long nice beach.

It is closer to Munich, which is a lot more practical. Especially if you consider the fact that in Munich itself finding accommodation is a big issue these days – it is very expensive to buy and very hard to find something to rent. Basically, after the tremendous influx of Ukrainian refugees finding accommodation in Bavaria has become an even bigger problem.

JACK SPARROW AND MORNING COFFEE

My mornings in Germany always started with a forty-minute long yoga session followed by a walk which lasted about the same – the necessary stuff for me to do after my longish "stay" in hospital in the intensive care ward and three days on a ventilator. I also went for a walk every evening, timing my strolls with the app connected to my fitness bracelet.

This way I also monitored my pulse which soared to at least 100 beats per minute after the hospital in a state of rest and jumped to 120-125 during my slow walks. The doctor assured me that it was a norm for my post-illness state and told me to keep sticking to yoga and regular daily walks. So I did.

Seeshaupt proved a perfect place for these walks and the local air was healing (or clean at the very least with a lot of trees and the lake around). Avoiding being nervous and staying calm was also a necessary condition for a proper recovery. The same "rules" were important to follow while in hospital in order to not kick the bucket. One of my wife's acquaintances was taken to the same hospital a week before me. She was having a period at that time and when her nose began bleeding hard in the intensive care ward under the ventilator, she had a rush of panic. The doctors put her into an artificial coma but that did not help – she died during the night, leaving a husband and two children – nine and six years old, a boy and a girl – behind.

So, here in Germany, unlike in Ukraine, I was able to avoid being nervous or worried – nobody would arrest me for being a Russian and/or beat the shit out of me if they consider me a spy. Here I did not have to worry about sirens or getting killed in many possible scenarios that could easily unfold if we had stayed in Ukraine.

So guess what the first place was where I went to stroll on the first morning in Seeshaupt. Exactly – Starnberger See.

The lake was literally across the road from the supermarket. There was a good view on it from there but to get to the shore you had to walk down an old stony staircase. I still had to stop and catch my breath after walking up any stairs (except the one in Tom's house).

There were a few wooden benches by the lake, grass covered the ground there. A small pebble stone beach on either side of the wooden pier reached out into the water. The wood it was made of looked dark and worn off from time and from people walking on it every day over the past twenty-thirty years at the very least – probably that was the last time it was redecorated or even rebuilt.

"Herzlich Willkommen to Seeshaupt," an inscription on a board above the entrance onto the pier said – "You are heartily welcome to Seeshaupt". Although it faced the water, not the bank. Later on, when I saw a tourist ship sailing towards the pier to let off some passengers and pick up new ones, I realized that this board was welcoming not those who came to explore this village from the land but to meet fans of boat trips on Starnberger See.

How come there was nothing like that at the train station, I wondered. Surely, more tourists come to this place by train or car rather than by ship from neighbouring Starnberg – this is where, as I found out later, these boat trips start. They were round trips but many people just get off at Seeshaupt or two other small towns on the Southern bank (Tutzing and Bernried) where the ship sails by and then take a train or ride their bicycle all the way back.

* * *

At first, living in Seeshaupt, I felt like I was a student twenty years ago when I went to university to study English. Back then, in my second year, I went to North Wales on a month-long English course. That was my first trip abroad (and even the first one beyond the former Soviet Union territory). And there have been no other trips after that until now, except when I went with my Chinese girlfriend to Kyiv and Odesa in Ukraine in 2008 and then moved there completely to marry my current wife Mary.

I was happy because I could practice my English in a country, where this language was native (albeit in Wales it was sometimes pretty hard to understand the local dialect) and that was something completely different from my life experience in Russia – you know, different culture, different people.

One thing is to practice English in class at a Russian uni or even talk to native speakers but still in Russia. But being in a place where everyone speaks only English, having to understand what people here want from you and make yourself clear to them is a totally different animal. Besides, that was my first time away when I left home for a whole month.

Anyway, when we moved to Seeshaupt, I began exploring this village with all of its pretty houses and cafes in the central area near the lake. For a few days, before I got used to the new place, I wished I had been a student of a German department, visiting this place from Russia to practice this language.

Just imagine – I would be twenty years old again, there is no bloody war, Russia is still more or less a democratic state with Putin (who had just become president) pretending to be cute and cuddly, with a whole life ahead of me (I know how to ruin it in a lot more creative ways if I could go back in time now, I have some fresh ideas about it – whoops, that was a bit of sarcasm).

Besides, I felt that German was quite interesting and if I had time and opportunity, I would be able to master it and enjoy the process, just as I did with English a long time ago.
Later on, that dreamy feeling wore off and life went on. I borrowed a book in English from Tom, a prequel (or rather a "sidequel" – a side story from the main one) of "The Pirates of the Caribbean" called "The Price of Freedom", quite a thick book, it can serve as a great tool to knock somebody out. I went off every morning for a walk, then ended up in a cafe near the lake, where I had a cup of coffee and read the endless book.

Near the place where I always had coffee in the morning, there was a small wine shop with windows full of wine bottles of various shapes, sizes and wine-making brands. Right in front of the entrance, stood a small table with a sakura tree spreading its branches above it. In spring, it started blooming and then later petals began to fall off the tree.

As I walked past that sakura a few times, I saw the table itself and the chairs next to it covered in rosy petals as if that was pink snow. They also covered the ground around the table. That was an enchanting site. I took a few photos of it and right the next morning the owner cleaned the table from that magic beauty and an old guy was sitting at the table sipping his coffee. Good things do not tend to last long, do they. A year later, when I visited Seepshaupt from another city, I saw that the tree had been taken down, alas.

It was during those morning trips that I began to pick up some practical German. Usually, I was sitting in the cafe, reading and also watching people buying coffee and pastry. German pastry is very good, by the way. I learned the name of the baked thing I liked a lot – "Nussschnecke". "Zum here essen oder zum mitnehmen?" which means "eat here or take away?"

Sometimes, for a change, I had coffee inside, then grabbed that Nussschenecke and went to read on a bench by the lake, right on the bank of it. The water in the morning was always calm, silent, and motionless. Sometimes people came there to walk their dogs.

A few times, I saw a rowing boat in the distance. A figure of a man sat there without moving and I could not figure out if he was fishing, meditating or just sleeping in a sitting posture.

That site seemed to be a quintessence of morning quietness. I wish I could stay in those moments for as long as I could, but then suddenly other lovers of sitting by the lake would start to arrive, often in companies of two or three, chattering loudly, so the whole magic of that quiet morning and sun reflecting in the mirror of the motionless lake was gone.

* * *

Back then, I also tried reading books in Russian I had brought with me but none of them went down well. I felt a strong rejection to reading fiction in Russian at that time.

I remained Russian and still spoke it but reading fiction books even translated into that language at the moment was impossible due to the fact that people who were attacking Ukraine and who potentially threatened myself and my family – their native language was Russian too and they were forcing everything Russian, the so called "Russian world", onto Ukrainians now. It took me a long time to distance myself slightly from that fact to save my mental state from destruction.

Otherwise, I was enjoying my morning walks along the lake – there was an alley that ran right next to it, along the bank, grown with trees and bushes on the sides, the lake to your right and old local houses and mansions to your left. I walked, I breathed the local healthy air, restoring my lungs, I read an easy-going book about the young Jack Sparrow and spoke English or a gesture-based German to the locals.

Once a woman from one of the restaurants saw me in the street walking from the supermarket. She asked me if I was from Ukraine and offered me a job in the kitchen. I thanked her and politely turned down the "generous offer", using a mixture of English and German.

I told her I was looking for an online job and washing dishes in a restaurant is not what I'm best at. She seemed disappointed as if expected that Ukrainian refugees are a lower sort of people who can do only low-qualified jobs. They are excellent managers, IT workers, psychologists, teachers. The only problem for many of them in Germany after evacuating is the language and the obligation to get their diplomas verified so they can work using their university degree.

In the centre of the village, near Rathaus (the town

administration) and the supermarket, the was also a big church (the local cathedral, I suppose) with a clock tower. The bell of that clock would ring every hour or so, but I especially remembered the bell going off in the morning and in the evening, during my walks.

Besides, this was a Catholic church and I imagined for a second I had travelled back somewhere to the times of the Middle Ages with monks who were about to burn some heretics or women they believed to be witches. Curiously, the domes of the church were shaped like onions – a similar shape to Russian Orthodox churches' domes but still, there was a distinct difference between them.

Near that church if you walked down the slope of the hill, stood a bar called "Servus" with tables outside right on the bank of the lake – the waves touched the ground just a couple of metres away from the tables. From the churchyard there was a pretty view of the lake, the bar, and rows of sailing boats next to it, slightly shaking on the water. That view is fantastic, especially at dusk when the sky turns violet and dark bluc with the daylight fading away.

But until May, the heavy chairs with metal carcasses outside the "Servus" bar were upset and put on top of the wooden tables. You could only sit inside in a nice big room decorated with elements of a ship – fishing nets, a ship steering wheel, etc. Overall, it was designed to give visitors an impression of a ship cabin.

The wooden walls and a fireplace with two armchairs next to it made the place feel very cosy to sit in and watch a storm raging outside on the lake, watching grey waves rise and then fall. I witnessed it once from inside with Mary, drinking hot mulled wine in April. The waters would not stop moving for a second, and the whole surface of the lake turned into a live, moving grey mass and looked like a giant ancient creature awoken by the storm.

The sound of the heavy rain beating against the windows, the noise of the storm and crashing waves would reach you through the walls, making you take another sip of hot mulled wine, happy and thankful that you are here inside and not caught by this horrid weather walking or bravely pedalling away on a bicycle somewhere between Seeshaupt and a village nearby.

GERMAN IMMIGRATION SERVICE. MAGIC WORD "TERMIN"

Kate helped us to arrange a "Termin", that's a German word for an appointment, with the Landratsamt of the area where Seeshaupt belonged. The administrative system in Germany remains a mystery to me with all these regions, districts, etc, so to make it simple I call this "Landratsamt" simply the immigration service for myself.

This word "Termin" proved to be quite deceptive. How do appointments work in Russia, Ukraine and, I assume, in the rest of the civilized world? You make an appointment, you come and you DO NOT wait (at least not for a long time, five or ten minutes maximum).

How does a Termin work in Germany? You have three attempts to guess that one, dear reader. This is how it works. You come at your time, doing your best not to be late, and – guess what? You wait...and you wait...and you wait... Often for half an hour or longer. Basically, you still wait in a live queue, regardless of your appointment.

If it were only related to the immigration service, that would be quite understandable – a load of people come to these refugee centres, Landratsamts, jobcentres, and the staff there are busy to the point when steam begins to rise from their ears. Naturally, the schedule of how you admit people there goes down the drain.

But this mess called "Termin" also applies to clinics ("Arzt Practice" in German, "Arzt" meaning a doctor) and, I assume, to all other public places where you come to interact with officials, doctors, etc. First, I thought this breaks the stereotype of Germans being obedient and order-loving. Then I realized that this mess with Termins does nothing but perhaps prove this rule.

Wherever you see a bloody long queue of people who came on an appointment at their particular time, they are sitting there, silently and obediently, and waiting without their faces showing even a shade of dissatisfaction.

They would be quietly reading a book or leafing through a magazine from the heap on the table without glancing at their watch and asking themselves why the hell were they told to come at this particular time and then they see other people being called to enter the doctor's (or somebody else's) office when it is your bloody Termin now and you took a few hours off work and nearly got your neck broken to be here on time. But there you go. Good gracious Lord, Germans even cross the road strictly when a green light switches on at the traffic light set. Even if there is not a single car in sight in sunny weather and they see an empty road for half a mile in both directions, Germans will not move until the red light changes for the green one. If you see somebody crossing an empty road at the red light, most likely that this is an immigrant or a careless person by their national judgment.

There are many things that just drive me crazy about the way things are organized in Germany.

Termins are certainly among them. However, it would be unfair to say there are no good things, let's be optimistic – they do exist. The glass is half-full. And even if it is half-empty, we'll get another bottle.

These positive things are pretty fundamental. But they are so closely interconnected with stuff that makes you mad that you probably just need time to come to terms with that. Time, beer, and sausages to help you adjust. Now the mystery of why there are so many beer-fests in Germany is solved. And it also seems clear why so many people attend them all the time.

* * *

Anyway, on the third day of our stay in Seeshaupt, we went to a nearby town called Weilheim (I think it was the centre of the local administrative region with all the immigration authorities located there). Kate had told us by all means not to be late as German officials in Landratsamt would take it as rudeness. Guess what – we were nearly late for our bloody Termin.

The problem is with lack of logic when it comes to trains in Germany. Before, I have told you about the confusing system of U-Bahn (urban trains) and S-Bahn (a hybrid of urban and suburban trains) in Munich.

Here is Seeshaupt, there were two ways of getting over to Weilheim – bus or S-Bahn (with one change). However, we ended up using the third, "universal" way.

I was accustomed to the fact that if there are two railway tracks, this means that one is for arrival and the other one is for departure. I remembered well that Kate and the three of us arrived at platform 2 when we came to Seeshaupt for the very first time. Therefore, I was logically expecting the departing train that would take us from Seeshaupt to Weilheim would run on platform 1.

Well, we got to the railway station, running out of breath, since Mary (like many other women on average) usually takes a long time to get dressed and get herself ready to leave the house. She always tells me that when she has an important meeting or event to get to, she sabotages it subconsciously and so leaves for it as late as she can.

Two minutes were left before the departure and we would have certainly made it...if the train indeed had departed from platform 1, which faces the direction of Weilheim.

However, instead, as if Murphy's law interfered all of a sudden, the train stood on platform 1. And we watched it go as that platform was the further one from us and you needed to use an underground passage to get to it.

"This is my luck!" as Jim Carrey's character said in "Bruce the Almighty" seeing that he would never make it to the meeting at work on time. "This is my German luck", I wanted to add at that moment.

There was an emergency way out, there is always one. I googled a local taxi service. Luckily, the person on the other side of the phone spoke English. The driver of a luxurious car, who came to the station five minutes later, also spoke pretty good English, so I managed to explain the situation to him and told him we were in a rush to get to Weilheim.

At the beginning of the war, Ukrainians got free train rides in Germany as I told you. If we had made it to that train the trip would be free but since we would also have had to change for another train on the way, we would have probably never made it on time for the Termin. Plus we also had to take an express Covid test in a lab in Weilheim before going to Landratsamt – that was an official requirement.

The taxi got us to Weilheim in about fifteen minutes (charging us 30 Euros or so) and there was still plenty of time to have the Covid test done.

Again let me say a few words about wearing anti-Covid masks. During the quarantine in Ukraine in 2020, I managed to avoid wearing masks, except when I went to the supermarket. Our flat was in the city centre, I worked online from home in my cozy little study, so I did not have to use public transport to get to the downtown with all the cafes and shops or classes for Dasha. All of it was within walking distance from us. And if not – we could afford a taxi.

But here in Germany, since the usage of public transport was inevitable, the whole thing seemed like a concentration camp with all these tests that are valid only for 24 hours and having to wear masks all the time when using it. The majority of locals took it for granted, though.

There are some people who hate wearing masks there too, but this only is related to Covid masks. When it comes to other public rules made for the sake of rules, they are obedient again.

Wearing a mask on transport (or in any other public place) was particularly difficult for me after the Covid pneumonia, since as an aftermath I often found it hard to breathe as the air came in through the nose with a slight difficulty – a psychological effect, I suppose. Therefore, a mask was sometimes a hell of a problem. So I began to roll it up from the bottom a little so that air would get it easier.

* * *

Having our tests done and seeing they were negative, we found our way to Landratsamt. It was situated not far from the city centre – a small modern building of four floors.

As we almost got there, we saw a family of five Ukrainians,

women, and teenage children, rolling their suitcases in the same direction. Judging by their talk, they had only just arrived.

When we found the place, a security guard walked out of the building and told us to wait outside. Mind you, we came maybe five minutes earlier than the time of our appointment. We waited for about half an hour or longer.

Finally, a staffer came out from behind the building and took us and the second family to an entrance behind, where about ten other Ukrainians were waiting. Nobody looked at our papers with the Covid test results. They just asked if we had done them and if they were negative, taking our word for it.

A while later, we were finally invited to go inside, our masks still on. It was a spacious hall with windows so big that they actually partly made up a glassy wall. There were several tables, and chairs, some of the tables pretty long as in a canteen, with benches alongside them. Fruit in vases and water in small plastic bottles were offered. Dasha took an apple and began nibbling at it, moving her mask down onto her chin.

At those tables, there had been already plenty of people talking to the officials, filling in forms, and answering questions with the help of one or two interpreters.

All the officials here were polite, they were smiling and doing their best to create a comfortable atmosphere for us all. When our turn came to answer questions, a German lady sat next to us with another one, who spoke Russian. But seeing that I could speak English, the interpreter went to help at another table.

The lady asked us about our names, dates of birth, when we crossed the border with Germany, how we got there from Ukraine, and how much money we had on us. The lady also asked where we were staying and I wrote down Tom's address in Seeshaupt. She kindly helped us fill in the necessary forms.

It is important to note that we did not ask for a status of refugees. We applied for asylum – this was specially allowed to people coming from Ukraine. The difference is that when applying to be a refugee, you have big obligations here.

The biggest one is having to live here a certain amount of years, like three or more, without being able to change your mind and leave back for Ukraine (whether the war is over or not – many Ukrainians felt really uncomfortable in Germany or Poland so they preferred to go back) or choose another country as a shelter.

Unlike us, people who flee Arabic countries or Syria, have to choose the status of a refugee since they are not eager to go back to their ruined houses or their home countries with totalitarian Islamic regimes, where you may be beheaded for a social media post, for wearing a short skirt rather than a long one or your wearing hijab in the wrong way.

Russia is far from that, Orthodox church high-ranking priests do not care as long as they can earn millions of dollars and drive expensive cars. However, an anti-war or anti-government post on local social media can get you a fine or a few years in jail these days.

When all the papers were filled out, a guy, called Andrey, came into the hall and told us in native Russian to follow him to an upper floor. We were each given a piece of paper with a number (sort of an ID card we had to carry while staying in that building) and we had to stick it to our chests.

On the third floor, we waited in a smaller room with chairs and a huge box full of stuffed toys for the children. Andrey smiled at Dasha inviting her to pick a toy or two from that box as a present, so she did not feel bored while we waited to get all the things sorted out.

She chose a small Teddy bear and that helped her relax a little, switching her mind from waiting in the stuffy room with just one small window open, with the noise and lots of strangers around her. Andrey then collected the filled-in forms from everyone and disappeared behind another the door in this room.

After maybe nearly an hour of waiting, we were given about four hundred Euros in cash and that was it. We had now been registered with the authorities and were free to go back. They told us we could already find a job, if we are lucky, and if/when we do, just let them know about it.

We were also not allowed to move to another region of Germany unless there was a very good reason for it – like a job there or something equally important. Therefore, we were required to stay in the Weilheim-Schongau area, in Seeshaupt.

Andrey also gave us a printed schedule of social payouts from April until June. The monthly amount for the three of us was around 900 Euros. This time we had been given around 400 EUR since half of March was already behind.
As we left, were saw that a lot of people had gathered in front of Landratsamt's main entrance by then, we heard Russian speech and other languages which I was unable to recognize. Refugees kept coming and Germany seemed to be bottomless to accommodate them all.

ROCK-N-ROLL OLD MAN IN WEILHEIM

In Landratsamt, we also got an address of a warehouse where refugees could go and get some essential stuff and clothes donated by local people. Since we came only with our winter things on (and some of them in our suitcases as well) and did not have enough cash for shopping yet, we decided to give it a go.

But first, we wanted breakfast – I felt really hungry after having only some oats with yogurt at Tom's in the morning. We found a coffee shop nearby with tables outside. Mary picked it and I did not really care. We ordered toast with ham and cheese and coffee. The bartender was a bearded young guy in his late 20s, with a bandana wrapped around his head and tattoos on his arms. He was polite and gave us a sincere friendly smile.

The toast was really good, so was the cappuccino. I asked for the bill then. Seeing that we were not local but I talked to him in English, he asked about where we had come from. Hearing that we had got there all the way from Ukraine, with a generous gesture he waved away my hand with the money.
"It's on the house", he said, "welcome to Germany."

That was certainly a nice surprise – it's not about the 15 Euros the bill required, it was about the attitude.

We decided to take a little stroll around the centre of Weilheim. Small streets paved with cobblestones, pretty-looking European houses of two or three floors. Dasha kept looking at stores with clothes since she loves shopping. On the square in the middle of the city, there was a church, again with domes shaped like onions.

Funny that the German word for onion "Zwiebel" sounds very similar to its Ukrainian analog – "tsybulya". I'm not sure, though, if that similarity is original or it was a late Ukrainian borrowing. Overall, there are many basic words in Ukrainian that sound like English or German, like English "cost", German "kosten", Ukrainian "koshtuvaty", etc.

After an hour of strolling and looking at the city, we then decided to ask for directions to that warehouse with clothes. After a few failed attempts (the local people had no idea if there was any bus that would take us there) I found an appealing pizza place and decided to try my luck in it. We ordered more coffee and a pizza. The latter was clearly not freshly cooked but rather just unfrozen in an oven for us. There was some sort of soft rock music playing in the bar speakers quietly.

I asked the bartender about the directions, showing him the paper with the address of the place. Obviously, he saw the line of text on the paper that was given out to refugees from Ukraine.

When I had looked up that route in Google Maps first, I saw that it would take us nearly an hour to walk there (and then the same long walk back to the city centre) and Dasha was certainly not up to that. Nor was I or Mary, to be honest. The Maps did not show any bus routes going that way.

The bartender was also pretty friendly, already in his late forties, with a beard and big muscly arms, looking a bit like a biker, with a ring in his left ear. In Germany, as I noticed later, a lot of men wear earrings – both left and right ones.

In Russia, bikers, rock musicians, and often artists too wear them in their left ears. A ring in the right ear is believed to often suggest a homosexual orientation but I think this is not the case in Germany. Anyway, asked a guy at the bar, who he had been talking to, about the place we needed – in German. That second guy looked pretty much like the bartender.

Next to him sat a man about over sixty, wearing a bandana with skulls and guitars around his head, he also had a pair of yellowish sunglasses on. He wore a leather waistcoat too. Were these two bikers as well? I wondered half-jokingly. A pizzeria run by the local version of "Hells Angels"? I wondered if they might have been under some stuff – like weed since they were joyful and laughing all the time.

But maybe at their age, all the harmful things they can get up to in Germany are beer and fried sausages.

What happened after that was pretty interesting and very much unexpected. The following minute that old man in yellowish glasses said he would drive us to that warehouse on the far end of the city.

I do not remember the make of his car but it was red and small with enough room for the four of us to sit comfortably. I casually asked him if it was easy to get a SIM card in Weilheim. I did it with no second thought, just for the sake of a conversation (while I still needed a SIM card, though).

It seemed that he was eager to be of help since he immediately drove us to the nearest mobile phone shop. It was lunchtime, so the place turned out to be closed. "Oh shit", our volunteer driver said heartily, when I shared this fact with him. I noticed this peculiar thing – when Germans speak English, they gladly use this popular English swear word, rather than use their own "Scheisse", which I think sounds equally juicy and emotional.

This love for English swearing seems to be a fine hint of the high degree of attraction German people have for the English language. Or perhaps this is just their desire to show how well they can speak it. I mean, the first thing you often learn when studying a foreign language, especially if you are twenty, is swear words. They make you feel curious as if they give a speaker some sort of magic power. Perhaps, no accident that "curse" (from American English) has a basic meaning related to dark magic.

Here's a good example. I cannot speak Chinese, but one of the first things I learned when I had a Chinese girlfriend ten years ago was how to say "fuck off" in their language.

Anyway, we then drove off to look for the warehouse. On our

way there, the old bandana man kept asking us about Ukraine, about the war, and told us funny stories from the days when he was young.

I was quickly translating all of that to Mary. Dasha was looking from the window at the city that was sailing past.

Finally, the man admitted to loving rock music and put on some stuff on the player. It sounded pretty good and I told him so immediately. I wanted to thank this man somehow and this was not a bad, albeit small, option, I think. He explained that it was a Swedish hard rock band. I wish I had remembered their name, so I could find their music on the Internet later on. It was cool indeed.

* * *

When we arrived at the address printed on the paper and got out of the car, I offered the old man some money for the ride. I mean, pensions are not too high even in Germany these days, are they.
He frowned at me and said: "Are you stupid? You'd better spend that money on your family". I thanked him and off he drove then.

We found ourselves surrounded by wide but not tall buildings that looked like big shopping malls, like IKEA or similar shops built outside Moscow in Russia since they take up a lot of space. There were no people outside here, the streets between these buildings were almost completely empty.

We just saw a couple of families with children who loaded some dissembled furniture into their cars and drove away. Cars were also parked in front of these buildings. A little farther off, by the motorway, there seemed to be a big construction site.

We found the address and it was indeed a huge warehouse there. Inside, there were a few staffers, three elderly women and one man. They smiled at us and said we could pick up things we needed – there were many metallic boxes made of grids.

Some were full of stuff for bathing and hygiene – toothbrushes, toothpaste tubes, bars of soap, packets with liquid soap, shampoo, etc. Everything here was donated, apparently, or bought with donations from local people.

There was a box with liners, pads, and tampon packs. At the farther end of the big square hall with a high ceiling stood grid boxes full of clothes – for adults and children separately. Jackets, coats, dresses, trousers, skirts – everything pretty much. In other boxes were shoes – winter boots and trainers mostly.

None of it was of the right size for me or Mary. And not many things were there that looked nice to wear anyway. My wife finally did manage to find a between-season coat, because she did not bring one from Ukraine. I picked a pair of winter boots.

We also found a couple of coats for Dasha, picked a bottle of shampoo, shower gel, and toothpaste with toothbrushes. That was it. One of the ladies who worked in that place told us we had come too late, all the best stuff had already been taken away by other refugees. She and her colleagues spoke fine English.

We thanked them and left. I then tried to find a route for us to go back to Seeshaupt. To do that, we first needed to head back to Weilheim's main station. Google Maps showed that we would have to walk for about forty minutes before we could catch a bus to take us there.

It was the same problem that we had faced in Weilheim earlier today when we wanted to get here. Now, it seemed a problem to get back. And this was for the sake of old but robust-looking winter boots, shampoo, and toothpaste, which we took just in case but we might as well have bought them in Seeshaupt.

We walked back to the warehouse and I asked the women if there was any bus back to Weilheim that perhaps Google was unaware of. They shook their heads apologetically.

Then one of them asked where we wanted to go. Hearing that our accommodation was in Seeshaupt, they looked at each other, signed sympathetically, and exchanged a few words in German. I explained to them that our daughter was autistic and would be unable to walk for forty minutes.

One of the women called an old guy from the back of the warehouse. He told us there were no buses to Weilheim from there but he would gladly give us a lift to Seeshaupt as he lives nearby anyway.

I suppose he added that just not to let us feel completely uncomfortable. But we did not feel that way at all, sorry. Call us cheeky bastards if you like but we were very happy and grateful. I was again amazed at how easily all these Germans we had briefly met on that day helped us out, indeed going out of their way to do that.

As the man let us off near Seeshaupt train station, I looked up how to say "you are very kind" in German in the translator app and said it to the old man from my heart. He seemed to be very pleased to hear this not in English but in his native language. He waved at us with a smile and drove off.

SHARING HOUSE WITH TOM

It was a long time since I had rented a room from a landlady/family, living in the same flat with them. Basically, the last time it happened was more than ten years ago. Since then, Mary and I had been living in rented flats in Kyiv, and for the past two years before the war we lived in our own apartment.

By that time, merely one thought of having to rent a room in somebody else's flat and living together with the owners, which of course included sharing the kitchen and bathroom, gave me the creeps.

But we were lucky since Tom's house was big enough and he lived on his own. The whole second floor was at our disposal. His parents rented a house far off, giving their son a chance to live by himself. Besides, Tom did his best to make our stay with him easy and psychologically comfortable for us.

When he was not at university in Munich (about forty minutes by train from Seeshaupt), he spent most of his time in his big room on the first floor, studying and playing games on his PC with a huge monitor. He loved rock climbing, so one of the walls there was turned into a rock-climbing exerciser with all those plastic things that look like rocks used for pulling yourself up and then for putting your feet on them as support to climb higher.

Dasha used to climb on such a toy wall back in Ukraine several times in entertainment rooms for children, so once or twice we asked Tom if she could use his climbing exerciser and he gladly helped her do that by holding her by the back, while she did her best to climb up.

In the morning, he was often off to uni, so the kitchen was all ours. Mary loved sitting there during the daytime watching YouTube on the phone or just sitting outside at the table on the mini terrace, writing her diary or just "mentally digesting" the new life: coming to terms with the war, with having to give up our settled and comfortable life in Ukraine to get to a completely new country. A country where we were brought down to zero basically and would have to start everything from scratch.

Sometimes, she and Tom cooked together – the kitchen was pretty cozy (with the cupboards coloured in red and yellow looking very much vintage and hand-made) and two windows – a regular one and a tiny window, through which you could see the table outside and the garage that Tom used for storing bicycles and bags with rubbish.

The path from the door in the fence near the road was also visible, so you could see through this tiny window (like through an arrow loop in a castle) if anyone was approaching the front door. Still, the kitchen, even though cozy, was very small, with space literally enough for two people moving around. Mary used gestures and a translation app to communicate with Tom when they happened to use the place at the same time.

Kate had told us that he might perhaps like Ukrainian food, so whenever Mary cooked borscht or salad, she always told Tom to help himself whenever he wanted. He always thanked her and seemed pleased.

Often, he went for a whole weekend to the mountains with his friends – they would ride their bikes and then do a bit of climbing or just climb without cycling. As he was about to leave he would always tell me: "Enjoy the free house!"

Sometimes when I saw him putting his gear into a bag, I would ask, "Tom, are you going climbing?" "Again," he would say with a proud smile, "and then again, and again, and again."

* * *

A couple of times, we had lunches together. We offered it more often but Tom then began to politely (the way Western people do) turn down our offers, saying that he had too much studying to do. Mary thought that perhaps Ukrainian food did not go down well for him, so we did not insist, nor did we take offense. After the first month, we began thinking that he got gradually tired of our presence in the house, although he never showed it or said anything.

When we only moved in, I asked Tom how long it would be okay for us to stay. He said that one month would be fine for sure and then, maybe, his sister would come over from the US where she was doing her PhD.

Later on, when we met Tom's parents, his father Robert told us very politely that they were considering moving to Switzerland if the government did not lift the Covid restrictions soon (since they were strongly against these measures). This would mean they would have to sell this house, Robert explained.

Their family was very religious, but it was true about the parents rather than Tom himself as it seemed to me. His father's small red Hyundai had a sticker on the boot, saying

"No Jesus – no Truth. Know Jesus – know Truth". Inside the house, as you entered the small corridor, you faced a big wooden cross on the wall between the toilet and the bathroom.

On a small table near the stairs that led to the second floor, there were two transparent plastic bags full of aluminum tokens shaped like coins with text on them, saying "Where will you spend the eternity?" Part of them was in German, and part was in English.

Tom and his family were not vaccinated against Covid (neither were we, by the way) as they believed that the obligatory vaccination restricted one's freedom and for other reasons as well. Because of this too, as Tom told us later, his sister decided not to come over from the States – she would be unable to go back there without a vaccination certificate.

While we stayed with Tom, Mary and I heard many stories about refugees from Ukraine who did not get along well with the families who accommodated them, not only in Germany. Sometimes, it was the fault of those refugees themselves, sometimes the families did not treat them well.

Russian media began spreading stories about a young Ukrainian woman who ran away with a husband (who was also a father of two children) in England, making him divorce his wife and other similar stories that gave Ukrainian refugees a bad name.

I'm sure many of them were made up by the "Troll Army" (that's the name of teams of content writers and bloggers hired by "Putin's cook" Evgeny Prigozhin – a story to follow later on – whose job was to spread anti-Western propaganda, including things about how Ukrainians are either suffering abroad or how locals sheltering them are suffering from those refugees).

There was, however, a pretty loud story, when a Ukrainian lady stole 30 bicycles in Denmark and then transported them to Ukraine (to sell them) through Germany. She was arrested while crossing the Polish border.

I have read about a similar case when a Ukrainian woman stole bicycles in Germany that were parked outside. When caught red-handed by the police, she said to the interpreter something like: "Germans are rich, they can afford to buy more". A new bicycle in Germany costs six hundred euros and more, just for reference.

Some Ukrainians indeed are quite nasty and they can give a bad time to people who let them stay in their homes. But there are nasty people in absolutely any nation, aren't there? This cannot be applied to a whole people in general. There are plenty of Ukrainians who are decent and respectful to Germans or to people of other countries who are giving them shelter and material support.

PART 4

BUCHA MANSLAUGHTER. ATOMIC STATION SEIZED BY RUSSIAN TROOPS

Mary and I kept reading news from Ukraine nearly every day. I subscribed to several Telegram channels that posted daily reports on how the war was progressing.

About that time, Russian troops had withdrawn from around Kyiv as a "goodwill gesture" but in reality, they wanted to focus their attacks on the Southern regions of Donetsk, Kherson, and Zaporizhzhia. The latter two are close to the Black Sea, so they are strategically important for Russia – to ensure a free land bridge between Crimea and the part of the Donetsk region controlled by Russians.

Besides, Kherson and Zaporizhzhia contain a lot of fertile lands, where hundreds of thousands of tonnes of wheat, corn, and other crops, as well as fruit, are grown in huge amounts every year. A lot of it was usually exported but there was always enough for Ukraine as well.

There is also the Zaporizhzhia atomic station, the largest in Europe. It is based in the town of Energodar and was captured by Russians in early March 2022. Russians then used it as a foothold to shoot missiles at the Ukrainian troops that surrounded Energodar to get it back, using the atomic station as a shield. This station is also an asset worth billions of US dollars, which is important to Russia.

Later on, IAEA inspectors were allowed to enter it. They found multiple violations of safety measures and required that the town with the station was returned to the control of Ukrainians. The atomic station was shot at several times by Russians – first, while they were taking it by storm and later, allegedly, to accuse Ukrainian troops of doing it to create an atomic catastrophe that could hit Europe.

The station now remains under the control of Russia and has been connected to the Russian electricity network, since that part of Zaporizhzhia formally voted to join the Russian Federation – with the results of the referendums most likely falsified.

People voted out of fear, seeing the military armed with Kalashnikovs (AK-47s) standing next to the women who walked around apartment blocks, knocking on every door to make them vote for joining Russia.

Later, stories were published told by Ukrainians about so-called Russian "filtration camps", which they had to pass in order to get out of the occupied regions.

To do that, they had to prove they had no connection to the Ukrainian army, that they had not criticized Russian politics and the war on social media and in personal messages in messaging apps. A lot of Ukrainian men were held there in awful conditions for months. A lot of them never made it out of them alive.

* * *

As the war started, Russians also took control of the forsaken Chernobyl city and its power station, placing their military in it, making them dig trenches to use that place as a strategic foothold for attacking Kyiv. Those trenches were dug right near the closed atomic station, where the radiation level is still pretty high. The soldiers who were there can be now almost guaranteed lethal health issues in the future. The troops were withdrawn from there later on as they continued with their maneuvers.
Dark-humoured jokes then began to spread around Ukraine that you can take Russian soldiers out of Chernobyl but there is no way you can take Chernobyl out of Russian soldiers.

Speaking again of natural resources, the Donetsk region contains 60% of all coal deposits in Ukraine worth around $12 trillion. There are small occurrences of natural gas, oil, and 20% of Ukraine's precious metals deposits there. This is another important reason why Russia conducted fake referendums in those occupied territories to add them to the Russian Federation.

The local Ukrainians were forced to vote "yes" with guns to their heads or with unvoiced threats to end up in a filtration camp, where "Nazis were to rehabilitate" and get a pro-Russian position about Ukraine. Many who managed to get out of those Russian camps told stories about regular beatings, often even getting tortured with electric shocks. At least that was said in reports by anti-war Russian media, prohibited by Putin now.

I find those quite easy to believe. Especially taking into account the fact that there are similar "rehabilitation camps" in China for ethnic Uigurs and everyone else who is not happy about the Communist Party reign and dares to express their opinion publicly. You can find videos of those Chinese camps on YouTube, where they are called "special schools". There people sing Chinese patriotic songs, smile, and get taught to think well of the government.

Some of those "students" were interviewed by journalists, and they said they had come there of their own will because the police or a social worker had recommended them to do it. They say they are happy but if you look at those people – they have eyes of imbeciles, since perhaps only they can justify their stay in those closed camps with high fences of barbed wire around them and smile, saying they are happy.

* * *

So, in March, Russian troops withdrew from towns and villages around Kyiv. When Ukrainian forces entered them, they found dead bodies of civilians all around the town of Bucha. Corpses lay in the streets – unarmed civilian men, women, teenagers, elderly people. Many bodies had their hands tied behind their backs, executed by shooting in the back of their heads. A lot of cottages and flats had been looted – jewellery, cash, even microwave ovens, toasters, and washing machines went missing.

Bucha is a wealthy place since a lot of people there work in Kyiv. Overall, many Ukrainians live better than Russians in provinces because they earn quite a lot in Poland or go to work on Western cruise ships and then send money back home.

Just to make it clear – a lot of soldiers that were thrown to Ukraine from Russia came from the poorest regions, such as Buryatia (Eastern Siberia). In Russia, all wealth is mostly concentrated in Moscow and St. Petersburg.

Go to small towns and villages and you will face poverty, unrepaired roads, toilets outside of homes that have almost fallen apart from old age and lack of repair, schools with no central heating, whole villages with no even infrastructure for supplying gas there, where people still use firewood in winter.

Many bodies of Ukrainian men found in Bucha had traces of torture, a lot of women and teenage girls had been raped. Dozens of bodies had been thrown into mass graves, basically just huge pits, and buried with no recognizable signs except man-made hills of earth, indicating that someone had been covering a massive pit.

The whole of Ukraine was shocked by this. I was shocked as well. I then recalled that back in 2015, when I worked for an IT company in Kyiv, I had a colleague who commuted from Bucha to our office every day. After hearing the awful news about the mass killings, I got in touch with him immediately.

Sasha responded – he was okay, staying in Kyiv with his parents, where he had quickly moved when the war only started; it proved a very wise decision. He did not get to witness all the horrible stuff that took place in the town when the Russian troops came in.

RUSSIA DENIES ACCUSATIONS. ITS PREVIOUS WARS IN CHECHNYA

Of course, Russian officials and the Russian media denied the manslaughter in Bucha and in a few other villages and towns that were de-occupied by the Ukrainian army later on.

The major argument Russians used to deny this was it was all "faked" and "staged". They claimed that the dozens of civilians in Bucha were killed by Ukrainian troops and then demonstrated to the whole world and their Western allies that allegedly cruel Russian soldiers slaughtered people who never held any arms, including women.

This has been one of the major arguments of the Russian propaganda – "we are not fighting against civilians or Ukraine's regular armed forces", they claimed, "we are fighting Ukrainian Nazis" ("Ukro-Nazis" as Putin and all those who support the war refer to them). As the war progressed, they began labelling all Ukrainian troops "Nazis", including the regular army.

In the autumn, after a truck exploded on the bridge that connects Crimea and Russia, Putin ordered to begin shelling power and TV stations (beginning with Kyiv and then moving those attacks to other cities), and then – residential buildings, business centres, supermarkets, concert halls.

He and all his officials kept claiming that Russia was only attacking "objects of military importance". Whenever a rocket or a drone hit a residential building, killing people in their sleep at night, or shopping malls, they claimed that these were the ricochet strikes of Ukrainian anti-rocket defense forces. Or that it was just "fake news" (thanks, Donald Trump, for this idiotic catch phrase). Russians have adopted the noun "fake" without even bothering to translate it.

The Russian anti-war media and their Instagram/Telegram accounts then published photos of those destroyed apartment blocks, supermarkets, and dead bodies lying on the floor amidst debris. They published photos of funerals where young mothers with their underage children or teenagers were being buried.

After those rocket strikes, pro-war Russian "Z" Telegram channels and chats were full of mocking messages, like "serves you right, you fucking Naziks", "let's keep shooting khokhlies (a derogatory word for Ukrainians used by Russians), and others of the same kind.

* * *

It is important to note here how Putin's rule in Russia started, and what happened before he was appointed as acting president by Yeltsin and then elected in 2000.

In 1998-1999, there were series of explosions in the entrances of residential buildings in large cities of Russia. Explosions took place at night, and Putin (before he became president but while he was the FSB director - the Russian Federal Security Service) then stated that it was done by "Chechen terrorists" – back then, Russia was still at war with Chechnya, who wanted independence, just like Ukraine now.

People around Russia began to gather in teams and stay vigil outside at the entrances of residential buildings every night to watch out for anyone suspicious.

My father and I spent a few nights on such night watches (it was my dad mostly, who stayed for most of the night, I went home to sleep after 1 a.m., I was about 18 then) near our "podyezd" – that's the door on the first floor through which everybody enters their part of a residential block, then takes a lift to their floor, there are usually four to five of such "podyezds" per each flat building.

Once an article came out that two suspicious men were caught at night by such a group of residents.

They turned out to be FSB officers with explosives. FSB then claimed that it was "an experiment" and that the explosive stuff inside the bombs was in fact sugar. But many thought that those explosions were ordered by Putin since he used that circumstance to strengthen his power in the upcoming presidential race. A lot of people still think so and they became even more confident in this now that the war in Ukraine has begun.

Putin then promised to chase Chechen terrorists and fight them wherever they would be caught, even on the toilet.
"If we catch them in the loo, we will bloody kill them there" – those were his public words which became a catchphrase later on – "мочить в сортире" ("сортир" ("sortir") is a Russian slang word for "toilet"). In The Washington Post article it was translated as "to rub terrorists out in the outhouse." It quickly became a catch phrase.

There were two Chechen wars. The first one lasted from 1994 until 1996. The second one went on from 1999 until 2006. Putin, who ran the second one, was unable to defeat Chechens since even when Russians started shelling their troops, Chechens would merely hide in mountain caves.

Russian soldiers were being killed in thousands. Chechen civilians perished in large amounts too, although Putin claimed there were no official statistics about that. The number of Russian soldiers named officially is likely to be significantly smaller compared to the actual figure. Russian troops then also started bombing civilian buildings in Chechnya, including apartment blocks, just like they are doing in Ukraine now.

Do you know how they ended? Putin found a pro-Russian leader, who gained power in the country back
then. First, it was Akhmad Kadyrov. During the first Chechen war, Kadyrov fought against the Russian troops. In 1999, he (and his son Ramzan, respectively) sided with the Russian Federation and started representing them in Chechnya. Some believe they were put on an FSB payroll.

Later, when Kadyrov senior became president of Chechnya in the early 2000s, Ramzan worked in the government in one of the highest-ranking positions close to his father. In 2003, he was appointed the head of the president's security service. He often negotiated with Chechen rebels, who still wanted independence, and convinced them one way or another to side with the Russian Federation.

There were several attempts to assassinate him. After Kadyrov senior was assassinated (an explosion in Grozny, the capital of Chechnya, in 2004) Ramzan continued to occupy high positions in the Chechen government, in particular spearheading the force structures. He was chosen as president in 2007 by the majority of the parliament after his candidature was suggested by Putin. By that time, Kadyrov was already the acting president anyway.

ZELENSKY ENCOUNTERS CHECHNYA'S PRESIDENT BEFORE WAR

Kadyrov dealt with everyone in Chechnya who still wanted to get separated from Russia; he convinced them to convert and start collaborating with the Chechen government controlled by Russia. Among those separatists, there were a lot of Kadyrov's relatives. All these materials are easily accessible on the Internet – feel free to open the Wikipedia.

Putin started sending to Chechnya big grants regularly to "help to rebuild" the republic after the war. Thus, Chechnya remained part of the Russian Federation but Kadyrov has been Putin's vassal since then. Chechnya's constant income is still coming from Putin's grants. Of course, Kadyrov and lower-tier members of the Chechnya's administration and members of their families control all that money, living lavishly well-off.

Now, Kadyrov is a famous authoritarian leader who strikes down all his political opponents. He has been doing it since he became president. Chechen bloggers and activists who are criticising his ruling are getting kidnapped in Chechnya and even on the territory of Russia, "arrested by local Federal Security Service or Ministry of Inner Affairs" as they call it and then they are taken over to Chechnya.

Nobody ever sees those people again. If you publicly insult Kadyrov on the Internet and this video or an article gets big public attention, and you are not a member of the Russian government or an oligarch, that is almost similar to signing your death sentence.

There was one media-covered case – in 2019, when Zelensky was still a stand-up comedian and ran his own show "Evening Quarter" (made and produced by his media company) before he became president, crying Kadyrov was shown during one of those stand-up performances with a voice commenting on that video, making jokes (they were not even targeted at Chechnya's president, the video was just taken as an illustration, sort of a meme).

This was part of a video clip where the Chechen leader was attending the funeral of a person close to him. That video was broadcast around Ukraine and got out onto the Internet.

Apparently, Zelensky was not involved in making that part of the show, since he only approved major scenarios and the business strategy overall.

However, when he got a phone call about that incident, he immediately apologized publicly to Kadyrov. He was accused of insulting the religious feelings of Chechen Muslims (an official accusation). Zelensky then apologised on TV and YouTube, stating that religion is a very "sensitive matter" and they never intended to insult anyone. The video was removed from the official YouTube channel of his show.

* * *

Kadyrov's troops now are taking part in the war in Ukraine and he supports Putin heatedly in this matter. If Putin loses power in Russia, Kadyrov will likely lose it in Chechnya – the maths is simple here. Putin and his regime cover up for all that – when people are kidnapped in Russia and taken to Chechnya for execution, Russian police do nothing and Putin's press secretary Peskov says that either "they do not interfere with Chechnya's inner affairs" or that this matter "needs to be checked thoroughly before any serious actions are taken".

In late 2023, Kadyrov's 15-year-old son beat an arrested Russian guy almost to death – for burning a Koran in a street full of people – pay attention here, please – the burning happened in Russia. Kadyrov's son beat the poor guy after he was taken to Chechnya. Kadyrov senior praised his son for that "deed" publicly. Peskov did not even comment on that. This is how the Russian government protects Russian people from Chechen Islamic gangsters who rule in Chechnya. But, of course, they must "save the Russian-speaking population" in Ukraine.

Since the second war in Chechnya ended, not only Kadyrov and his close circle became "sheiks", all the Chechen mafia in Russia, especially in Moscow and St. Petersburg, were given a lot of preferences.

So were average Chechens in Russia, since they have a Chechen expat community in every Russian big city. Now, Chechens often commit violent crimes in Russia, but then they get off easily – either get a small prison sentence, court rulings are made in their favour or pretty often the police do not even accept legal complaints against them.

Chechens run large and small businesses, like food and clothes markets (those were popular back in the 1990s), selling shaurma (rolls with grilled chicken and vegetables, very popular fast food in Russia (something close to Doner Kebab)) and owning casinos.

There is a classic Russian movie "Brat" ("The Brother") shot back in the 90s about that decade that you can watch (I'm sure you can find it on the Internet with English subs if you want to). It is about Russian and Chechen assassins, gang fights taking place to the accompaniment of a soundtrack made by a popular Russian rock band.

This movie is loved by Russians, and it illustrates pretty well life in the country back in those years.
This is an iconic movie for the majority of average Russian people, and the main character is believed to be something like a national hero. His name is Danila Bagrov.

He is a former military who came back from Chechnya to his provincial hometown. After getting in trouble with the police on the first day upon his return, he decides to move to St. Petersburg, where his elder brother is a prosperous assassin, although their mother is not aware, thinking that he just became a "big boss" there. A "freelancer", in the original meaning of this word, is a knight with a lance who fights for those lords who can offer the highest payment.

Then Danila takes over and begins killing people on his brother's orders. He also kills two gangsters to save accidental victims among civilians.

The idea was to show him as some sort of a Robin Hood but in reality, the main character of the "Brat" movie is merely a brat, for whom killing or injuring anyone for the smallest reason is not a big deal at all. Perhaps the popularity of this film and this Danila Bagrov character is one of the reasons why Russia is attacking Ukraine now.

What you read and watch ultimately impacts you, often in a

way that you do not realize it at all, like hypnosis.

There was also an iconic Russian film serial "The Brigade". It was about three guys who were friends since childhood and then they formed a gang after the USSR was gone, and then they also fought for "the truth and justice" using their own illegal methods. This was shot in the early 2000s and it looks like a Russian version of "The Scarface" movie a little. The actor who had the main role in "The Brigade" is actually very talented and by now he has become almost an icon in Russia. He supports the war against Ukraine, alas.

The majority of Russians are so easily manipulated with the ideas of "fighting for the truth/justice", of "protecting the weak" (thinking they are protecting the Russian-speaking population of Eastern Ukraine, while they are simply killing the Russian-speaking people in this country), "standing for the good against the whole world turning bad", etc.

BUREAUCRATIC HURDLES IN SEESHAUPT

Anyway, let's go back to our new life in Germany. As we began to settle in Seeshaupt, we faced many bureaucratic issues to solve. For example, we had to register in the Rathaus in Seeshaupt, go to Weilheim to provide piles of papers to Landratsamt, fill in tonnes of forms to continue receiving social payments and then also to start receiving Kindergeld (250 euros monthly paid to help parents to take care of their children until they reach the age of 16 in Germany).

Since all these papers were in German, we had no choice but to ask Tom and his father Robert to help us with that. They translated these forms for us, helped us fill them in, made phone calls to Landratsamt since only few workers speak English there and they were never around when I called.

Actually, we were lucky that Germans had done their best to simplify all these procedures for refugees from Ukraine – when people flee Iran, Syria, Afghanistan, or other countries with wars or religious authoritarian regimes, all this bureaucracy can last for years for these poor people. But we were lucky to receive a temporary residence permit for half a year with an opportunity for prolongation and you were allowed to get a job immediately.

Besides, all Ukrainians were required to enroll in integration German language courses, so that afterwards they could study a new profession or begin working with one they had in Ukraine.

Some Ukrainians began getting low-qualified jobs, like working as waitresses, dishwashers. Those were mostly women in their forties or thirties. A lot of men took to driving trucks, fixing water pipes, electric wire, or redecorating flats and houses – things they did for a living in Ukraine before the war.

* * *

Before that, even when moving to Ukraine I had never faced having to fill in such a huge amount of papers. Mary and I had to write there about our education, previous work experiences, how much we used to earn, to say if we had been ensured privately in Ukraine or not and other similar kind of stuff.

Then we had to get ourselves medical insurance because otherwise, it was impossible to visit a doctor in Germany. Later on, when we moved to another town, I had tonsillitis with a high fever and was hardly able to hold on to my feet. Nurses in a local clinic refused to let me in until I showed them the number of my medical insurance card, which was in the process of being issued.

My landlady, who was with me then, had to call the insurance company right there standing in front of that small rural hospital on a cold November day, a clerk told the number to the nurses and only then did they let me in to see a doctor. The doctor gave me an indifferent smile and said that without that insurance number, this visit would have cost me around 300 euros. That's capitalism, there is nothing you can do about it. All of these things required sending a lot of emails, making phone calls, filling in papers (and then filling them again), sending them by post, then sending more papers later as more details about us were necessary to submit.

I had to arrange the medical insurance myself, while as we found out later, the jobcentre was supposed to do that. So it turned into a kind of mess – I got myself, Mary, and Dasha insured with a branch of a popular insurance company in the North of Germany, then their Bavarian branch told us we had to be insured with them and Mary still uses a paper-substitute with her insurance number because the card has not issued even a year after our registration with them.

I was surprised to discover later that Germans have insurance for nearly all aspects of their lives – if you accidentally scratch somebody's car or cause damage to another property that belongs to somebody else, you need insurance to cover that. If you want to use the services of a lawyer, you need other insurance (unless you want to pay a hefty hourly fee by yourself). If you die all of a sudden, you need another type of insurance (but we have the same thing in Russia and Ukraine too, although the compensation is low), you need insurance to get proper dentist treatment (which goes beyond the basic one covered by regular medical insurance).

The problem is, as I was told, that Germany was already used to only "slow-coming" refugees from the aforementioned countries. They were not prepared to embrace such a huge inflow of people coming from Ukraine now. Hence the mess and bureaucratic chaos. But at least they provided accommodation and social payouts for people pretty quickly, which was very efficient for them.

Then we had to get Dasha to a local school. Tom's dad kindly offered his help with this. In Seeshaupt, there is a primary school where children go from the first to the fourth form. Tom told us that he and his sister had attended that school and then went off to study in secondary and high school in Weilheim, riding a bus there and back home every day.

Robert went to the Seeshaupt school with us. He explained to me that it would be a lot more efficient and faster if he did the talking since his children had attended that school already and so the teachers would be more open to him (a local person would be more welcome anyway), rather than if I went there by myself and tried to settle the matter.

Besides, since Dasha is autistic, she needed a special school regime – in Ukraine she got tired quickly from too much emotional pressure at school because of a lot of people around and tasks that were too difficult for her. So back home she attended school for three days per week. We hoped to arrange more or less the same easy schedule here for Dasha, also because she would have a language barrier here.

Robert succeeded with that and he too seemed amazed at how easily the school principal agreed to take on Dasha without any paperwork at all, without any local confirmation of her diagnosis, and allowed her to attend two or three days a week. We had a medical certificate about Dasha's diagnosis from Ukraine but still had to be confirmed by doctors in Germany.

I'm putting a special focus on Tom and his parents here, because their help to us went truly beyond any limits, while other refugees did not get even one-third of such assistance and sympathy from the people they were staying with. Robert and Claudia (Tom's mother) also went as far as to help us find a second-hand bicycle for Dasha (although, she has been unable to ride it yet) and invited us to celebrate Easter with them in April 2022 in the backyard of their house. I can certainly say that they accepted us almost as if we were part of their family.

AIR-RAID SIRENS – WHAT THE HELL WAS THAT?!

Once about noon, when we were in the house, I heard an air-raid siren go off very loudly. That sound made me shudder. It was clearly in Seeshaupt, somewhere close to Tom's house. So I went to another room where Mary was knitting a plaid for her sister's newborn baby in Canada.

"Oh my God!" she exclaimed, her eyes wide open with fear and alert. "What's happening?! Do we have to run down to the basement?!"
The siren gave me the creeps but Mary looked way more than just slightly worried.

As I was shivering a little and my heart was pounding, I went out of the house to get a look around. Everything was calm and quiet, as it always was here – vintage white cottages with roofs of dark brown, and chopped firewood behind fences lying along the house walls. Yards outside the houses around us were empty but I spotted a neighbour in the yard of the house right next to ours.

I went out, came up to their fence that was just up to my waist, and asked her in English what the hell that siren was about.

The middle-aged lady gave me a friendly smile, then said: "Well, that's either an air-raid alert or there is a fire somewhere in Seeshaupt or near it and they are summoning the fire brigade. Most likely, it's the latter."

I thanked her and went back to the house. When I passed this explanation on to Mary, she breathed out, calming down and cursed this way of announcing a fire, sarcastically saying that she had nearly made a puddle because of that.

Just in case, to be completely sure, I wrote to a German friend of mine on Facebook. She used to study at Cambridge in the UK and now she lives and teaches there subjects to do with Russian literature, telling students about Pushkin, Dostoyevsky, and Soviet dissident writers.

Josie confirmed that this was indeed most likely a fire siren, nothing more. I asked her why Germans were so innovative as to use an air-raid siren for summoning a fire brigade. As it turned out, this practice was usual in small towns and villages where firefighters work voluntarily, basically.

I wondered, if they do not get paid and cannot go to put out a fire anytime it is necessary, and it is like a hobby for them, what happens if they are at their daily jobs when a fire starts? A guy is in the middle of negotiating a one billion contract with customers and he gets an alert that he is wanted right bloody now to extinguish a fire in a village twenty kilometres away from his office...

Small towns and villages in Germany seem to be doomed to get burned down one day, I thought then. Later on, I found out that this was quite a practical system that exploits local men's desire to do good deeds, charity and simply to get some adrenaline.

There is a special app, which notifies all the volunteers when there is a fire nearby. Those who are not busy, let the fire brigade know they are coming and so they are heading there to put the fire out. This is done in Germany instead of keeping a whole fire brigade on a payroll. I suppose it helps save a lot of a city's budget.

But there was a funny advantage to those sirens howling which I figured out later. When more Ukrainians began to arrive in Seeshaupt and they started panicking when a fire siren went off, I casually told them that they should relax – nothing was threatening them, no need to grab their emergency bags.

The same story was in the Telegram chat for Ukrainians in Germany. From time to time, somebody who is new in the country, asks what those sirens mean and whether they should be running down to the basement immediately.

I seemed to be the only one who responded to that person in the Telegram chat room, telling them that it was about a fire somewhere in their vicinity.

This information sort of made me knowledgeable and made me feel a little superior to refugees who had just arrived. And next time, I heard a siren go off in Seeshaupt, Mary and I also jumped nervously but it was more of an instinct and we quickly relaxed even without having to change our pants. Gradually, we got used to that and even went a few times to see a local fire brigade practicing in Seeshaupt.

BRIDGES BURNT: RUSSIAN CULTURE AND LANGUAGE CURSED BY UKRAINE

During the first couple of months of our stay in Seeshaupt, Mary and I felt on the one hand that we were safe being far away from the war zone now. On the other hand, I still felt awfully sad about my home country attacking Ukraine – the country which had also become home to me – and invaded it on a totally made-up pretext with specific purposes, though.

I was torn between thoughts that I was Russian who hated this war, that my countrymen practically tried to kill me, my wife and daughter (and our friends who remain in Ukraine), and the fact that I was basically betrayed by my own homeland. The Motherland, as government officials say pathetically when they want you to believe they are doing something extremely important and good, whereas in reality, it is the other way round.

I suppose it is much easier to be a Ukrainian in this situation

– you are just scared of the war, worried about your country getting invaded and destroyed, about your men dying in fights. You can just hate Russia and you will not be torn between the two feelings which in a way contradict each other.

You are on the side of Ukrainians because it is them who are being attacked, residential buildings getting levelled, civilians killed, women and girls raped in occupied towns and villages, and men who have military relatives are executed because they are believed to be spying for the Ukrainian army.

At the same time, you are crushed by the feeling that this is all being done not by aliens from a faraway galaxy but by your countrymen with whom you share basic cultural values and who have them same background and native language. All of these three aspects are hated in Ukraine now – the Soviet past, the Russian culture, the Russian language. Even by those in Ukraine who preferred to speak Russian before the war. Even if they continue to speak it, they have stopped using it on social media as it may cause hatred from their friends and subscribers. They are using it in public places now too, instead of Russian.

Playing Russian music in public places is prohibited (many modern pop and rock singers support this war, although there are also those who have made their pro-Ukrainian position clear and left Russia, now giving concerts to huge Russian-speaking audiences around the world). Selling Russian books is forbidden in Ukraine now. I expect that if anyone is caught listening to Russian music or reading a book in Russian there they will be at the very least taken to the nearest police station and questioned as to what the hell were they doing keeping a book written in the language of the occupants.

This is what Putin has done to the great language of Dostoevsky, Tolstoy and Pushkin, to the culture which is valued and studied in all major parts of the world.

This war has managed to achieve something that all Ukraine presidents failed to do before – unite Ukrainians really tight, giving them a sort of national idea – to get independent from Russia and to leave behind everything to do with it, condemning everything to do with Russia and its culture.

Putin has prevented the entrance of Ukraine in NATO for the time being but Finland (it has a border with Russia longer than Ukraine does) has become a NATO member and Sweden is in the process of joining it too. It is the right time to question whether the prevention of Ukraine joining NATO was the true reason for the invasion.

GERMAN "BOOSE FESTS" AND "SEXY" SHOP TITLES

During the first months of our stay in Seeshaupt, Mary and I did not feel well psychologically, especially Mary. We read the news every day to be aware of how the war was coming, hoping to see signs that it was going to end soon or reports about negotiations coming. Alas, we saw none of that.

We began drinking beer pretty often in the evenings, sometimes those were several evenings in a row. Mary felt very sad as she read a lot more news than I did. But I also kept checking what was happening in Russia, about celebrities – musicians, actors, film directors – protesting against the war.

Musicians, stand-up comics, and writers, who were pro-Ukraine and voiced their position openly on social media, left the country, heading for Israel mostly, or to the Baltic countries. Old school actors and directors were getting fired from famous and prestigious theatres; many were also forced to leave Russia or decided to do it themselves.

Some of my friends in Russia wrote to me to ask where I was

now and how I was doing. They told me about their shame about what was happening and their fear to say anything to oppose the invasion.

In the meantime, hundreds of people began to gather for protest meetings in the central squares of various Russian cities. A lot of them were arrested. Later, laws were passed that stating that speaking against the SVO (the "special military operation" as it is still hypocritically called by officials) and taking part in such meetings could get you up to 15 years in prison.

People began to get charges for "discrediting the Russian army" in their anti-war posts on social media, for speaking against the war, or publicly calling for peace in Ukraine.

A woman was taken to a nearby police station for coming out to the central square of a town (that is traditionally called Lenin Square since there is a monument to this guy) holding Tolstoy's "War and Peace". A ten-year-old girl made an anti-war drawing during her class at school. Her widowed father was arrested for that and the girl was sent to an orphanage. This is just a very short list of famous anti-war cases that have taken place in Russia recently.

People sharing their anti-war or pro-Ukrainian positions publicly began to be reported on by their colleagues, relatives, and friends. Those reports became more and more frequent over time, returning the country in the times of the late 1930s under Stalin's rule when thousands of people were getting reported on by their friends, colleagues and neighbours for any sign of "anti-Soviet" behaviour or criticism/jokes about Stalin or high-ranking Communist Party members.

All those people were then arrested, executed, or sent to labour camps. The status of those people in those times was "the enemy of the Soviet people". Now it has been replaced by "foreign agent".

First, it was given to organizations only, then it was spread to individuals too. Russian high-ranking officials close to Putin claim that this term was borrowed from the US, which sounds like "it was not us who began using it" or "if they can call their people that, so can we". This does not change the essence of the matter, though – repressions in Russia have come back after approximately 70 years of absence.

Sometimes, these people are not arrested but they are fired, and face difficulties finding new jobs. If they are bloggers or celebrities they are obliged by law to add the warning that "the following material is published by a foreign agent who is being funded by foreign anti-Russian organizations" (the quote is not an exact one but it shows the precise spirit of that message).

So, Mary and I drank beer in the evening at home or went to the seasonal cafe "Servus" (a word used for "hello" in the South of Germany and Austria); I have mentioned this place earlier. There we had Curry Wurst (cooked sausages with curry and potato chips). They cook it very tasty in Seeshaupt. With that, we would order a pint or two of popular local larger called "Helles" (or simply "Hell", a true name for beer in English when you have a bad hangover) and Weissbier – beer brewed from wheat. We drank it watching white swans swimming near the shore and looking at small waves splashing against the pebble stone beach.

The bartenders already began to remember us, knowing we were from Ukraine. One of them spoke perfect English, which made communication easier for me and allowed me to make some small talk while ordering beer or coffee. A young bartender in his twenties, whose name I never found out, asked us how we liked it in Germany, how we liked Seeshaupt and other similar things.

The sound of the splashing waves of the lake as we watched

them while getting anaesthesia from alcohol, made us let go of the worries, fears, and anguish. It gave us a bit of relief from what we felt about the war, Ukrainian soldiers and civilians dying there. About the old life going into the past and fading away. "The world has moved on", as gunslinger Roland in Stephen King's Dark Tower books say.

Once, a week or two after we came to live in Seeshaupt, we saw a small local beer festival dedicated to Ukraine, whose goal was to raise money for it. I'm not sure where this money went exactly eventually – to help refugees or to buy humanitarian aid for Ukrainians who chose to stay in the war zones. But I think it was the former.

The Ukraine Fest it was called or something like that. This was the first time that we saw what famous German "fests" were like. There are huge tents with long tables and benches inside full of people. The guests drink lots of beer, eat stakes and fried sausages (white and brown ones), talk, laugh a lot loudly, dance to live music, and sing. I started calling these events to myself "bukhlofests".

"Bukhlo" is a Russian slang word for "boose". Since such events never go without seas of beer, hence the "bukhlo" element. A funny fact – there is a town near Munich called Buchloe, which is pronounced basically as the Russian word for alcohol above (in German 'ch' is read as [kh]). Seeing this town's name on trains heading through it made me smile for the first couple of months, but then this reaction gradually faded out.

Anyway, during that fest in Seeshaupt, the big tent was full of people, a lot of them were teenagers. The air buzzed with happy voices of people talking, many of them a bit tipsy, but none seemed to be drunk to the degree when they were unable to stand.

When the bartender selling beer outside the tent heard my request in English, he asked if I was "from Ukrainian people".

When I nodded, he generously waved away my hand with money, insisting that I take the beers free of charge.

The price of beer was pretty high at that fest – four or five euros per bottle. I saw the same price policy during other beer fests later on, I thought it was a norm here to overcharge people for beer which can be bought in supermarkets for about 1.5-2 EUR.

However, during Oktoberfest, they sell casked beer, which is a lot tastier and is worth the money charged for it – about 10 EUR per litre mug. Often, here in Bavaria, during these gatherings, they wear traditional costumes.

* * *

A few words should be said here about these traditional Bavarian costumes ("Trachten" in German). Germans in Bavaria wear them not only during beer fests but also on various national and public holidays, and on days when big football games take place.

Men wear a "Lederhosen" – trousers (or rather shorts down to their knees) made of leather and decorated with various embroidered patterns. Often those are held using suspenders. Men also wear checked shirts with those leather breeches and sometimes waistcoats made of similar kinds of leather, also with embroidered patterns. Sometimes, a hat with a big feather sticking in it completes this costume on a man. Overall, these Lederhosen look pretty cool.

Women in Bavaria (Austria and Switzerland too) wear a "Dirndl". Here is how Wikipedia describes it – "A dirndl consists of a close-fitting bodice featuring a low neckline, a blouse worn under the bodice, a wide high-waisted skirt and an apron." This type of national clothes also looks very pretty and interesting.

The thing is that the word "Trachten" (plural for the German for "national costumes", pronounced as "trakhten") can raise certain associations for a Russian person – sex, to be precise. "Trach" (read as "trakh") in Russian is a sexual intercourse. "Trachten" looks like a verb ("en" is a verbal ending used in German) – to have sex. In German "trachten" as a verb means "strive" or "aspire". The second one is close to the Russian meaning to some degree, I would say.

There was a famous showman and actor Roman Trachtenberg (a stage pseudonym), who used to tell a lot of dirty jokes on TV and the radio in Russia until his sudden death in 2009 right during a radio show.

In Seeshaupt, there is a nice-looking building (designed in a folk style) with a big sign above the door which says "Trachtenheim". "Heim" is an element from Scandinavian mythology used as part of names of worlds – like Hellheim. It can mean: "land of", "world", "house", "safety haven", etc.

When I saw that place for the first time, I could not help laughing – the name sounded like a "brothel" to me. I realized that it could hardly be that but the title brought the name "Trachtenberg" in my memory. "Berg" is also strongly associated with Germany for Russians (it means a "mountain").

Anyway, it took me some time to find out what "trachten" means in reality. This may seem like silly stuff, but there's nothing you can do about it. I thought about telling Tom about this shop and about the associations it brought up but I doubted he would appreciate this.

There were similar cases in Ukrainian – some language elements that made me chuckle (because of their similarity to strong Russian swear words) when I came to live in Ukraine and so it took me several years to get used to them. They were actually written on hoardings and I heard them from local people. I suppose that is a global situation with languages of neighbouring peoples that are very similar to each other when it comes to vocabulary elements and phonetics.

MARY HIRED WITHOUT GERMAN KNOWLEDGE

Viktor Frankl was a Jewish-Austrian psychiatrist who founded logotherapy, a school of psychotherapy that describes a search for a life's meaning as the central human motivational force. In less professional circles, he is famous as the author of the book "Say Yes to Life In Spite of Everything", which Frankle wrote while he moved from one German Nazi concentration camp to another during WW2 and spent there several years, being one step away from death in many of its forms every day.

The main survival principle when you are locked in concentration camps he came up with, watching his cell-mates, was the following. First to die are those people who believe that the awful situation they are in will come to an end soon. Those who believe that it will never end lose life motivation and so they die fast too.

People who come back to their everyday lives, who busy themselves with chores, etc, are the ones who manage to survive in the long term. Frankl survived because he kept himself busy writing his book.

So after spending several weeks drinking beer in the evenings, visiting local bars and reading the news from Ukraine, Mary and I decided to try and come back to everyday life. Mary started filling in her CV, I translated it into English for her, then her sister Kate found a company that was hiring skilled psychotherapists with a knowledge of Russian and Ukrainian languages.

They were offered to distantly work with the victims of the war who left for Germany or remained in Ukraine, providing these people with professional psychological treatment. That was a free-of-charge platform that lived off governmental grants and private donations.

So after a series of online interviews, Mary was accepted. She was happy because she did not know a single word in German (apart from "Termin" and "Danke" by that time). That indeed was a big stroke of luck since 99% of refugees who come to a new country first need to master the local language. Only then do they go and do some low-qualified and low-paid job in a supermarket, restaurant, or something like that.

This company hired about twenty Ukrainian psychotherapists and then said it would teach them how to use its own patented method to treat refugees within merely five to seven sessions.

The founder of the platform, a German person who had previously worked with Afghani refugees, had created her own express method of bringing them back to a state of resourcefulness. This "crash course" would take a few months, then an exam was to follow. During all this time, Mary and the other accepted candidates would be paid a minimal monthly salary.

So, she had something to get herself busy with and had a prospect of earning money in the future in Germany. Dasha had begun going to the local school. As for me, I continued my daily walks in the morning and evening, trying to explore

Seeshaupt since you don't get to live in a famous resort place in Bavaria often. I wanted to make the most of that opportunity.

BREAKING "QUIET HOURS"

I began to help Tom around the house a little. First, I needed to get myself busy with something, and second – I felt it was the right thing to do since Tom had kindly allowed us to stay for free and was very friendly and patient throughout the whole time we spent there.

So I took out the rubbish, learning how to sort it – the paper rubbish was to be put into the big plastic bag outside, and the plastic rubbish went into another bag.

There was a special container for organic rubbish and a separate one for things that were not disposable – batteries, liners, old clothes, etc. Following Tom's instructions, when bags with paper and plastic garbage got full, I put them into the garage with a plane painted on its front door.

Another thing I found I could do for Tom was chop firewood. Near a symbolic fence that separated Tom's house from an empty square of land next to it (the one grown with high grass and weeds), there was a line of round wood chunks. That was the wood Tom's father bought and it all had to be gradually chopped into smaller pieces for the winter. I noticed that many houses in Seeshaupt had small log pieces neatly put along their walls.

Often, there were separate stacks with a roof for keeping that firewood dry when it rained. Tom had such a stack behind the house right next to the bicycle shed. Wood had been also piled along the back wall of the house, up to the waist in height.

So nearly every day, I went out in the yard and chopped a chunk or two, sometimes three. Then I would take a cart on two wheels, throw the chopped pieces there, and wheel it to the wood stack, where I then took them out.

A couple of times all three of us - Robert, Tom, and me - together did the chopping. That was fun and some good exercise outside.

Rules of good behaviour and existence for neighbours in Germany required that the time between midday and two o'clock should be quiet. The same goes for Sundays and it is called "Ruhezeit".

This means no music outside (however, I seldom heard music played outside in Seeshaupt at all, even beyond that "quiet period"), no chopping wood, no using electric lawnmowers, etc - nothing that can disturb your neighbours.

The time between 10 p.m. and 7 a.m. is also included but that goes without saying, doesn't it, since this is a universal rule not to switch your lawn mower on at night and let others sleep.

Before I found out about that "quiet time" during the day, I had a few times chopped the wood during those "Ruhezeit" hours but nothing happened - nobody complained or called the police, and the sky did not collapse. Probably I was lucky with Tom's neighbours who decided not to complain, who knows.

I also mowed the lawn outside the house a couple of times. Tom was having a hard period at university anyway, so he did not have the time to do that and I was glad to be of help.

TRAVELLING AROUND SOUTHERN BAVARIA

Throughout all those weeks, we tried to relax in Seeshaupt and its vicinities to restore ourselves psychologically. I was practicing my poorest German, Mary had begun working; Dasha was busy with school and learning some basic stuff in German, so she could make herself understood in class.

Those were phrases, such as "I feel bad", "I'm sad", "Could you repeat that please?", "I need the toilet", etc.

Soon, more people from Ukraine began settling in Seeshaupt; I began hearing Russian speech in the streets and supermarkets more and more often.

We did a bit of travelling near Seeshaupt, too. Some of it was driven by necessity – e.g. I went to the town of Penzberg two train stops away farther South. I went there to open bank accounts for myself and Mary, so we could receive the social payments directly to our bank cards. Besides, Mary needed a card to receive her salary.

Penzberg was much bigger than Seeshaupt and it had a large

pharmaceutical factory in it. As you walked along the streets in the centre of the town you could see mountains really close – so close that in some parts they rose to cover a big part of the sky.

Later, Mary and I visited that town together and she said she felt like moving there, since for her it was not as quiet as Seeshaupt. She loved the place where we were staying but often wanted to move somewhere more lively than our village. She thought that Dasha would like it better too – my wife was sure that we could find some childcare places there, where Dasha would perhaps love spending time with other children.

In Penzberg, there were also more places to go and more ways to spend time than in Seeshaupt. I did not argue but I felt that I would like to stay in Seeshaupt – I liked the place, I loved my strolls along the lake and it was the quietness of the place that attracted me at that time.

One weekend, Kate and Andrey took us on a trip to Kochel am See – the final station on our train line if you head South past Penzberg.

This is a village for tourists with plenty of cafes, shops, a pretty mountain lake, hotels and inns with beautiful views, lots of hiking routes, and a cable car to crown it all. Lots of people go there in the summer with their mountain bicycles or just stroll around this pretty village and then walk up along the mountain trails.

As the train took us there, we went past cows and horses grazing in the pastures, past farmhouses with mountains standing huge and tall right behind them (and wood sheds, of course), and I recalled TV commercials of washing powder that I saw as a teenager in the 90s. Those commercials promised that your washing would smell of "Alpine freshness", "freshness of a frosty winter morning in the Alps" or something like that. There were also commercials advertising chocolate with cows grazing near mountains, eating bright green grass under their hooves. I had never seen the Alps until then in real life, especially so closely.

At that time, we still had to wear masks on public transport. You could more or less avoid it on buses, but on trains, it was mandatory as a conductor always showed up to check your tickets and check if you had a mask on.

We saw a very beautiful lake called Kochelsee. It looked like a gigantic mirror on the ground surrounded by mountains with snowy peaks. The mountain peaks surrounding it were reflected in the water. We lunched on the grass on the shore, watching ducks making their way on the water slowly near the bank. The water was so clear that you could see through it down to the rocky bottom with small fish swimming right under the surface.

END OF HOSTILE TRAIN CONDUCTOR

As I mentioned before, when Ukrainians entered Germany, fleeing their country, they had the right to receive a sort of "welcome ticket" – a free train ride towards their destination.

Still, later on, there were no clear rules regarding tickets for Ukrainians (as there were no clear rules regarding all other aspects of their stay in Germany).

For this reason, each time we travelled somewhere, such as to see Kate and Andrey near Munich, we would just show our Ukrainian IDs and the conductors just would say "Danke" with a smile and move on to the other passengers around us. However, there was one particular lady conductor who, it seemed, decided to declare war on me and Mary. And that was not only related to tickets.

At that time, she worked on our route and we often bumped into her as we went from Seeshaupt to Munich and back. She was in her fifties and seemed to be a hardliner.

First thing she did was to refuse to speak English to me when checking our tickets. By her responses to my clear English phrases, she would insist aloud that I should speak German to her. Even with my awful German skills, I could understand that much of her angry talk.

"We are in Germany, right? So you should be speaking German," she would say in German with a formal angry smile. Okay, what the hell, I thought, I'll play your way. She seemed satisfied hearing my broken basic German and went off to check the tickets of the other people in the carriage.

That was not it, however. A few times, she made us buy tickets, even though the regular rule goes that tickets should be bought in advance and if you get caught ticketless on the train/bus, you're in for a 60 EUR fine no matter what.

Well, at least they do not throw you out of the nearest window, saying "Aha, you have no ticket!", like Indiana Jones did in the "Last Crusade" movie. It seemed, though, that she would be happy to do that, but the law would definitely be against her.

Still, speaking German and knowing that we could not understand her, she made us buy tickets from her, giving us something which seemed like an explanation made up on the spot.

Once, when Mary was going back from Munich with shopping bags (that was clothes from a second-hand shop), that lady again began blabbering away and pointing at those bags, demanding that Mary buy a ticket as if the shopping was the reason. We told Kate about that later on. She asked me for details and wrote an email to the railway company.

It turned out we were not the only "victims" of that lady conductor. Once we again took a taxi from Seeshaupt to Weilheim and I shared that experience with the driver, telling him about that old bitch, but making it sound like a half-joke. To my great surprise, he told me that he had also bumped into that woman and she made him pay a fine for no clear reason. The driver wrote a formal complaint to Deutsche Bahn.

The important thing here is that he got a refund for that fine and a promise that the conductor would receive a reprimand. That made me more confident in thinking that we could after all bring that nasty lady to justice.

After another time she confronted us on then train, I asked Kate to write one more email to the railway company. After she had sent a formal complaint, we had never seen that vicious conductor again. Nevermore.

Maybe she was fired. Maybe they simply moved her to another train route, who knows? But it was quite satisfying to see such a prompt reaction. This would hardly be possible in Ukraine and definitely impossible in Russia, where they would just rudely tell a complainer that he/she is free to stop using their services if there is something they are unhappy with about their work.

Our "train battles" were followed by the introduction of a 9 EUR summer ticket (just as an experiment, according to the news headlines, as the government tried to make transport companies reduce the ticket fees). Now, rather than paying a fortune for travelling, you could go anywhere in Germany for merely 9 euros per month (excluding first-class trains, such as ICE, though).

Apparently, that was partly a decision for Ukrainians as anyone could afford to buy that ticket, even asylum seekers who live off social payouts.

Trains then became literally full of people, though, every day, and often you had to sit on the floor – there were that many folks wishing to take advantage of those train ride discounts.

Still, that was better than having to pay 4 EUR to travel just two or three train stations as Tom had to when going to university in Munich, and having to change several times on his way there and paying for that accordingly.

PART 5

RENTED HOUSE NEAR DACHAU

It was time to leave Tom and his family and rent an accommodation of our own. Besides, Mary was seeing Kate every weekend (sometimes I came along) and travelling from Seeshaupt to Neufahrn or even to Munich and then back home was pretty long and tiresome.

Also, we felt like starting to live by ourselves. Tom and his girlfriend Eva were great company but they were students and sharing a house with a bunch of other people for a long time was okay with them. As for us, we had concluded that we would like to live on our own. We wanted our own kitchen and bathroom. Our own fridge and house.

Robert showed me a few mobile apps I could use to try and find a house to rent. The problem is that, unlike Ukraine and Russia, when you want to rent accommodation in Germany, most often you would have to move in with your own furniture. You would be lucky to have a furnished kitchen at the very best. Basically, Germans charge rent for bare walls and the roof. In Ukraine and Russia, flats that are rented out most often come with all the furniture.

All the houses that I managed to find were in deep countryside but we needed one with a school close by for Dasha. All the cheap houses were in the middle of nowhere, somewhere in the farmlands, where you would need a car even to visit a supermarket or to the nearest train station.

Otherwise, you were in for an hour of riding a bicycle there. And again – they were equipped with hardly any furniture.

Finally, Kate found a flat for us near Dachau – a town near Munich, famous for its large (and the very first) Nazi death camp, where tens of thousands of prisoners were kept during WW2 and even before that, beginning from when Hitler came to power and started locking his political enemies away.

The flat (actually the whole first floor of a house) was in a village called G., about twenty minutes from Dachau by bus. Dachau is half an hour away from Munich by train – that was much closer than Seeshaupt, hurray.

Among several candidates, the landlady luckily picked us. So, as July began, we moved our stuff there. Before we did that, we had to receive official permission from the jobcentre in Weilheim. We motivated our transition with the fact that Mary had to travel to Munich several times a week for work and that also her sister lived nearby. That seemed to convince the officials in the jobcentre and they let us go.

Tom kindly helped us bring all our stuff in his van from Seeshaupt to G. Before that, his father, mother and himself gave us a nice farewell lunch outside their house on the terrace.

They and Eva had become very close to being our family back then and we loved staying with them, having chats almost every day. Dasha loved Eva too as an older friend and she adored the vegan ice cream Eva often cooked from frozen fruit. But we had to move on and Tom needed a break, I reckon, even though he loved to live with flatmates.

After that, I took several trips back to Seeshaupt (sometimes, taking Dasha along) to see the Russian-speaking family doctor and dropped by to visit Tom and Eva.

* * *

Our landlady in G., Helga, was married to a Mexican guy called Juan – both energetic, lively people, who adored life. Both retired and grey-haired but always in a good mood and very optimistic, with smiles on their faces. I very seldom see them feeling down.

Juan used to be a musician in an orchestra in Dachau and he was very good at playing the guitar.

During summer evenings, their adult children came over, they would sit at the long table outside, having dinner with grilled sausages and beer, playing the guitar, and singing songs until dark.

The atmosphere was very friendly and family-like. Helga had a big heart and she practically included us in her family. It was not that she made an exception for us, this was their natural way of treating tenants as she had told us before we moved in. She warned us about that, asking if their family-like and a bit chaotic atmosphere would suit us. We did not mind at all; on the contrary, that promised to be fun.

Helga owned three houses which stood next to each other. She, her husband and her sister lived in the biggest house; her daughter Margo occupied the third one. It was the second house that was rented out to us. We got to live on the first floor – two rooms with a big terrace, a kitchen and a bathroom. Every room was spacious and most importantly the rooms and the kitchen were fully furnished.

Helga even gave us some extra furniture – a gorgeous ancient-looking (at least fifty or seventy years old) desk with drawers and a huge wardrobe. On the day we moved in from Seeshaupt, we found a basket full of food products from a supermarket in our new kitchen.

Inside there were spaghetti, sausages, cheese, fruit and vegetables (a bottle of red wine) and a card, saying "Ivan, Mary and Dasha, willkommen". Mary and I found it very touching and cute. It was also very much to the point since we did not know yet where the supermarket was. Dasha was happy to have moved to a new place. She had become a bit bored with Seeshaupt – the girl loves big cities and she dreamed of us moving to Munich or Berlin eventually.

Another tenant, Rob, a small, dark-haired guy, moved into the smaller flat on the second floor a couple of months later. He was in his early thirties. He had found a job in Munich and so he had to move closer to it. We got on okay.

He also loved D.I.Y work and next year in the summer he found himself a hobby of converting his small van into a trailer inside. Every weekend, from my window I heard loud sounds of a drill working and various types of music playing too – from hard rock to retro stuff.

He was obviously breaking the rule of "the quiet hours", but nobody around seemed to care or complain about that noise. Helga did not mind it either.

G. AND DACHAU VS. SEESHAUPT

Compared to Seehaupt, G. was not pretty at all, to be honest. Helga's house and the house where we lived stood right by the motorway, so buses and cars often whooshed past it. Over time, though, I got used to living there and felt at home in G.

There were no mountains here to be seen even from afar, and no pretty lake. There was river Amper, though, flowing in the woods near the house. A few walking bridges in the forest as well and a small dam were nice to look at for a couple of times when we had just arrived. But I stopped my daily walks since there was nowhere to go for lengthy strolls here.

A few times I did walk along the motorway that led to Dachau but I did not think that it was particularly good for my lungs. The scenery was okay, a rural one – fields of corn and other crops along the motorway but I got bored from seeing that every day pretty soon, so I eventually gave up on those strolls.

The good thing was the closeness to Munich as I mentioned above. Two or three buses that ran
several times per hour on weekdays took you to the Dachau train station within about twenty minutes. There you could either catch an S-Bahn and get to Munich in around half an

hour or take an RB- train and you would be standing on Munich central station in ten minutes already.

I was surprised to learn that Dachau was in fact older than the Middle Ages, the first mention of it goes back to the 800s – that's even before Prince Vladimir baptized Kyiv in 988 A.D. Back then, Kyiv and the lands around it were called "Kyiv Rus'" – this is where the name of Russia originates from, according to one of the popular theories. Kyiv is a lot older than Moscow anyway, that is a historical fact. This is another indication of the deep mutual cultural and historic roots of Ukraine and Russia which are being broken in the current war.

Going back to Dachau, the name of the town, according to one theory, goes back to the Celts who came to live here around 1,000 B.C. before Germanic tribes arrived. "Dachau" is believed to originate from the Celtic word "Dahauua", which can be roughly translated as "a loamy meadow". Others believe that the etymology of the town's name is Germanic after all and comes from "daha" meaning "clay", and "ouwe", which means "water overflown land". The name of the Amper river is believed to be rooted in the Celtic word for "water". As I said before, for many Russians the primary association with Dachau is the Nazi concentration camp, not ancient Celts. There is a memorial of it on the outskirts of the town. I will share my experience of visiting it later here. Stay tuned.

BORSCHT AND BAVARIAN CHURCHES

Dachau was something in between Seeshaupt and Munich – a village and a megapolis. It seems to have been built on a classic Medieval scheme – a castle surrounded by houses where peasants lived and worked. Dachau indeed has a castle on the hill (the Dachau Schloss) with the so-called old town spread around on top of the hill.

All the pretty old streets are up there. Roads paved with cobblestone, lots of small and cozy-looking bars, cafes, and restaurants waiting for locals and tourists, who wish to sit outside in the summer watching sprays of water rising and falling within small iron fountains. One part of the main street in the old town has many old houses painted in different colours standing right next to each other, making you think like you have found yourself in a classic fairy tale by Hoffman or Hans Christian Andersen.

On the same street, right as you emerge from a road leading from the downtown, you bump into a Medieval cathedral. It stands near the local Town Hall ("Rathouse") and its domes are shaped like onions, like everywhere else in Bavaria.

I did not go inside since I had visited a similar church in Seeshaupt and Frauenchirche Cathedral in the centre of Munich (that's one of the tourist attractions, a cathedral in Marienplatz with two tall towers which made it first look like a mosque to me) – they are all built based on the same architecture scheme and look very similar inside.

Often enough, the size of the building is the only difference between them. However, I have not yet seen Catholic churches in Germany have the same creative variety and local national spirit that Orthodox churches in Russia and Ukraine can offer.

Ten years ago in Kyiv, when Dasha only was born, Mary and I lived near a street with two churches standing almost opposite each other – one belonged to the Ukrainian patriarchy, and the second one was part of the Moscow patriarchy. Those were two completely different churches both inside and on the outside. The Ukrainian church inside was decorated in a folkish style, with lots of grass – yes, you read that right. Being inside that church, you felt as if a witch from a local old fairy story was coming to get your soul and you would have to protect yourself here throughout the night by saying prayers and surrounding yourself with a magic circle on the floor (that's a popular fairy-story by a Ukrainian writer Gogol, who moved to St. Petersburg in Russia and died there in the 19th century. Along with Leo Tolstoy and Dostoevsky, Gogol's books are part of the school curriculum in Russia).

Russians consider him their local classic since he is famous not only for spooky fairy stories about Ukrainian cossacks, witches and other folklore stuff but also for his classic novels about Russian landowners and state bureaucrats – the novel "Dead Souls" is known in the UK and US too and is studied as an exemplar of Russian 19th-century literature. Ukrainians insist that he is a Ukrainian writer.

But these discussions about what cultural heritage belongs to which country have now reached the peak of ridiculousness on the side of Russia. Many celebrities and average people there now claim that borscht (a famous beetroot soup with cabbage that become widely popular in Soviet Russia and remains sort of its carte-de-visite even now) is a Russian dish, although it initially came from Ukraine.

Anyway, the Russian church in Kyiv stood almost opposite the Ukrainian one and was based inside a train carriage with no wheels and stood right on the ground. It looked pretty neutral inside and right next to it there was a site where a proper building for that church was being erected. Before I moved to Ukraine I had seen very pretty and peculiar churches in Russia too. You need to bear in mind that Orthodox churches are also meant to be brighter and more beautiful inside than Catholic or Protestant ones. The goal is to attract the congregation to make them feel "God's presence" through all the icons with golden frames, etc. That beauty was an initial idea when back in 988 Prince Vladimir of Kyiv conducted a forceful Christianization for the people in Rus' under his rule. It was made basically out of geopolitical motives.

As for Germany, it is enough to visit just one church there and it will save you time, which you can spend on visiting other sites for tourists.

GRAVEYARDS IN GERMANY, RUSSIA AND UKRAINE

In the old town, I bumped into a graveyard that looked really old. I had only seen similar graveyards somewhere on the Internet on a "list of beautiful graveyards of the world" among those "worth visiting for tourists". I bet those tourists have a non-typical set of mind if they like spending time gazing at graves, even though pretty ones (perhaps imagining themselves in the afterlife boasting to each other – look my grave is more expensive and it's prettier than yours, you loser!).

If you enjoy that kind of thing and believe that a cottage in the UK countryside with windows looking out on graves 300 years old near an ancient church is a gem worth the fortune charged for spending a weekend there, then come to Dachau, pay a visit to that cemetery and saturate your aesthetic sensitivity.

Russian and Ukrainian graveyards are different. They are mostly ugly, often with litter thrown around, memorial headstones made of cheap metal. Time makes them deepen inside the ground or fade out, and the paint starts coming off in small pieces. Famous places, like Vagankovo Cemetery in Moscow or similar ones (Novodevichy Cemetery in the centre of Moscow, next to a well-known old monastery), where famous artists (Russian musicians, singers, actors, etc) and politicians are buried, do not look pretty either.

Tourists (especially people coming from the West) often go there to see the graves of Russian/Soviet celebrities of the past. But an average person cannot get a burial spot there, since it is only for the elite. Still, even these two graveyards are totally different in style from German ones.

Gravestones and monuments in those Russian graveyards look quite stern, severe, bearing the spirit of, it seems, struggle, discipline, obedience and all those values that the Soviet Union cultivated in its citizens. They sort of emphasize the strictly negative, mournful and atheistic attitude to death.

German cemeteries on the contrary look and feel relaxed, cozy, they are bright in colours as if the dead people there have gone to a well-deserved rest and might still indeed be alive somewhere in an invisible world as the religions tell us.

Also, German graveyards look like parks protected by UNESCO, like postcards with views of Swiss mountain resorts – all clean, pretty, and well-looked after. No wonder about that – my landlady Helga, for example, paid 750 EUR to rent a spot for her parents' grave for fifteen years.

Besides, those who rent grave spots, need to look after the graves after the funeral and make sure they stay clean and pretty.

Helga said that this is a sort of social event for her as she talks to other people in the cemetery who come over to clean the graves of their dead relatives. "Talking to the Oldies", she called that. Often, these are people she had never met before.

FUNERAL INSURANCE - CHEAPER WHEN YOUNG

Funeral and everything related to it is a perfect business in Germany. Perhaps, in such countries as the US, the UK and the rest of Europe the situation is similar but I am in Germany now, so I will be talking about the local funeral business.

The price of the cheapest funeral in Germany starts at 2,000 EUR and then goes up to 13,000 EUR, according to Statista data. In the meantime, in Ukraine, you can organize a funeral for $2,000 and this will not be the lowest price. In Russia, the cheapest funeral costs around 500 EUR.

The more expensive one is priced at 2,000 EUR. Elite funerals' price list starts at 3,000 EUR and can go into infinity, especially in Moscow or St Petersburg, where all the financial and political elite reside.

Germans are quite inventive, if I may say so when it comes to burials. Cremations now are the most frequently chosen option here – it will save you 750 EUR for fifteen years for a rented spot on a graveyard (this price can go way higher, depending on the part of Germany you are in).

People can choose to bury an urn with the ashes in a forest under a specially reserved tree. They can scatter the ashes or drop an urn with it to the bottom of a lake. That takes its roots from sailor's burial in the past, I guess, when a ship crew would simply throw their dead shipmates over the board.

These are all cheaper options, I guess, than the 13,000 EUR mentioned above. Burial is one of those ultimate things you cannot avoid, and it puts the funeral business into pretty much the same niche as the food and pharmaceutical industries.

It's for this reason, I guess, especially in Germany, this is not a cheap procedure. Besides, it is not only this that comes so expensive – simple things like getting your coat or shoes repaired come also highly-priced.

Once I had a slide zipper changed and the shop charged me 40 EUR for that. Good Lord, in Ukraine it costs 20 hryvnas – 0.5 EUR. This kind of work is referred to as minor repair, you know. MINOR. I was told that in Germany, these small businesses have to pay high taxes, hence they charge high fees for their work. Well, what can I say, lower the taxes for these people then, because the German government is not just taxing the business here, it taxes customers in addition to the pretty high income tax (up to 40%) they have to pay already.

Who knows, perhaps, the same high tax scheme works for funeral businesses. Luckily for Germans, their national rationality has found a way out. Do you remember I mentioned various types of insurance policies earlier?

Well, German people have also come up with funeral insurance – "Sterbegeldversicherung". Try not to disjoint your tongue, when pronouncing that. This will cover up to 10,000 EUR of funeral costs. So some people are paying a certain amount of money from every salary monthly to be able to afford a funeral in the future. I was told that if you start doing it when you are young, it comes cheaper. Looks like a hell of a bargain.

Beginning to set money aside, when you are still twenty-five or thirty and in perfect health? Sounds like a pretty rational approach to life (and death), doesn't it. Still, Germans do not seem to be bothered about buying funeral insurance until they get into their 50s, so everything is cool with them on this side.

Overall, when I hear about high funeral bills I recall a scene from "The Big Lebowski" movie, when Dude and Walter came to pick up the remains of their late friend Donny from a mortuary. The bill for the urn with the ashes was $180 – the film is set in 1998, so that was a hefty sum. That was the "most modestly priced receptacle", since they "range up to $3,000", according to the manager. Walter told this guy that if they are bereaved that does not mean they are idiots.

There is one method of an expensive funeral that I think is worth the money spent – modern technologies allow turning the ashes of a dead person into a synthetic diamond. This way, at least you can always carry this jewellery with you in a ring or necklace. This way, you would feel that the diseased close person indeed stays with you.

In Russia, agents from funeral companies are often referred to as “vultures”. Because as soon as somebody dies in a residential block, here they are, emerging from nowhere to offer their services, sometimes competing with each other, often treating dead people as nothing but assets to earn money on.

These days, funerals in Ukraine are taking place nearly every day because of the war. Think of the profits this industry is making, even if they are selling the cheapest packages. Aside from arms dealers, funeral parlours are also among the biggest beneficiaries of any military conflict. Since the war started, both in Ukraine in Russia prices on coffins, funerals and everything to do with them have soared.

Graveyards are being quickly filled in both countries now. But Russians keep coming to fight in Ukraine with stubbornness and energy that could be certainly used for much worthier goals.

GERMAN RED TAPE VS OUR LANDLADY

Yes, the local bureaucrats caught up with us even in G. First, the local Landratsamt demanded proof from Weilheim that we were indeed allowed to move from there. The problem is that a jobcentre and a Landratsamt in Germany are two completely different beasts when dealing with refugees. German bureaucrats seem to love making their work more difficult than it is already, perhaps for them, it turns life into a brighter experience.

But anyway, we got permission to move here from the jobcentre, forgetting about the Landratsamt.

It took a few weeks to settle that problem, with Helga constantly making calls for me in German, talking to all those officials, sometimes driving with me to their offices, and translating there German for me. Helga spoke perfect English.

I would like to emphasize her help with this red tape and with filling in tons of documentation later on. That went beyond any limits and would have been impossible without this nice and very kind lady. I often sincerely told her that she was a real star. All she did was laugh amiably in return, refusing to accept money or presents that I offered for her constant help.

Aside from helping me with papers and phone calls, Helga also treated Dasha like her actual granddaughter Liz (who was a few years younger than Dasha) – Helga gave her Christmas presents, a 20 EUR bill upon receiving a school certificate after she finished the first year in it, and even gave her some money to go to the Dachauer Volksfest to enjoy various types of merry-go-rounds and buy some treats. Once, Helga even brought her a present from "a tooth fairy", when one of Dasha's teeth fell out.

Anyway, there were papers to fill in so we could continue receiving social payouts. These were inevitably followed by phone calls to the jobcentre. Then came papers to fill about our medical insurance – what I did in Seeshaupt proved to be not exactly the right thing and now we had to arrange it all from the start.

Now, you might get the impression that I'm being critical here of German social institutions. Not at all – I'm deeply grateful for the regular and long-term financial support they have been providing to all Ukrainians.

I have to give it to Germany – no other country in the world is doing that. Or if it is, like Romania or Ireland, for example (I have a friend who picked Ireland rather than Germany because he had fluent English), it is on the verge of being cancelled.

Besides, in Germany, Ukrainians with children also receive Kindergeld – "children's money" – for every child in the family. 250 EUR per month until a child is 18, this is the same as what native Germans get. It takes time and knowledge of German to apply for this Kindergeld, though. And it takes plenty of nerves if you do not speak German.

I guess, if there is any criticism that may be spotted in the book is my emotional reaction to the fact that it could all have been organized a little differently. With less hassle for both German social workers and refugees.

However, what German jobcentres could definitely do is become more progressive and begin using email. I have asked them several times about it – please send me your letters by e-mail so I can copy the text and paste it into Google Translate. I'm sorry I do not understand your language yet, it is not a native one for me and I'm learning it. But their response was they are sorry but this is impossible. Why on earth??!

It is 2023 already, nearly a quarter of the 21st century is left behind, ChatGPT and Midjourney have been invented, while Elon Musk is launching test rocket flights aiming at Mars in the future. And you guys still prefer paper letters to emails.

This means that I, same as Helga and any other German citizen, have to keep tons of paper documentation at home just in case it may be required by the local tax authorities, the jobcentre or any other governmental body one day in the future.

I guess when a person passes away in Germany, the funeral is soon followed by a bonfire where "truckfuls" of papers get burned that the deceased will not need anymore. Still, I would not be surprised if the relatives prefer to keep storing all those papers for a few years longer – just in case the authorities decide to make a final check at some point in the future, you know. Helga then confirmed my concerns – you do have to store those papers for five years after a person passes away. And so do the authorities.

Germany targets reducing the usage of fossil fuels and preserving the environment. Why don't they begin by reducing the usage of paper and thus save a lot of trees for a start?

DASHA'S PROBLEMS IN DACHAU SCHOOL

Before we even moved to G., Kate helped us find a school that might suit Dasha both now and in the long term. It was a Förderschule Schule based in Dachau. This type of school specialises in children with mental development delays, autism spectrum syndrome and similar things.

The German system of education cares for such children, giving them a chance to adapt to society and receive at least a basic education in accordance with their abilities, which was very good in our case. Curiously, Germans call autism "ASS" – Autismus-Spektrum-Syndrom. When we began dealing with all the papers to do with this issue for Dasha, it turned out to be an "ass" indeed, a real bummer.

Besides, if we decide to stay in Germany after the war (if we are allowed to), this school would still be a plus – there are many children like that in the country and these schools, where the curriculum is adapted to these kids, allows them to develop with no bullying or fun-making at them from mentally normal classmates. They grow to become people who can adapt to society and support themselves financially by mastering a profession that suits them and cope with their mental state.

Another thing here is that often children can outgrow small mental development impairments as s/he turns into an adult. In Germany, all children go to a primary school with a more or less similar curriculum for everyone. In secondary school, they get divided, depending on the score they get during the final tests, and move on to a normal school for average children, to a gymnasium (for those who pass the tests with flying colours), or to a school for kids with the lowest marks.

The first group has a high chance to go to universities and get degrees. The second perhaps can make it there too. The third one in the future would work in factories and in other low-qualified jobs. Still, German authorities do their best to take care of children with various development levels, which is great, you've got to give it to them, they deserve praise here.

Anyway, I arranged a meeting with the school psychologist. She said there was a place and they could admit Dasha. Then the psychologist tested her via a method which if used back in Ukraine (in Kyiv only, perhaps, in a top clinic) would cost us a minimum local salary.

Here, in Dachau, it was done free of charge, merely as part of testing a child and appraising his/her mental abilities before admitting to school. Dasha proved to be of a "medium intellectual level". That was good news. It is easier to develop the mind of a child with a medium level rather than a kid with a low level of intelligence.

When we lived in Ukraine, Dasha watched a lot of video blogs on YouTube and kept telling me, as I walked her to school every morning, that she dreamt of going to school on a special school bus. Well, here her dream came true – children of first and second forms get to be picked up at bus stops not far from their houses, transported to school and back. All the parents have to do here is take their children to the bus stop where they get picked up.

Our daughter was provided with the majority of the books necessary for school, but we had to buy some particular exercise books for various subjects mentioned by the teacher too, as well as stationery and things like that. Plus, we had to get a vaccination against chickenpox done for Dasha.

What was a first for all of us here is the law (not even a rule but an actual law) that children are obliged to go to school every day without any exceptions. If they happen to fall ill, the parents have to take them to the doctor and provide a paper confirming to the school secretary that the child indeed is ill.

If you want to take your son or daughter to visit a grandmother in another town or take him/her along on a vacation, you have to ask the school for permission.

What a nightmare after a Ukrainian school where nobody gives a damn if you miss a day or two for a substantial reason without having to ask the director for permission. Teachers in Ukraine have better things to do than drill children's parents' brains, as we say in Russia, about a couple of absences in school.

My first reaction to that was – gosh, is the close location of the Dachau KZ (concentration camp) impacting your heads that much here, guys? Unlike the school in Ukraine or even in Seeshaupt, Dasha was not allowed to attend two/three days per week here, she had attend lessons every single day here.

Mary and I did our best to talk to the teacher to explain that Dasha would get tired easily and then start falling ill. The teacher smiled as if hinting that she would not listen to us like she was certain that we were just trying to make life easier for our daughter. Apparently, this strict rule exists because Germans want to teach their children to grow up self-sufficient and independent.

The moral here is that they will have to do a lot of unpleasant things every single day when they turn into adults. Forcing them to go to school is a dress rehearsal of that. Germans try to turn this into a habit for them starting from an early age. In Ukraine, we have a saying that life makes you swallow frogs and you'd better swallow one frog every day. Otherwise, if you miss a week or more, one day you would have to swallow a whole bucket of frogs in a single day.

Still, as we warned the teacher and the secretary (I went to talk to her as well, but it was no good – all I got was polite "no's" accompanied by a cold smile), during the first several months, Dasha kept falling ill nearly every two weeks. That was her typical reaction to school and all the noise from a lot of people in it, from too many emotions and intellectual work on subjects too difficult for her.

She started getting a sore throat and runny nose easily, was unable to understand German and so she could not make contact with her classmates. This really stressed her out. So the doctor would listen to our explanation, be sympathetic, and would allow her to stay at home until the end of the week. Luckily, the teacher and the secretary spoke fluent English, so we were able to communicate and discuss all that in detail.

According to German laws, a child can stay at home for three days without bringing proof from the doctor, if they are ill. We followed it and took her to the doctor on the fourth day.

However, after a few months, one day we received an official letter from the school, requiring that we take Dasha to the doctor on the very first day of her illness since she had missed school too often.

Unaccustomed to such a treatment of children with an autistic diagnosis, I was enraged. Thoughts that the German "censored past" (they hate to be reminded about the fascism period and this is even punishable with a fine) had not disappeared but was converted into the new ideology started buzzing in my head – extreme bureaucracy that binds your hands and legs really tight, leaving just your throat and mouth free so that you can still breath, nod and say "yes" when required. You are not allowed to say "no". WTF?? We respect the laws and customs of the asylum country, but that is too much. Like old men showing their privates to teenage girls on the beaches.

If you disobey, the system in Germany will crash you with rules, make you pay a fine, or even worse – send Jugendamt (children's social service) reps to your house to see if you are a worthy parent and whether your child should not be taken away. Bloody hell. Those were my first thoughts.

Teachers, leave the kids alone, don't turn them into another brick in the wall, you know.

I gave my opinion on this to my landlady, trying not to get too emotional about it. She agreed that the school here may be hard for Dasha but she was convinced that the rule of attending every day was justified.

Okay, she is right at the end of the day, I admit, it is a great idea to teach your kids to swallow those bloody frogs when they are young. But, gosh, why do you guys have to do it in a hard way? No sympathy for their own children. "This is not madness, this is Spart...Germany!" In the US a catchphrase says that nothing is certain except death and taxes, in Germany you can easily add strict school attendance to this.

I thought that if I got that attitude at school when I was little or even a teenager, my life would have turned into hell and I would have hated everything to do with school - I needed a day's rest once in a while, aside from the weekends. At least, unlike Russia, Germans are doing their best to make classes for children as interesting and attractive as they can.

In that particular school where Dasha went anyway (in Seeshaupt and Dachau), I cannot speak for other schools –

everything is done playfully, the teachers do not tell them off if a child fails to do his/her homework. That's a major advantage. Still, if a child fails to do that for a week or longer, the teacher will first initiate a conversation with his/her parents about it. If nothing changes, prepare tea and biscuits for people from Jugendamt when they come over to check why you do not care how your child does at school.

SCHOOL FINALLY GETS BETTER

Dasha kept getting tired of daily visits to school without any breaks. Things turned so bad that she began crying before going to bed – too many emotions, too many people, the language she was unable to speak and understand, hence no friends in there.

I submitted a letter and a translation of her autism diagnosis to Jugendamt, asking that they provide Dasha with an assistant who would sit with her during classes and help her with the language and the tasks she does not understand. They told me that they would try to help but it may take up to half a year or longer since there are not that many school assistants for children with mental disabilities who can speak Russian.

Dasha ended up finding a school in Munich with a Ukrainian class (she found the exact address on Google herself) and kept telling me and Mary that we must move there. She loves Munich anyway and dreams of us moving there permanently. At the very least, she asks that we go there at weekends, walk, visit the huge local toy shop and buy her ice cream, hot chocolate, and pastry. The latter is excellent in Germany.

I kept talking to the teacher about her problem but she continued to tell me that children are often ill during this season (it was November-December 2022 already), and that people in general often catch colds in the autumn and winter. Mary and I made "an agreement" with Dasha, saying that we could not move to Munich or go to a different school right now but we promised her that we would try and get her a Russian language assistant for classes soon. That seemed to do it, she continued to go to that school, waiting for an assistant to appear.

Weeks passed, though, and Jugendamt still did not give her any assistant-teacher, saying the same thing as before – this is a difficult task to find a Russian-speaking teacher for this job. They would have to hire somebody additionally for that – there were just a couple of teachers from Russia at school but they were busy with their jobs. One girl I knew wanted to work with Dasha but she would not do the Covid vaccination. Without that, the path for her was closed there.

Finally, we decided to help Dasha begin to learn German and found her a young Ukrainian teacher – a girl in her early twenties called Lolita. Her name first brought up strong associations with Nabokov's novel and I thought like "What a name to give to a girl". I have never heard of women with this name in Russia (except the famous pop singer but Lolita is her stage name) since Lolita has become a noun to name young teenage girls described in the Nabokov novel. Still, I got used to the name. Lola was a nice person and more like a friend to Dasha, who helped her master German in a playful form.

After that, miraculously, the problem with the lack of an assistant or with the school itself began to dissolve. First, we arranged with Dasha's teacher that once or twice a week she would take her to a pre-school class where a Russian lady taught.

A month later, Dasha forgot about that as she grew to like her German classmates and classes too. She learnt to play simple games like tick-tack-toe or hide-and-seek with them during the breaks. The children there were friendly to her, which was very good for Dasha and made me and Mary feel calm about her.

Gradually, Dasha began to pick up German words related to school subjects and to learning in class.
The teacher gave her and the other children homework, which included working with new vocabulary (where she had to match pictures of objects with the words and other similar stuff).
When spring arrived, Dasha stopped crying in the evenings before school and stopped falling ill. The issues with the school related to that seemed to be over. Yay!

DACHAU KZ MEMORIAL

As I mentioned above, for many Russians, the name Dachau is first of all associated with the famous (the very first one set up in Nazi Germany) concentration camp. When I heard about Dachau many years ago, I, like many of my countrymen, did not even realize this was first of all a town much older than Hitler's regime and the camp there was built only in the 1930s.

So I thought, since we live near such a famous site, it would be a real miss not to go and see it. My wife was not interested, she does not like that sort of thing, and I would not take my daughter there either.

I suppose my interest in such a place was more of a boy's thing coming from childhood. As children we used to play war in the courtyard of our apartment block, chasing each other with toy pistols.

That was back in the 1980s, in the Soviet Union Russia, so a pistol was easy to make from a piece of tree branch or plywood by giving it at least the rough shape of a weapon with a kitchen knife. Those children who had wealthy parents sometimes turned up with toy sub-machine Kalashnikovs made of plastic and painted.

This was partly a heritage of WW2, I suppose. Nowhere in the world are war games as popular with little boys as they are in Russia. Some opposition journalists there now believe that these games in our childhood have partly prepared the country for the current war with Ukraine – for some soldiers, it started as a game, like paintball or Lasertag, and Russian men were raised on these games; this acceptance and longing for fighting required to be unleashed sooner or later.

Add to that the cult of WW2 victors, which was again activated by Putin after 2014 (and before that – beating the Mongol-Tatar hordes – first Chenghis Khan, then his grandson Batu, thanks to which Western Europe never had to fight them) and you get a furuncle that would burst open sooner or later.

Anyway, as children we loved everything to do with cars and war. Not only did we play the latter, but we also collected used bullets and empty bullet shells. For some reason, those were often to be found behind the apartment block my friends and I lived in – the side of it where there were no entrance doors and windows merely looked onto small gardens with flowers, and trees on pieces of land with nothing but weeds and some garages.

Aside from bullet shells, we could sometimes find some interesting items there that people would throw out of their windows – elements of devices or mechanisms – radios that did not work, some pieces of bicycles, engines, cigarette lighters, etc. That was one of the coolest pastimes of my Soviet childhood – go and look for those things with my friends.

Often, we would imagine or try to guess what our findings really were, part of what bigger and more complex things they used to be before they got thrown out as rubbish. Any piece that seems junk now back then was like a real treasure for us.

We would then keep those things as collectibles and proudly show them to our parents and often trade them with each other. Sometimes it was our parents who recognized what those things really were and told us to throw them away. Ah, grow- ups know nothing about treasure, do they?

Sometimes, we found empty cigarette packs ("Pall Mall", "Magna", "Marlborough", "Camel" and they had to be hard packs, not soft ones; those were good collectibles for some of us since locally made Soviet cigarette packs looked plain and dull and would only raise the interest of a smoker) or empty cans/bottles from foreign beer brands (some of us collected those too since in the Soviet Union beer came only in plain looking glass bottles (like cheap Helles in Germany now) that you could only bring back to food shops for recycling and get some change for them; Germans are still using this Pfand system but in Russia and Ukraine this is not as popular now and mostly bottles, once empty, now become regular garbage thrown onto a dump).

When I was a child, an invitation to go for a walk "behind the house" from a friend sounded like one to go and visit a secret place, a treasure island, or something like that.

* * *

Anyway, back to Dachau. Now, there is a concentration camp (KZ for short) memorial – a local site where a load of tourists come all the time. It is on the outskirts of the town and a bus runs there on a regular basis from Dachau central train station. The journey to the site took about ten or fifteen minutes. A lot of tourists rode with me on the bus – not only Germans but also people from the UK and the USA, I could also hear some Chinese people speaking their language, which sounded a bit like singing with the four tones it has.

After you get off the bus, you walk to the tourist centre, get a map of the site and a portable audio guide in several languages. To obtain the guide you leave your ID and it stays there until you bring the device back. Plus you pay 5 euros for the rent. I found there an audio guide in Russian. Then I walked towards the KZ site itself, following crowds of people who had tour guides, explaining things to them in English.

On the gate door made of iron, I saw a phrase in German, which I had certainly heard of before – "Arbeit macht frei", which means "labour makes you free". In the Soviet Union times, curiously, this was used in other forms. There were popular sayings (and still are, by the way) about labour dignifying a person or labour turning apes into humans a long time ago. That's a fact but in Russia or Ukraine, you mostly hear these phrases from bosses who want you to do some extra hours in the office or persuade you to work at the weekend without extra pay.

The site where I came, according to the booklet, in the past had been only a small part of the camp, where the prisoners lived. There used to be barracks here, with only two of them reconstructed now. But behind those two there were long lines with the squares on the ground which marked where the other "living blocks" used to stand.

I started at the buildings where now there are museums – lots of black and white photos under glass on the walls about 1930s Germany, newspapers with headlines about the economic crisis after WW1 lost by Germany; about Hitler coming to power and people trusting him to "save Germany" from the chaos that only the national-socialist party claimed to be able to handle while communists and the other parties failed to do that.

There were rooms with prison bars on windows, big halls with white walls, shower rooms where the floor damaged by bullets from machine guns when Nazi soldiers shot the prisoners was preserved. In boxes under glass panels, you could see passports and some personal belongings of the prisoners – very old-looking forks, spoons, pocket watches, black and white photos, and other stuff. Among those, I saw a passport of a Ukrainian prisoner.

Another interesting thing I saw there was a map on the wall. On each European country's image, there was a figure – the total number of prisoners from that country who passed through the camp. To my surprise, the second biggest country here was...Germany (Deutsches Reich) with 31,456 people sent to the Dachau death camp. The first place belonged to Poland – 40,395 people. The Soviet Union came third – 25,113 prisoners (aside from Russia, that included Ukraine too, as you understand, Belarus, Georgia, and other countries). The USSR was followed by Hungary – 21,124 prisoners. Most likely, the majority of them never made it out of these walls, and "labour made them free".

Prisoners here produced weapons and other things necessary for the German army back then as it marched around Europe, invading one country after another easily.

It should be said here that no matter how bad the post-war USSR looks now from the distance of history, it never surrendered to German Nazis, lost nearly 20 million people in that horrible war, and did every single thing to achieve victory, eventually taking down the German flag on Reichstag in early 1945 and replacing it with a Soviet red one. It was the USSR that resisted the strongest and made the end of the war closer, even with the land-lease help from the USA.

It is peoples' lives that are the most valuable. And Russian, Ukrainian, Georgian, etc, people were the ones that perished most while trying to stop Hitler's troops from conquering the world. Soldiers of the Allies always had their countries to return to. Soviet soldiers did not – they defended their country with their lives. All the countries in Europe together with the USA did their best to beat the Nazis ultimately.

Inside the barracks, there were rows of hard wooden bunks. One bunk above another, three altogether standing in one section, and nine of such "three-storey" berths standing together in a single block. Two of such three-storey lines of berths stood together with 54 beds in total. 54 people lived in big a single room...

A long table with a bench stood by the windows. The toilets and the room for washing were the worst. No showers, as you can imagine. Instead, there were two basins with small fountains, where the prisoners washed every morning. Each of them had ten minutes for that and for using the toilet.

Anyone who took more time would have been punished. The WC room contained two rows of iron toilets, six in each row by the wall. No booths with doors to give you privacy, and no plastic seats in winter. Imagine the rush in the morning with everyone doing their best to wash and use the toilet within the provided time, the atmosphere of doomness and fear (reigning about the whole camp), let alone the smell. Only the strongest survived it, as well as they survived the daily hard work that followed with three miserable meals they got per day.

You can read all about it (and also about how prisoners felt, what they dreamed and thought of during their stay in those camps, how they communicated with each other and how they tried to survive every day not only doing the hardest work in the toughest conditions (poor clothes, poor health, just very basic medical treatment) but also tried to avoid being killed by the guards and kapos) in the book by Viktor Frankl that I mentioned here earlier.

There was also a building with a prison in it – a prison inside the camp. The prisoners called it the "bunker" and were scared to death of getting there. SS tortured them during interrogations in the room with walls designed specially to muffle screams and other loud sounds.

Along the corridor of this one-storey building now tourists walk taking curious looks inside the small cells through partly opened (and fixed in this position) doors with windows in the upper part of them. Some of the cells contain stands with photos of famous prisoners, who also included Germans – those who criticized Hitler or were claimed to be foreign spies – with their short bio on a sheet of paper under glass.

In the yard of the "bunker", they would execute prisoners – put them to the wall and shoot them dead. The wall was made of special material to hold bullets that were extracted after the war. There were also a few standing cells, 80 cm by 80 cm each, for those whom the SS decided to give the hardest time there.

* * *

The next place I went in the camp was the crematorium where bodies of prisoners were regularly burnt. The audio guide, along with the photos with captions near the place told me that the crematorium never stayed idle – there was always work for it, literally every single day. That was a death conveyor, as was the whole camp.

There were two buildings – an old one, which was smaller and only contained two furnaces – and a new crematorium built a few years later. The local "staff" needed a new, bigger crematorium since the amount of bodies they had to dispose of grew rapidly and one small crematorium was just not enough.

The latter was maybe three times as long as the first one and it contained four big furnaces. It had "shower rooms". When a new group of prisoners arrived, those who looked the weakest and/or ill, as well as children and the elderly, were sent to those rooms to take a "shower" after their travel.

You probably know why I used inverted commas to describe those "showers" and what happened next – the people went into those small rooms which indeed looked like ones where you could take a shower, except for a few things – there were no showers inside. Instead, you could see special holes in the walls from where legal gas was coming into the room full of people. You can read/watch Stephen King's "Apt Pupil" to get an idea of what happened there.

In the black and white photos on the walls covered by glass, you could see that their clothes were put in piles by the entrance outside. Then the workers of the place would burn them as well, perhaps picking some of the valuable personal belongings from the clothes to keep them. The same thing happened to the bodies – the four furnaces could work faster than just two but still, they were unable to get rid of all the bodies quickly. These days, one corpse in modern crematoriums takes one or two hours to burn down completely, depending on the weight of the body (the amount of fat it contains) and the material the coffin is made of.

Sometimes bones do not burn down to ashes so they have to be crushed with a cremulator. I guess this procedure was the same back in the times when thousands of bodies were getting burned in concentration camps in Nazi Germany, only they were incinerated without coffins, so my blind guess is that it took roughly an hour, if a person was not too overweight. That makes it around seven bodies per day for one furnace. 32 bodies at maximum but I doubt that were able to burn more than 28-29. Still, no wonder that those crematoriums ran non-stop (except perhaps for nights) and there was always black smoke rising from the chimneys.

These days, there are also other ways to cremate bodies, these are especially relevant to those who care about the environment. One method is called resomation – "water cremation", using water and alkali-based solution when a body is basically gets diluted.

The remains look similar to ashes after they are processed. The second one is promession, when a body gets frozen to the temperature of minus 18 C and then put it into liquid nitrogen. The organic powder that is left after this gets the liquid absorbed out of it and the remains, resembling ashes, are passed to the relatives of the deceased. This is sometimes used in the UK, the US and Europe but poor countries, such as India, mostly use regular cremation. They actually burn their dead right outside on traditional pyres, regardless of what it does to the atmosphere.

Leaving the crematorium behind, I visited four chapels with memorials dedicated to the victims of Dachau KZ – Catholic, Russian Orthodox, Jewish and Protestant ones. Each memorial had a different exterior and interior design with elements that keep reminding the visitors of the KZ – barbed wire, prison cell bars, high walls of stone – several times higher than an average person. The crosses in the chapels (except for the Jewish one) were also big as if likening the victims of the camp to Jesus Christ and his Golgotha Cross.

* * *

The final thing I'd like to tell you about regarding the KZ is the big memorial (a memorial inside a memorial, so to say) devoted to all the victims regardless of their religion. It was in the middle of the square not far from the entrance. You will see why I think this is particularly important and is closely related to the subject of this book.

This small memorial symbolizes the whole path that prisoners went through starting from their arrival at the camp and finishing by their death or liberation at the end of the war.

A guide walks groups of tourists from start to finish through it. This memorial contains two monuments – you face the first one after you walk between two not very high walls standing wide apart so that a big column of people could move between them. Then you face a monument that features huge barbed wire made of stone or metal, whatever, and posts on which barbed wire used to hold that surrounded any concentration camp – they look like lamp posts basically but with the tops bent towards the observer – to make climbing over the fence with barbed wire a next to impossible thing to do.

After that, you turn left and walk towards the end of the "prisoner's path" – a memorial that says "Never again" in several languages, including English, German and – Russian. “Never again”. “Nie wieder”. “Никогда больше”. The inscription in Russian can be removed now since it goes against what Russia is doing now.

It was Hitler who began the war against Europe, believing that the whole world had turned against Germany. He then began destroying Jewish, Slavic people, and gypsies as inferior nations, striving to keep the "clear nation of Arians".

Now, Russia is in the same position as it is attacking Ukraine, hitting civil objects with missiles and drones – not only concert halls, supermarkets, cafes, and theatres but also residential houses. They are killing military Ukrainians and a lot of civilians too. Those who were captured in the occupied cities had to pass through severe checks of their opinions and beliefs regarding Russia (their mobile phones, messenger apps, and social media accounts were checked too).

Anyone who had relatives in the Ukrainian army, especially men, was beaten till they bled, kept in "filtration camps" in the city of Mariupol (on the bank of the Azov Sea in the South of Ukraine, which was almost 100% destroyed as the Ukrainian army held on to it tight and the last defenders stayed in the Azov Steel factory, striving to defend it, while the rest of the city was captured by Russians), in Zaporizhzhia and other cities occupied and now stolen by Russia through fake referendums. Lots of stories of Ukrainians and their photos, who themselves or passed through these camps or it happened to their relatives, can be proof of that.

Russia keeps saying that they are hitting only strategic military objects and never damage civilian buildings, claiming rockets hit the residential blocks as a result of the Ukrainian army's actions – either the wrong shot of the air defense forces or deliberate shots to give Russian troops a bad name by making up these "fakes".

Oh, by the way, likening the Soviet Union to Nazi Germany is now punished with big fines in Russia. A guilty arse always feels a boot heading to kick it.

The worst thing, as I said before, is that Russians believe they are again fighting Nazism, while Putin and those around him are trying to keep their power and write themselves down in history as the leaders of the "victorious Russian army".

Many average Russians are beginning to believe that too, seeing their army as "Motherland's defenders". Russians worship their ancestors, making the victory in WW2 an iconic event. Z-patriots believe that Russian people are better morally than the rest of the world (slamming the liberal ideology, same-sex marriages and many people changing their gender in the West). They think that they are surrounded by enemies from all around...

As for Germans whom I saw in the KZ memorial, there were families with children under ten years old, a lot of teenagers and it seems they were sent there on a mandatory school excursion. I remember seeing their bored glances when they were inside the barracks, listening to the guide, smirking at each other, and laughing at their own jokes told in whispers in the back rows. When I was at school, I had similar feelings about ballet, the world-famous "Swan Lake" by Tchaikovsky where we were forced to go and see with school.

It was not only me who felt bored there, that is a well-known fact that during the Soviet times whole classes of teenagers were taken to see "The Swan Lake" several times to "make them more cultured". But the actual effect was the opposite one – they hated ballet, especially men.

There is one more thing that should be said about "The Swan Lake" here – it was broadcast on TV in Russia during the early 90s when there were political coups. Since then, everybody in Russia knows that should a regular broadcast on TV be interrupted by "The Swan Lake", then something is surely happening at the very top of the government – the President is most likely being replaced. So now, all the people who wish Putin to get lost are making jokes on social media about how they are looking forward to the "Dance of the Little Swans" being shown across all Russian TV channels – the sooner it happens, the better.

When I returned home from Dachau KZ, I decided to watch "Escape from Sobibor". This is a film based on a true story with Rutger Hauer playing a Soviet officer who lead a riot and an escape from the Nazi Sobibor camp in Poland. It operated from May 1942 until October 1943.

For Russians who were born before 2000, Rutger Hauer is an iconic and one of the most loved Hollywood actors of the 80s. Classic films "The Hitch-Hiker", "Flesh and Blood", and others in which he starred were watched by millions of Soviet and post-Soviet people in the late 80s and early 90s and got a high appraisal.

"Escape from Sobibor" starkly illustrated how prisoners lived and were treated in death camps like Dachau. In particular, it also showed the work of the "shower rooms" and crematoriums.

In the film, as soon as the train with a new party of prisoners arrives, all the elderly people, women, the sick, and some children are separated and taken "to have a shower". The rest of those who arrived never saw them again but they all could see black smoke rising fiercely from the crematorium chimneys.

PART 6

"PUTIN'S COOK" PRIGOZHIN AND HIS "TROLL FACTORY"

Now it is time to tell you about the further course the war had taken. It is useless to describe here what was happening in Ukraine, because...how can you describe hell in detail? I'm no Dante who descended there, then returned and wrote a poem about the nine circles of it. Besides, this would turn the book into chronicles of the war in Ukraine and that was not my goal.

So now I will describe what was happening in Russia during the start of the war and how Russians reacted to it. Also, you will get another proof that this war was declared not only on Ukraine but on average Russian people too, their lives and welfare.

Let's begin with The Wagner Group and its founder, Evgeny Prigozhin, also known as "Putin's cook".
Private military company (PMC) Wagner ("CHVK Wagner" in Russian; also known as Wagner Group in a more business-like context) became well-known during the war as it took an active part in it.
Founded by Prigozhin about ten years ago, it is believed to have

been participating in the unannounced war against Ukraine in its Eastern rich in coal territories of Donetsk and Luhansk since 2014. What Wagner does is hire mercenaries, sending them to Africa, Syria, Ukraine, and other places where military conflicts and full-scale wars are taking place to represent Putin's interests and help overthrow the local leaders, suppress or conduct riots in those countries, provide security services to the presidents, high-ranking politicians and so on.

Prigozhin is a former convict, who spent two years in prison for robberies in the late 1970s. In the late 1990s, he began running the most expensive elite restaurants in St. Petersburg. Putin liked going there and Prigozhin himself served on him, his wife, and guests at the table. Born in 1961, Prigozhin was 62 in 2023.

After that, Putin allowed Prigozhin's company Concord Catering founded in 1995 to begin supplying the Russian army with food products. The same company later founded PMC Wagner which has been funded by the Russian government. Before creating Wagner, Prigozhin showed his talent as an organiser and manager by working in the sphere of pro-government media and state propaganda. Over time, he grew closer to Putin.

Prigozhin's name is also associated with the so-called "Troll Farm" (officially called the Internet Research Agency) based in St. Petersburg. The "farm" is believed to have attempted to influence the results of the US elections, when Donald Trump came to power. Its existence was first revealed in 2016 by journalists. Workers of the "factory" were also involved in promoting the interests of the Russian government and oligarchs and in impacting governing decisions made by them in Russia via fake online media, forums, and discussion boards on the Internet.

After the recent "mutiny of Prigozhin", Putin during a meeting with the top members of the government admitted that over the past year (from May 2022 until May 2023) the government paid Wagner Group 86.262 billion rubles ($940,255,800) – that was the money for military payouts and incentive awards. More than 110 billion rubles were paid to Wagner Group to cover their insurance payouts ($1,199,000,000). The date comes from a fresh Putin's talk made to the government broadcast on TV.

Aside from that, during the same period, Concord Catering earned 80 billion rubles ($872,000,000) on supplying food products and catering for the Russian army. When the company only started, it "just suddenly" began winning numerous state tenders for catering services to high-class people from the government, including Putin himself. This included banquets and catering for schools and government workers.

PRIGOZHIN RECRUITING CONVICTS

Soon after the war was unleashed, the presence of PMC Wagner in Ukraine and its active participation in it was announced. A while after Russian troops failed to take Kyiv by storm "within three days", Prigozhin at Putin's permission started going to various prisons (including those with a high level of security, in Russia they are called "prison colonies") to offer convicts to join Wagner and go to fight in Ukraine.

He talked to them personally in each place as the prisoners gathered in the inner yard, explaining the contract terms to them – the same salary as regular Wagner mercenaries earn, "honour to protect the Motherland" and the major bonus – they will be pardoned after their contracts expire. They began offering to recruit even those, who they would not have hired before – the worst of convicts, slime of humanity – rapists and murderers. Hundreds and then thousands of convicts joined them. That number later increased to tens of thousands.

Prigozhin's political influence surged as the war started and Wagner Group began receiving increased funding from the state, as well as military airplanes and other things necessary for successful fighting. In the course of the events that I will describe further on, the total count of Wagner mercenaries grew, by some estimates, to 50,000 and basically, it turned into Prigozhin's personal army.

“Native" Wagner mercenaries started to refer to the "convict troops" as "penal units". Notably, among those convicts were those doing long prison terms – twenty years and more. There is a famous case of entrepreneur Alexander Tyutin, who was sentenced to 23 years in jail. On his order, in 2005 his business partner, his wife and his daughter were killed – shot from a Kalashnikov gun, all three of them. They were then finished off with an axe, a Russian criminal tradition, I suppose, rather than shooting a bullet in their heads.

Tyutin was arrested in 2018 when the murder of his niece (over her inheritance) was prevented and he got caught red-handed as he was hiring a killer (an undercover agent of the Inner Affairs Ministry).

This guy joined Wagner to go to Ukraine after spending three years in prison when he was 66. Six months later when his contract was over, he went back to St Petersburg and flew to spend a holiday in Turkey, Antalya, to recover both from prison and from the war in which he supposedly took part. Thus, Wagner gently helped him to remove 19 years from his prison sentence.

You may of course believe that he "served" and took part in actual fights, but if you want my take on this – Tyutin is a businessman with a criminal past, and Prigozhin is a businessman with a criminal past and present.

I do not see, why they did not have a deal for a few million rubles, and Tyutin likely spent those six months in a safe place in Wagner positions away from fights until his contract expired. Then Prigozhin just let him walk away, "pardoned" by

Putin. I bet this was not the only deal between Wagner and wealthy prisoners, but this was certainly the one about which the word was actively spread by journalists.

Another similar case reported by the media was about the former deputy Alexander Khakonov from the Krasnoyarsk region of Russia. In March 2022, he killed his wife and secretly drove her body out to the woods. Some random people stumbled on her corpse a few days later, and Khakonov admitted to committing the murder. The judge sentenced him to nine years and eight months in prison with the highest security level. Before being moved to the actual jail, he stayed in the detention centre. There, Khakonov was recruited by Wagner representatives and went to the war before he even started to do his time.

Is he really taking part in active military actions or is he just having an easy time, hired by Wager just formally for a bribe to Prigozhin? Who knows. Give me your best guesses, if you like.

People on social media went furious, naturally not wishing all these convicts to come back after their contracts are done, armed and with fresh battle experience. Having killed other people and coming back free from prison they would hardly become law-abiding citizens but would likely get back to their old criminal ways, civilians feared.

Grounded fears often tend to come true. A 28-year-old Ivan Rossomakhin came back from the war to his native town as he got some time off Wagner service. Four years ago there he had been sentenced to 14 years in jail for a murder and had served four years of his time before he was recruited by Prigozhin.

Locals began complaining to the police that upon return he was often seen showing aggressive behaviour – in particular, he walked around the village drunk beyond repair with an axe in his hand, hacking cars parked in the streets and shouting out threats to those who even looked at him sideways.

He ended up hacking an elderly woman to death, coming inside the yard of her house. He then went to the police to surrender and plead himself guilty. This was a loud case, so Prigozhin commented on it publicly for the media – he said it was a shame that the guy committed a crime again and recommended that if anyone else saw former Wagner soldiers behaving aggressively, they should contact Wagner Group through one of their business centres. He promised that in that case they would take those guys away and send them to the fire line immediately.

Notably, when average people began writing complaints to the public pages of Prigozhin and Wagner on social media about them hiring convicts and thus endangering society, Prigozhin responded: "It is either them or your children, the choice is yours."

As the war kept unrolling and the Wagner Group turned into a buzz word, a lot of Russian Z-patriots started praising them, calling them "Wagner musicians", "Wagners" or simply "the musicians". Shops started selling their merchandise, such as tee-shirts saying "Wagner orchestra on tour" depicting tanks and armed soldiers. A lot of people began to buy and wear that stuff in public.

WAGNER DEFECTOR PUBLICLY EXECUTED

One notable thing took place when one of Prigozhin's mercenaries decided to change sides. Evgeny Nuzhin – initially, he had a 20-year prison sentence to do but then Prigozhin recruited him during one of his visits to prison camps.

Nuzhin went to the war, then he managed to escape from Wagner's positions and surrendered to Ukrainian soldiers. On October 12, 2022, he gave an interview to Ukrainian journalists in Kyiv. He told them that from the very beginning, he was against the war, planned to surrender and that he was willing to fight on the side of Ukraine.

Nuzhin also shared details of how former convicts recruited are treated by Wagner senior soldiers and officers. If you quarrel with an instructor, they "bring you down to zero", which means they shoot you down. He also shared many other details of how things stood within Wagner troops. He called on other Russian soldiers to leave their battle positions and either flee or surrender to Ukrainians.

This man somehow was captured by Wagner soldiers after that interview. Some sources say he was exchanged by the Ukrainian side for 10 or 20 of their soldiers who had been held captive. Both Russia and Ukraine exchange captives regularly. However, others say that it was a kidnapping. As for Nuzhin himself, in the video I will be talking about a little lower, he said that somebody hit him on the back of his head in Kyiv and then he came to it in a basement, where Wagner men told him that he was to undergo a trial soon.

It does not matter in the end, how he was brought back to Wagner. What's important is that his execution was recorded on a video and published on one of the popular Russian Telegram channels. His head was crushed by a sledgehammer against the wall where the man was sitting.

Prigozhin commented on that video in one of his interviews. He refuted claims that it was done on his orders, however, he said that if it had been done by his men, then it was a really neat job, suggesting that Wagner does not let off defectors and traitors.

Later on, another video was published in which a sledgehammer with a Wagner logo and sham blood stains on the handle was shown. It was supposed to be sent to the European Parliament which wanted to declare the Wagner Group a terrorist organization.

Since then, a sledgehammer became strongly associated with the Wagner Group and Prigozhin until Wagner PMC ended after his death.

PARTIAL MOBILIZATION; ARMY DODGERS AND "LAW-ABIDING" RUSSIAN MEN

"We thought we hit the rock bottom but then we heard someone knocking from below." - Russian saying

After it became clear that the tens of thousands of convicts conscripted by Wagner failed to make a turning point in the war and get any noticeable advantage for the Russian army, Putin did something that had not been done in Russia since WW2 – at the end of September 2022, he announced partial mobilization.

Putin's press secretary Peskov stated that the goal was to draft 300,000 men. Things had turned bad for the "victorious" Russian army in Ukraine, contract soldiers were dying by hundreds, same as conscripts (when the war started, Putin stated that active duty soldiers were not taking part in the war). However, when the flagship of the Russian fleet, "Moskva" sank in the Black Sea on April 22, 2022, it turned out there were many conscripts on it after all.

The vessel was hit with Neptune anti-ship missiles by Ukrainians. Then other reports followed, when conscript soldiers either started fleeing the front line, trying to get back to Russia or mothers of those guys began making public complaints to the Defence Ministry about their sons being thrown into the massacre in Ukraine.

The parents of those who were on the "Moskva" flagship begged to know what had happened to their sons but the Defence Ministry would not admit they were dead, saying just that those soldiers had gone missing after the explosion and the ship sinking.

Back then, Putin made a public statement on TV, saying that the cases of active-duty soldiers participating in the SVO would be investigated and the guilty parties would be penalized. Opposition online media and the Committee of Soldiers' Mothers in Russia spread the word that when young people were conscripted in 2022, they were forced or tricked into signing contracts to join the soldiers fighting in Ukraine.

News reports began to emerge saying that some soldiers who signed their contracts before the war preferred to resign from the SVO, even when threatened with prosecution on their return to Russia.
Many of them got critical assessments when they resigned, which vilified them as "unreliable on the battlefield", claiming they had betrayed their comrades-in-arms and their "Motherland" overall.

* * *

The September 2022 mobilization was a shock to many in Russia. Still, quite a lot of people took it as their duty to "defend their Motherland", even though they hated the idea that they may easily get killed. They made themselves go to the military commissariat's offices ("Voenkomats" in Russian), their wives and children either seeing them off proudly or weeping, not wishing to let them go. Those were mostly men in their late 30s and older.

However, since both the Russian healthcare service and the Russian army have been turned basically into paupers by the government after the Soviet Union collapsed, the conscripted soldiers (and those who volunteered, too) did not get any bulletproof vests, munition, or any other necessary things.

They had to eat tinned food, often it was past the use-by date. The military chiefs told those people's wives and parents to buy everything themselves, including warm socks and thermal underwear. Billboards began emerging in the streets offering to take a bank loan in order to send your husband/ father to the SVO. Before that, similar adverts offered loans to buy everything for your child to send him/her to school after the summer holidays. A perfect and happy way to live in "the greatest country in the world", isn't it?

Some of the drafted soldiers began to publicly complain about the lack of munition. Besides, those people were often transported in trains that were initially designed to carry cargo, not people.

Many of those soldiers had no army experience at all, or no actual experience of participating in military conflicts. When they arrived in the East of Ukraine (the Donetsk and Luhansk regions), they were just given Kalashnikov guns, sometimes rusty ones, and thrown into the midst of a battle. A lot of them were killed during the first weeks of their "military service".

Several trains that carried newly conscripted soldiers exploded or went off the rails as they moved closer to Ukraine as a result of internal attacks. Another nasty thing is that Putin began conscripting people in the "newly joined" territories, annexed from Ukraine, making them fight their countrymen.

* * *

Back to army dodgers. As more and more people began avoiding the reception of draft notices and hid behind the doors of their flats, Voenkomats began sending those notes to the offices to be delivered personally to the people whom they failed to find in their homes. A lot of IT workers, engineers, and people from other spheres important for the economy were demanded to go to war (read – get killed in Ukraine for Putin). Even though, the law says that university students are not to be conscripted until they graduate, many of them also began receiving draft notices, even PhD students. University teachers, including professors, were also demanded to go to Voenkomats and join the army. They were eventually sent to war to serve in the firing line.

Oddly enough, cases were reported by the media when disabled people (literally with no arms or legs) were given draft notices. So were those who were diagnosed with illnesses that usually would make them free from having to join the army. Relatives of some of them spread the word about this through the media, and eventually, those people with disabilities were left alone.

Now, you may think – why is he telling us about the problems of Russians during the war, when it is Ukrainians who have suffered most during it? That's true, things turned out the worst for Ukrainian people as their land, their homes, and families were being attacked and destroyed; bodies of civilians often torn to pieces by rockets and drones. But I would like to show both sides of the war.

When Putin sent troops to fight Ukraine, he also started war against Russia – those are people, many of them are friendly to Ukraine, who like this country and have nothing against its people.

They are pro-peace, they want friendship with Ukrainians and open borders as it was before the war broke out.

This war ultimately impacts average Russians. Putin, his close circle and government officials remain well-off, despite the multiple sanctions. Besides, none of them or their children have been sent to the firing line so far.

What is more, the adult children of these people keep studying or living abroad, in the USA, and Europe. They are publishing reels/photos on Instagram showing them on luxurious yachts somewhere in Dubai or the Mediterranean.

MOBILIZATION-DODGERS FLEEING EN MASSE

"Mogilization" – this is what name this mobilization got among Russians who were against the war.

"Mogila" means "grave", hence the verbal noun made up by people who began to be massively conscripted (often forcefully) to make "a refill" for the troops who stayed to rot in the Ukrainian ground by the end of September 2022.

"(Mobi)gravization", "cemeterization", etc, feel free to choose your own English neologism for this. Hopefully, you will never get to use it in real life in your country, though.

All of a sudden, all those Z-patriots, who rigidly support the war, calling the soldiers fighting in Ukraine "Motherland defenders", and are who proudly putting "Z" letters on their social media avatar and their cars' windshields and who are wearing tee-shirts with that letter, got a great chance to prove that they were not just blabbering about talking "patriotism".

These people since the annexation of Crimea in 2014 have been putting stickers on their cars that said "1941-1945, we can easily repeat it" and then applauding when yet another rocket or armed drone hit a residential block in Kyiv or another Ukrainian city with civilian people dying, including women and children, far away from the firing line.

Men who wanted no part of that, especially those from sixteen to thirty, began to grab tickets to leave Russia to avoid receiving draft notices – once one is issued on your name you will not be allowed to cross the border.

Seeing that a lot of young people were not taking those notes from the couriers, they started issuing draft notices and "invitations" for people to come over to "solve minor issues unrelated to the mobilization". The advice that all anti-Putin bloggers and attorneys gave to people on the Internet was to avoid going to Voenkomats by all means.

The first rule of a draftee, as they say now, is not to accept "mandatory invitations" to Voenkomats, not to sign papers to confirm their reception and by no means actually go to the conscription offices.

Logically, you should not open up when you hear the bell ringing in your flat and look into the peephole in the door to make sure you will not see enlisters accompanied by policemen waiting outside your door.

As a lot of people began to do that, recruiters started tucking these notes under apartment doors. A few times in Moscow, in flats where people who were to be conscripted did not open up, the military and the police sealed the doors of their flats from outside.

* * *

The number of people rushing to leave Russia jumped to 800 hundred thousand in total, some sources name one million – this includes not only those who tried to avoid the mobilization but also people who began to leave Russia after the war began.

European countries quickly closed their borders to Russians even as tourists and began to only accept those who had criminal records for "discrediting the Russian army" or for criticizing the war/Putin. These were mainly journalists, activists, and other public figures. They would have to provide proof that they had been prosecuted in Russia and that their life was jeopardized.

Some Baltic countries stopped issuing visas for Russians, stating that they should protest against the war in Russia rather than flee it. Therefore, with Europe closed, Russians headed en masse for post- Soviet countries, such as Georgia, Armenia, and Kazakhstan.

Lines of cars to cross the borders were endless; many were turned back by Russian border guards – they checked their database to see if draft notices had been issued on their names and they made a lot of men turn back. Some did not want to wait and crossed borders on foot, walking thousands of kilometres until their legs and feet were sore.

According to top-tier media, Putin was indignant, personally offended, by the great number of people who chose to leave Russia – that number had surpassed the amount of immigrants in the early 1990s after the USSR collapse. Therefore, he thought of a "genius method". Draft notices began to be issued electronically. There is a government online platform "Gosuslugi" (translated as "State Services"), which was launched in 2011. Through it, Russians gain access to services provided by state bodies online, e.g. registering a new car, getting a driver's license, changing one's passport, etc.

The Gosuslugi portal was initially constructed exceptionally badly. Registering an account there was a real challenge and so was using it, so the site became a target for stand-up comics and a subject for memes and jokes.

Now that the majority of Russians are finally registered on that platform, draft papers began to be sent directly to their Gosusligi accounts. The trick here was that account owners were not notified about this and Putin's decree now stated that they must themselves check their inboxes from time to time to monitor this matter.

If a man received an "invitation" to a Voenkomat through Gosuslugi but did not know about it, he still automatically became a subject for conscription. Getting such an electronic note, even with you being unaware, automatically makes you unable to leave Russia.

By the end of 2023, the Russian government went even further – people who were forbidden to leave Russia, mostly those who received draft notices, had to hand in their travel passports to the authorities for custody storage for the period during which they were banned from going abroad.

OLD FRIEND GETS IN TOUCH, FEARING MOBILIZATION

A lot of programmers left Russia – mainly those who had a chance to switch to a distant job with the company they were working for already. Others were so eager to escape the grip of Voenkomats that they simply left the country without thinking about how they would make a living in the future.

Many of those later went back to Russia – either because it was too expensive to live abroad or because they quickly ran out of the money they had. The latter went back much quicker. Some also came back because of their families who had stayed behind.

A colleague of mine left St. Petersburg with her husband for Bali. The husband was not a subject for conscription but they just refused to support the war. After a few months, she told me they were going back – Bali was too expensive (although it was a nice and exotic location); besides, they had a mortgage to pay in Russia.

Another colleague of mine first left for Thailand with his wife, but after half a year, he also had to return to take care of his elderly parents. After I got back to work in September, we started writing articles together for the same website. Another guy I work with has immigrated to Montenegro but he had decided to do it before the war broke out. So when it all started, all the paperwork had already been prepared and he just left for that country with his wife and no intention to come back.

In an interesting turn of events, as the "mogilization" started my old friend from Moscow wrote to me on Instagram to ask how I was doing. We used to work together for a Chinese company in Moscow in the late 2000s. A few years after I moved to Ukraine, she got married. Over the past few years, we have been just sending birthday and New Year greetings to each other.

But here, Ann messaged me in a panic to say he was afraid that her husband Vova (short for Vladimir) may be summoned and sent to Ukraine. By that time, they had two children, a boy and a girl, the daughter may be one or two years younger than Dasha.

Vova was head of the IT department in a large Russian company in Moscow. Ann said that she thought a lot about me and my family when the war started but, she told me, you don't realize how the war impacts other people until it begins affecting you directly. That is true – I did not hear a word from her when the war began; she did not even write to me to ask if me and my family were okay.

I told her that Vova should leave ASAP or their children risk remaining half orphans. Ann agreed, saying that he could basically switch to a distant work mode, at least for a few months and he would manage to keep his well-paid job.

The problem was that Vova did not think this whole situation was serious, "people in Leningrad and Rome think that death is something that happens only to others but not to themselves", as Brodsky wrote. I began to send her the news about how the situation kept unrolling, what new things Putin's government came up with to drag more men into the massacre in Ukraine.

So Vova would not go unless he was able to keep his job. The second thing was that he planned to return afterwards as he liked Moscow and did not want to spend the rest of his life outside Russia. Well, I thought, it is your life at stake, mate, not mine.

This was the period when the police began to seal the doors of apartments of those who would not open up to receive draft notices. The police stood by entrances into underground stations, forcing men to take those notes and confirm the receipt with their signatures. Some people were taken to police stations for refusing to accept those papers.

Vova stayed at home, working distantly and trying to avoid bumping into Voenkomat people or police in the street, he would not open doors when somebody rang the bell.

A few weeks after the mobilization began, the opposition media and Telegram channels began spreading rumours that the government was about to issue an order that the borders be closed for men of fighting age. I recommended Ann to hurry up with the departure. They found a ticket for Vova to Kazakhstan but there was a week or two before the flight date. Flying earlier would cost a lot more, like a few hundred thousand rubles. So Vova waited. And he waited and he waited.

In the end, he was not conscripted, and I'm glad he was not – I know him in person, I respect him and Ann, they are nice folks. But after everything calmed down for them, I never heard from them again, we only exchanged minor comments on social media.

I guess that was yet another proof of the universal law – if your friends are not in touch with you that means they are doing fine. But once in trouble, they are ringing the bell of your door, asking for help or at least for sympathy.

MONGOLIA AS “POPULAR DESTINATION” FOR ARMY-DODGERS

Mongolia became a very popular destination, along with Kazakhstan, for those who fled the conscription. Since the war started, the number of direct flights to that country from Russia surged by 7,580%. Previously, Russian tourists did not value that place much as there is nothing in particular to see or do there, apart from going to the steppe or, perhaps, mountains. But in 2022, Mongolia became a way out for those who wanted to avoid killing Ukrainians or getting killed for Putin's imperial ambitions.

You do not need a visa to go to Mongolia, so within 2022 alone, the number of Russians who dashed there reached 138,300, according to statistics from online open sources. If you compare it with the data from a year before, you will see a striking difference – in 2021, this number was merely 1,800.

NEW AGE "PHILOSOPHER'S SHIPS"

In September of 2022, it was a hundred years since the "philosopher's ships" sailed from the USSR, taking away several hundred representatives of Russian intelligentsia who were exiled from Russia on ships.

Back then, this was a measure of "social protection" for those people provided by the Soviet government after Lenin had initiated a campaign against "the negative inflow of bourgeois ideas". All radical opponents of Bolshevism were just wiped out but as for intelligentsia, Lenin decided to get rid of them softly.

NKVD (later it became KGB, these days it is the FSB (the Federal Security Service)) went to the houses of around 200 or 300 doctors, scholars, university teachers, agriculturists, professors, musicians, actors, etc, and told them they had to leave the country without a chance to return. If they returned, they would be arrested. The Soviet government sent an official request to Germany to accept the exiled and give them shelter. To that, Germany responded that their country is not Siberia and no exiles can be sent there just like that. However, they added that if the Soviet citizens were to write their own letters asking for asylum, Germany would help them, of course.

A lot of those people did not like Bolsheviks but they had come to terms with the revolution itself, accepting the fact that their country had changed radically.

The ships sailed from Petrograd (the name which was later changed to Leningrad and then to St. Petersburg these days but before Petrograd, it was also called St. Petersburg) on September 29, 1922, taking those people away. Some of them returned later and they were put in labour camps.

As for 2022, a lot of intelligentsia people left Russia of their own will – mostly actors (young movie actors and old-school theatre legends from the Soviet times), popular fiction writers, rock musicians, top stand-up comedians, lawyers, and journalists.

Among those actors and musicians, there were great names who began singing underground back in the early 1980s and the 1990s of the last century. These people are now touring the US, Canada and European countries with concerts for the Russian-speaking audience, who either left Russia in protest too or had immigrated in the early 1990s or 2000s. These musicians are donating part of their profits to help Ukrainian civilians.

Many of them are giving interviews, openly stating their highly negative attitude towards not only the war but also Putin and his government. Many are saying that fascism has taken over Russia.

The majority of these artists have been declared "foreign agents" by the Russian government for the above-mentioned reasons. In the past, especially in the times of Stalin, they would have been officially called "enemies of the Soviet people". Some of these people are known not only to Russian-speaking audiences.

Dmitry Glukhovski's books, for example, have been translated into a dozen languages, including English, German, Polish, Japanese, etc – "Metro 2033", "Metro 2035", "Futu.re", "Text" are the most famous ones.

In Russia, an arrest warrant for him has been issued and he is also a "foreign agent", along with the leaders of such ultra-popular rock bands as "Aquarium" (Boris Grebenschikov, aka BG and sometimes also called the "Russian Bob Dylan"), "The Time Machine" (Andrey Makarevich) (these bands are the two very first rock groups who began playing in the Soviet Union, writing rock songs in Russian, often inspired by Western music, but without using balalaikas), and many others. The legend of the Soviet pop music stage, the "prima-donna" Alla Pugacheva also left for Israel with her family.

The other half of Russian intelligentsia, not surprisingly, has sided with Putin and supports the war. Among them are rock musicians of second and third tiers, top modern Russian actors, and the majority of Russian science fiction writers, including Sergei Lukyanenko. His books have also been translated into English and many European languages, one of his novels was even bought by Netflix, but once the war started, the film series production was frozen.

ARMY-DODGERS HEADING FOR ALASKA

The media described an interesting case when two Russian men (Sergei and Maxim, no surnames were disclosed) sailed to Alaska in a fishing boat, escaping from Voenkomat people. It was also reported by The Anchorage Daily News and The Economist. They sailed to St. Lawrence Island, overcoming 300 miles through the Bering Sea from the Russian mainland (an urban-type place called Evgekinot). They were detained for three months by Alaska's Customs and Border Protection service, being interrogated and passing various checks. Ultimately, they were allowed to stay in the USA.

Sergei and Maxim later publicly shared that they had spent three months in a big room with 70 other prisoners, got rice and beans for meals and read all the Russian books that the librarian brought them twice a month. They were finally bailed out by a Ukrainian priest, who later also helped them to find accommodation. By now, they have both received work permits.

Sergei told the journalists that he and Maxim decided to escape after people dressed in military uniforms several times came over and knocked on the doors of their flats. They did not open up and stayed quiet inside.

They packed bread, sausages, boiled eggs, coffee, biscuits, packs of cigarettes, plus enough fuel to last them for 300 miles, and sailed off. When they arrived in the town of Gambell, they asked for political asylum. It was ultimately granted to them after months of waiting.

HISTORY REPEATS ITSELF: STORIES OF PEOPLE WHO ESCAPED FROM THE USSR, RISKING THEIR LIVES

There were several documented cases of people who managed to escape the USSR forever, putting their lives at stake as they mostly escaped by water with nothing but swimming trunks or bikinis on them. I think it would be interesting for you to read about them briefly here since this is pretty much along the lines of people escaping from Putin's Russia now.

THE RED BIKINI GIRL

One of those "defectors" was Liliana Gasinskaya, also known as the "red bikini girl". She defected from the USSR in mid-January 1979. She worked as a waitress on a Soviet cruise ship "SS Leonid Sobinov". Liliana was only 18 but she had dreamed of leaving the Soviet Union for many years by then.

She had no guarantees whatsoever that "the other side", when she got there, would grant her asylum and not transfer her back to the Soviet authorities. In case such defectors were returned, they were either sent to labour camps or got forceful psychiatric treatment.

At night, when there was a big party on the ship for the passengers, Liliana put on her red bikini and jumped over the board, swimming to the coast of Australia. It took her forty minutes.

Australian officials had heated debates as to whether they should send her back or allow her to stay.

However, she did get a political asylum after all. Besides, the story says that Gasinskaya promised to kill herself should they send her back.

Liliana became a model for the Australian edition of Penthouse magazine, earning $15,000 as its first-ever nude centrefold.

Another famous escape from the "socialistic camp" (this is what it was often called in official speeches in which the USSR was opposed to the "capitalistic world" of the West; a pretty truthful comparison with a pinch of dark humour, if you see what I mean). Another loud escape which involved swimming over a long distance, happened five years earlier, in 1974. It was pulled off by Slava Kurilov.

SLAVA KURILOV'S ESCAPE

Vyacheslav (Slava for short, translated from Russian as "glory") Kurilov (1936-1998) was a Soviet oceanographer, who dreamed of travelling to see the entire world. After he escaped, he became a writer as he published a book about his escape when he lived in Israel. It was published both in Russian and Hebrew. Later, it also came out in English, called "Alone in the Ocean".

Back in the USSR times, the easiest way to leave the country illegally was to walk over the Gulf of Finland on the ice – this is what Lenin did before he returned to spearhead the revolution. However, Finland and the USSR had an extradition treaty, so anyone who escaped to Finland would have been sent back. This is why Soviet dissidents had to think about countries lying farther away and he decided to swim to get there.

Just like Liliana Gasinskaya, Slava Kurilov jumped over the board of a cruiser liner called Sovetsky Soyuz (that's translated as "The Soviet Union"), which was following the route "Vladivostok – The Equator – Vladivostok", without entering foreign seaports.

Slava swam for three days in the ocean until he was able to reach Siargao Island which belonged to the Philippines. He jumped into the water on December 13, when the weather in the ocean was stormy and he had just a snorkelling mask and fins on him. Kurilov was a sturdy man as before the escape he had practiced yoga for a year, up to 12 hours every day, which made him physically strong and enduring.

He was picked up by a Philippine fisherman who saw a man in the water clinging to the side of his drifting boat. Kurilov spent half a year in the Philippines, while the authorities checked if he was a Soviet spy. Only after that, he was allowed to leave for Canada. After living there for ten years and travelling a lot, Kurilov moved to Israel, where he got married and wrote his book.

He died in 1998 in Israel in a diving accident on Lake Kinneret, where he got tangled up in a fishing net underwater and got out of the air.

In 2022, Russians planned to start filming a biopic based on his book with one of Russia's top actors. However, the war with Ukraine never made it happen. Besides, the anti-USSR topic is not favourable in Putin's Russia anymore.

PYOTR PATRUSHEV – A SWIMMER ESCAPING BY SEA

I will not exhaust you with a lot of these escape stories, this is the last one. Pyotr Patrushev (1942 – 2016) trained as a professional swimmer in the city of Tomsk in Siberia. He was a backstroke champion and so he took part in multiple swimming contests in Moscow and other Russian cities. Before he escaped, he even trained for the 1964 Olympics. In June 1962, he managed to swim from the Georgian city of Batumi to the coast of Turkey (35 kilometres) without any special gear on him but flippers. He went for it at night to have better chances to stay invisible to the military ships on the border with Turkey.

He had to dive several times to avoid getting into the beams of the searchlights on the border guard ships. He managed to avoid getting caught in nets spread in the border waters, he avoided military motor boats that were patrolling the waters; he stayed out of sight of the patrolling airplanes too. The detailed story of his escape based on the book he wrote about that is now included in the curricula of intelligence services in many countries around the world, according to Wikipedia.

In his book "Sentenced to Death", he said that after he reached Turkey, the local authorities thought he was a spy and put him in prison, where he spent a year and a half. Young Turkish investigators practiced all forms of interrogation on him, including sleep and food deprivation and fake execution by shooting him with blank bullets.

Later on, he got an anchor job with BBC, where he was able to set up his own radio programs, during which he talked about things he was deeply interested in – environment protection, psychology, human's inner world, Oriental philosophy, professional sports, etc.
He published several other books, including the one called "The Nirvana Project. How the Cold War Was Won".

Apparently, the story of Patrushev's escape inspired Russian film directors after the USSR was gone. At least one movie seems to be partly based on his story. In 1999, a Russian-French feature film Est-Ouest was released with a Russian celebrity actor Oleg Menshikov (who also played the main character in Nikita Mikhalkov's Burnt by the Sun, a film about Stalin's repressions shot in the early 90s, which won an Oscar) and Catherine Deneuve.

In 1990, Patrushev came to Russia for the first time to visit his relatives. His death penalty was cancelled a few years before the USSR collapsed. Still, Patrushev was held in the Russian airport, detained for eight hours and then released with no explanation provided. But the KGB officer told him: "You see, Perestroyka works indeed now".

I just cannot imagine what these two men (Kurilov and Patrushev) felt when they were alone in the middle of a huge body of water, having to constantly swim (day and night, on adrenalin, deprived of sleep and then overcoming great weariness, resting as they swam, saving the remnants of their energy) not only to get away from the abyss under their feet but also from the ideological abyss of the USSR they had left behind, swimming towards a new life – to countries where they would even probably feel lonely until the end of their lives but remain free.

A curious fact – Pyotr Patrushev is the namesake of Nikolai Patrushev – former head of FSB and a top government official close to Putin, who is also connected to the war in Ukraine. I wonder if these two Patrushevs are related somehow.

* * *

Russians are famous for having a great mental connection to their homeland. At least this was true in the past – when the first waves of immigration from Russia occurred after the revolution in October 1917.

Back then, a lot of not only intelligentsia but also Russian army officers left for France and other European countries. Many of them soon blew their brains out because of strong feelings of nostalgia. Not to mention the fact that they had to earn their living by washing dishes in restaurants or driving horse cabs after living wealthy lives of respected people in high-ranking positions in their homeland.

I have great respect for them – their spirit was very strong, their intention to leave the country where you cannot criticize your government when it does awful things, spills seas of blood, the country where the ruling higher class deliberately keeps the population poor as part of the state ideology, claiming that they all live in "the best country in the world". Therefore, all those immigrants (they were far from those who are referred to as "economic refugees" these days) from Russia had three major stress factors – the change of the political system they could not accept, having to live away from their homeland, often among people whose values were not close to them and having to work low-qualified jobs to survive.

Learning a foreign language is another major problem, but it is more of a modern one at the moment – back in the late 1900s a lot of Russian army officers and intelligentsia spoke French or English fluently (or both of these languages).

If we just for a moment go deeper into the history of the 19th century, French was the language of the aristocracy in Russia. Sometimes, Russian aristocrats hired Russian nannies so they could live with them and teach their children to speak proper, native Russian.

This was also the case with the German language after Peter The Great's rule. Just think about this high degree of Russian culture depending on that of France, Germany and other European countries. Before Pushkin started his writer's career, Russia had no poetry in Russian, it was mostly French or written by Russians in French.

No wonder that in the US Russian and Ukrainian immigrants came up with a radical solution to at least one of these problems – they settled down in Brighton Beach, calling it Little Odessa. You are surrounded by Russian native speakers there and you have literally everything in Russian – newspapers, schools, shops, restaurants, cafes, supermarkets, radio stations, TV channels, etc.

This area boasts the biggest Russian infrastructure in any country outside Russia and (perhaps formerly, the one in Ukraine). So if you are fleeing Russia for either political or economic motives, you are welcome there. By the way, I'm curious how Brighton Beach residents feel about the Russian-Ukrainian war now – they have a lot of people from both countries there, at least there are plenty of their descendants.

According to the census, as of 2010, Little Odessa had 23,431 people living there officially.

However, since a lot of people prefer not to take part in a census and rent flats without official contracts, thus letting the owners dodge taxes, the ultimate size of the Russian-speaking population there is a lot more than that.

In Germany, the Russian diaspora is a very big one too but many Russians over here are pro-Putin, unfortunately, and even have made several automobile rallies with Russian flags to support the war.
In Berlin, they have brought lots of flowers to the remains of a Russian tank destroyed in Ukraine, which is set near the Russian Federation embassy. However, these people are not in a hurry to go back and live under Putin's rule for some reason. As we say in Russia, they want to both eat the fish and ride on the dick, meaning to strive to benefit from all the possible options, which often contradict each other. Or you could use an old Russian joke to describe their attitude – "From certain distances you find your homeland the most attractive place in the world". "Your love for the homeland grows proportionally to how far you are getting away from it".

It sounds a bit opposite to what I said earlier about Russian officers shooting themselves in immigration but, come on, dear reader, the times have changed and if the former were forced to leave Russia, they were deeply religious and had their own honour code (like the Samurai), the latter do it of their own will and they are "economic refugees" already.

To finish off with the topic of making escapes, I'd like to tell you a story just to let you rest from the pieces of the harsh Soviet history a little.

When I hear the word "escape" as a noun, I always recall the title of a popular movie based on Stephen King's book – "The Shawshank Redemption". This is a typical association for Russians – we love that movie.

Once during an interview, King told a story when he was in a supermarket and an old lady approached him, saying: "I know who you are! You are Stephen King, the horror story writer. But I detest your books! I like stories like "The Green Mile" or "The Shawshank Redemption", they are so hearty and have much more light in them, unlike your stories."

King told her: “Ma’m, you know, I wrote these too.” “No way!” the lady responded and walked off indignantly.

PRIGOZHIN'S "MUTINY"

Moving on, I think that one more thing worth mentioning here is the so-called Prigozhin's mutiny.

On June 24, Saturday (it was the weekend, so the whole of Russia could watch this short-lived event without any distraction from work), Yevgeny Prigozhin and part of Wagner mercenaries went from Ukraine back to Russia. They entered the city Rostov-on-Don, which is very close to the border with Ukraine, and took control of the key military facilities and administration buildings. Prigozhin claimed they did that without a single shot fired.

Military vehicles, including tanks, stood in the central square of the city. A lot of local civilians came out and started yelling at the Wagner mercenaries, telling them to piss off (this was exactly the expressions they used in Russian, judging by the videos from that square in Rostov-on-Don published on Telegram) because otherwise, they were afraid that the Russian army would start shelling the city to destroy the Wagner people.

"Get the hell out of here!" a guy shouted at Wagner soldiers in the TV report. "Did you hear what Putin said? Because of you, they will level the city!"

On the morning of that Saturday, Putin addressed the nation on TV. He spoke about the "mutiny", calling people who were doing that in "the hard time for Russia" traitors and stated that all the guilty parties would face severe punishment. Putin also referred to the mutiny as a “strike in the back” of Russian people targeted at an inner split of the society.

Curiously, he did not make a single mention of the Wagner Group and did not speak about his "cook" Prigozhin directly. He just used words like, "traitors", "enemies of the Motherland" and similar ones.

The whole country was watching those events as they kept unrolling. So were Ukrainians. I bet all of them and a lot of Russians, including myself, were hoping that Prigozhin had a good chance to win this one, overthrow Putin, and end the war after (hopefully) getting the presidential chair. Prigozhin stated that what made him come back from the Wagner positions in Ukraine and take Rostov was air strikes made by Ministry of Defence forces at his positions in the East of Ukraine.

Also, photos emerged on Telegram with Prigozhin in Rostov having a fresh scar on his cheek, so rumours began to spread that perhaps whether those air strikes had been real or not but somebody had attempted to liquidate Prigozhin, perhaps even his major enemy Shoigu – the Russian Minister of Defence. Shoigu’s public affairs service denied that there was any air strike and called these statements of Prigozhin a provocation.

Prigozhin demanded that General Gerasimov (head of the SVO) and Minister of Defence Sergei Shoigu were to be taken from their current positions and replaced with somebody "more competent".

Before that, Prigozhin had already started public conflicts with them, addressing Gerasimov and Shoigu in his videos

published on the Internet and spread around wide by the media.
In those videos, he demanded more shells to be delivered from the Ministry of Defence as Wagner soldiers had 'ammunition hunger'.

* * *

Prigozhin had recorded a lot of videos, had given multiple interviews in which he slammed the two aforementioned commanders-in-chiefs, claiming they were unable to lead the Russian army to victory in this war and were only making things worse in the fireline. Prigozhin also stated that a lot of his mercenaries had been killed because of the 'ammunition hunger' and the MinOborony (the Ministry of Defense) would not send them the requested ammunition.

What was curious is that Prigozhin began publicly stating that Ukraine had not intended to attack Russia. Per his words, it was the Russian army that started it all, invaded Ukraine, and began killing everyone there.

What is more, he clearly said there were no Nazis in Ukraine. Wagner, he stated, had to follow orders and do their best for Russia during this "hard time" but now it was the Russian government, basically represented by Gerasimov and Shoigu, that stood up against them. In his video interviews with pro-war Z-bloggers, who visited the Wagner positions in Ukraine, he kept saying that a load of his people were getting killed but they were doing their job better than the regular Russian army.

It all looked like Prigozhin was criticizing Putin, although he never used his actual name, nor did he say "president" a single time. Prigozhin referred to "dedushka" ("the old man"), saying phrases like "What if the dedushka is an arsehole and we are all dying here in vain?". Everybody understood his hints, since “Ded” (pronounced similar to "dead" but the vowel is a little softer) is what people unhappy with Putin’s politics and war call him for his old age and for him holding onto the presidential chair with a tight grip. These are also the reasons why a lot of Z-patriots in Russia are criticising Biden and making fun of his handshakes with invisible people.

Opposition media began writing that these actions Prigozhin began to look like he was running a presidential election campaign and was trying hard to earn a high political score with the electorate.

Anyway, Prigozhin said that he was leaving some of his mercenaries behind in Rostov-on-Don, and along with roughly two thousand other mercenaries he headed for Moscow on a "March of Justice".

With all this, "Putin's cook" kept saying in his public audio messages on Telegram and YouTube that his "march" was not aimed against the president and was not intended to be a coupe. All Prigozhin was after, as he put it, was justice and getting the head of the SVO and the Russian Minister of Defence replaced.

On the one hand, it all looked like a real mutiny. Pushkin described a Russian mutiny through a character in his novel "Captain's Daughter" as "pointless and merciless". This phrase ended up as an aphorism. This Pushkin's story (which is part of the school curriculum in Russia, by the way) was set in the times of the well-known rebellion of Cossack Yemelyan Pugachev against the rule of the empress Catherine the Great. It must be noted that eventually Pugachev was betrayed by his closest war-lords, surrendered to the government, and executed publicly in Moscow. A similar fate befell the leaders of all other rebellions in Russia in the past.

However, a lot seemed fishy about the whole thing, since Putin did not accuse Prigozhin and Wagner directly. And Prigozhin did not accuse Putin either, nor did not say that he was going to become the new president. The intention to "find justice" sort of turned him into a favourite of average Russians who thought they were suffering not from Putin but rather from the incompetence and greed of people in his close circle. As they say in Russia – "the tsar is good, it is the boyars that are bad and evil". Boyars is the Russian plural word for court nobility.

Since all Wagner mercenaries were average Russian people (with convicts among them), it all was made look like Prigozhin wanted justice for all average Russians, not only his soldiers but for civilians as well – he frequently stressed the fact that many parents had lost their sons, fathers, and husbands in the war, fighting as part of Wagner Group, because of Shoigu and lack of ammunition.

* * *

As Prigozhin and his mercenaries headed for Moscow, he posted a video, in which he claimed that some people in the closest circle of the president had been deliberately misinforming him, giving him reports with inaccurate data about the war and about losses that the Russian troops are suffering in Ukraine. He also urged average Russians to join his mercenaries on this "March of Justice". A criminal case was quickly initiated against Prigozhin and he was charged with inciting an armed riot.

Prigozhin and Wagner battalions passed through the Lipetsk and Voronezh regions easily "without any shot fired or Russian soldier killed", he claimed again. However, MinOborony began sending armed helicopters to attack Wagner columns with military vehicles as they were near the city of Voronezh, which is roughly 600 kilometres south of Moscow. Wagner people had air defense rockets and launchers on them, so they shot down one plane and six helicopters sent against them. Fifteen people, including pilots, soldiers, and officers on the board of the plane, were killed. In the course of these fights, a petroleum base in Voronezh caught fire. The local fire brigades were unable to extinguish it for several days.

Several regions of Russia around Moscow, including Moscow itself, declared a state of anti-terrorist operation. This means the police and the military had unlimited power to check the ID of any person at any time in the operation area. They were allowed to enter any buildings, including private residences, offices, etc. The Internet connection began to get weaker and sometimes it was shut down completely to deprive the approaching mercenaries of connection. They had the authority to confiscate personal vehicles from citizens, and move them out of their flats in case of military necessity.

Government officials close to the president began leaving Moscow on their planes one by one, heading for St. Petersburg. Among them was former president Dmitry Medvedev, who has been actively supporting the war, threatening the West with nukes and claiming that the US and EU were pushing the world towards WW3 by supporting Ukraine with weapons.

Bloggers who were able to track the president's personal plane using special apps stated on the Internet that Putin had left Moscow for St. Petersburg too. However, his press secretary claimed that the president remained in the Kremlin, working as always no matter what.

Army battalions began to set up defence around Moscow – they prepared heavy trucks for blocking the roads, and set up roadblocks made of sacks with sand and blocks of concrete. In Voronezh, Lipetsk, and Moscow regions, they began to blow up bridges and roads in order to slow down the advance of the Wagner troops.

I guess it is worth mentioning here that Voronezh (the city

where Peter the Great built the first ever Russian fleet) is my home city I have close relatives there and I was a little worried about them at that time. Besides, that was the first time Voronezh emerged in international news.

Then suddenly, when Wagner battalions and tanks were 400 kilometres away from Moscow, the mutiny stopped. The President of Belarus, Lukashenko, was able to persuade Prigozhin to stop, promising him immunity from Putin and presidential pardoning for him and the Wagner soldiers who took part in the riot. Per news reports, Lukashenko and Prigozhin had known each other for many years. Therefore Belarusian president allegedly volunteered to make a peace talk with Prigozhin.

"Putin's cook" agreed to that and posted an audio message on Telegram, which was then spread and commented on by multiple media resources and popular bloggers with huge audiences. He stated that now as the Wagner troops had come close to Moscow, a lot of blood of average Russian soldiers could be spilt and he did not want it to happen. He again claimed that he had no intention to overthrow Putin and so the Wagner troops are turning around and heading back to their positions in Ukraine.

Still, some Wagner soldiers made jokes in interviews that even though they had stopped just 400 km before Moscow but they had managed to scare the crap out of half of the Russian capital city's population. Imagine, they said, what would have happened if we had managed to enter Moscow.

PRIGOZHIN'S FAMOUS NAMESAKE

The mutiny made a shock wave in the top of the Russian government but it also created a huge wave of memes. The Internet remembers everything, as the saying goes, and so memes and jokes about Prigozhin's "crusade" started to emerge one after another. Among them was a meme featuring a book called "How to Fuck Up a Coup Within 12 Hours. Beginner's Guide".

Many people, especially in Ukraine, watched all that "circus" with fingers crossed, hoping that even though in theory, Prigozhin would even make a worse president than Putin, he still was able to overthrow him and stop the war.

However, the Wagner founder retreated into the bushes. The following day, I saw a fake Netflix poster on a Telegram channel where Prigozhin was depicted as an over-muscly bold black guy – it was a fake advert for a movie with a title quite in the spirit of Stallone's "Disposables".

Then a screenshot of a post in Ukrainian language was published, where a girl disappointedly confessed that this was the first time she had "watched a porn video where people fucked each other but none of them eventually cummed". Others wrote comments, saying that "the bald one had been jerked back and forth totally in vain" ("jerking the bald guy", as you've probably understood, is the Russian analog of "bashing the bishop").

However, the biggest "victim" of Prigozhin's mutiny (of course, except for those dead Russian pilots) was the music producer with exactly the same surname, the husband of the pop singer famous under the stage name Valeria – Joseph Prigozhin. He is also bold as a woman's knee. It became clear that a lot of Russians did not even bother to look up the difference between those two and began writing to Joseph on social media, in comments under his photos and in direct messages to him.

"Why the hell are your troops moving to take the Kremlin?!", one comment said on a screenshot published by an anti-war Telegram channel.

"Joseph, why are you doing this? Stop heading for Moscow please!" a woman commentator wrote.

Curses and hate followed, of course. The producer later confessed that he was spending that weekend with his family in the country. Then he saw those comments and his hair stood, even though he was zero bald.

He commented on that misunderstanding on the phone to a major state online newspaper, saying that he was glad that his name could make people happy and served as a basis for memes, since memes and humour help one to live through bad and difficult times, such as Russia is witnessing now.

Memes began to emerge about him. In one of those a famous pop singer Valery Meladze (with an anti-war position) asks Joseph to let them join Wagner and the producer tells him: "You've got the wrong Prigozhin, mate". A hell of a time for a guy who has a surname like that these days.

The best joke that was born after all this is a "new church

holiday" in Russia. In August, the Russian Orthodox Church celebrates the Apple Feast of the Saviour, when the summer begins fading into the autumn, and people bring apples to Orthodox churches to have them consecrated. In Russian, it sounds as "The Apple Saviour Feast."

Now, on June 24, new memes declare that Russians will celebrate "The Potato Saviour Feast" (also meaning "The potato guy saved it"), since Lukashenko, who supposedly stopped Wagner's prompt advance to Moscow, is keen on agriculture. He often makes it into headlines proudly showing huge carrots grown in Belarus under his valuable guidance. As for potatoes in particular, Belarus is famous for growing tremendous amounts of them and importing them to Russia (to other CIS countries as well before the war began).

PUTIN REACTS TO MUTINY

After the fake riot of the "fake Pugachev" was over, experts began to actively discuss it in the media, basically trying to grasp what the hell that was. Prigozhin and his mercenaries, who took part in this show, got off really lightly – none of them were arrested, and everybody got an official immunity from Putin. Prigozhin was supposed to head for Belarus with all of his private military company now. However, it did not happen at once. The Belarusian president during the first couple of weeks after that stated that he did not know where Prigozhin was – maybe he was in Moscow, he said, but not anywhere in Belarus anyway.

When the Wagner troops were wrapping up their military vehicles and temporary defense constructions in Rostov-on-Don, videos on the media and Telegram channels showed Rostov people praising them as heroes – Rostovians gave them loud applause, shouted things like "well-done guys!", taking selfies with them. When the police arrived after the troops were gone, the crowd shouted "Disgrace on you!" at them since they had retreated as soon as the Wagner soldiers took over the city at the very beginning. The cops did not even dare get out of their cars now that the Wagner mercenaries left.

The media claims that after the mutiny, Prigozhin had a private meeting with Putin. Any other person, who would have attempted such a brave undertaking in Russia with Putin in the president's chair, would have already either been arrested, shot in the process of the mutiny or they would be found after committing a "suicide".

But not "Putin's cook", no sir. He is safe and sound. Besides, after the whole thing was over, he gave journalists quite a different reason for his "rebellion" compared to the initial one. This time, he did not say anything about the Ministry of Defence hitting the Wagner camp with rockets. What he said was "I flew off the handle". Just like that.

As he led his troops in the "march for justice" to take Moscow, his mansion was searched, tonnes of cash, gold, and guns of various types were found. The police also came across multiple wigs and other ways for changing an appearance, including several passports with citizenships of different countries, which Prigozhin had used under completely different names as he had changed his looks for each of those passport photos and when he had been to those countries with his mercenaries.

Minivans with billions of rubles in cash were found near the Wagner offices in Moscow and St. Petersburg. Prigozhin stated that he had used that money to pay salaries to his mercenaries and for compensation payouts to the families of those who got killed – cargo 200 (the Russian military code word for dead soldiers being transported back to Russia from hot spots). All of those billions were returned to Prigozhin after he "surrendered" and ordered his soldiers to head back to the field camps in Ukraine. Politics and military experts, including couch-based ones, came up with a more or less similar opinion – after Prigozhin's "prank", no real mutiny can be possible in Russia within at least the next few years.

According to a major opposition Russian media organization

Meduza, more than a dozen high-ranking officers from the army and FSB (who worked with or had any other connection with the Wagner Group) were taken in custody.

If we look at conspiracy theories, this mutiny seems like an "exhibition performance" to check the system of defense for weak points in case something like this happens in reality later, to unveil people in the army who would eagerly support such a riot and to see the reaction of average people.

When I was a teenager, I read a story about Ivan the Terrible who once brought all his boyars together in a chamber and started telling them that he was thinking of becoming a monk and leaving the throne to somebody "worthy". He began asking the boyars what they thought about it and who would be the best candidate to be the new tsar.

The boyars knew their tsar's character too well and that it was most likely just a loyalty check. So they began interrupting each other to tell Ivan the Terrible that he was the best and the only tsar they wanted. It indeed turned out to be a test for them. The right answers saved their lives.

A similar thing may have happened with Prigozhin and Putin. They are old companions, after all, and have been collaborating for many years. The Wagner Group got financial support from the state, even though Putin after that publicly said that PMC Wagner does not exist as a legal entity, since there is no law about private military companies in Russia. All of this can be found in Google (in Russian, though), besides, there is a video with an extract of Putin's speech on Twitter and YouTube.

It seems there was hardly any better candidate to perform a fake mutiny and at the same time make it clear that if such a thing happened indeed, the initiators would not make it as far towards Moscow as Prigozhin managed to. However, critics of Putin's regime are certain that the mutiny was for real and it revealed massive holes in the defense system within Russia itself.

Speaking of Lukashenko and Wagner, now, as I am finishing writing this book in July 2023, the Belarusian president has been telling Putin that Wagner soldiers are eager to go to Poland and that the Polish army is being moved towards the borders with Belarus to "prepare for a potential attack". Lukashenko told Putin he could show him on the map the place where the Polish army was gathering.

A lot of memes about the start of the war with Ukraine featured Lukashenko, who after the war began, told Putin that he would show him on the map from which spot exactly the Ukrainian army allegedly planned to attack Belarus, as well as it allegedly planned to attack Russia. The same memes are now re-emerging but this time they are about Poland.

A Hollywood aikido ex-star, whose name you can easily guess, often visited Russia and Belarus after the war in Donbas began in 2014 and Crimea was annexed, meeting both with Putin and Lukashenko, expressing his total support. Their mutual photos were published on the Internet, where Lukashenko is showing the actor huge Belarusian carrots.

Russian memes with the aikido actor eating those mega-sized carrots say “Driven to destroy this” or “Hard to eat” in line with the titles of his action movies. Somebody even made an ironic sticker pack on Telegram with this man and his feeble attempts to speak Russian in his films. Those also include him eating Lukashenko’s monster-sized carrots. It would be nice to find out what this guy from Hollywood thinks about the current outright war of Russia with Ukraine but all of a sudden he has stopped visiting both Russia and Belarus. I wonder why, I wonder why.

Here’s another funny fact: on June 29, Putin had a closed meeting with Prigozhin and some of the top Wagner commanders that lasted for three hours. After practically referring to them as “traitors of the Motherland” three days before that. Also, Putin’s rating surged to 90% after the way he handled the “mutiny”.

PRIGOZHIN LIQUIDATED

The payback came exactly two months later. On August 23, a private jet Embraer Legacy which belonged to Prigozhin exploded in mid-air.

Prigozhin and the second co-founder of PMC Wagner Dimitry Utkin were on board according to the official lists of passengers. The explosion took place in the Tver region, not far from Moscow after the plane took off from one of Moscow's airports and headed for St. Petersburg. There was a short video circulating Telegram channels in Russia, where two girls in their early teens, by the sound of their voices, saw the plane beginning to fall like a rock – they began swearing badly and screaming from shock. The jet then hit the ground behind the woods, the explosion was not visible on the video.

All eight people on board, including three members of the flight crew, got killed. Their bodies were burned so badly that Prigozhin and Utkin were identified by DNA tests. Prigozhin had one of his fingers missing, and Utkin wore Nazi tattoos on his body – these signs were also used to identify them. Like Icarus, Prigozhin tried to get too close to the "sun" and he literally got thrown down from the sky with his wings burnt.

Putin made an official public statement on that, confirming

the death of Prigozhin. He said that the results of the tests confirmed that the identified bodies matched the list of the passengers of the plane.

An investigation then was opened with people viewing video cameras in the Vnukovo airport where the plane had taken off, the remnants of the jet were studied thoroughly. The result which came later stated that the jet crashed because of "deliberate misdeed", which resulted in a structural failure of the plane in the air. In his later comments, Putin said that a hand grenade exploded on the plane, causing the crash.

Opinions of average people and commentators on social media split here – while Prigozhin is officially dead, many believe that the Wagner founder did not get killed and that the whole thing was a staged accident.

The media also stated that Prigozhin on that day took off in another private jet from the same airport, while he registered to fly on the one that crashed. However, that was not confirmed afterwards.

The reasons why some people continue to think that Putin has just allowed his "cook" to go into hiding are the supposedly good business relations between him and Putin and the fact that those two had known each other since the late 90s. Although, Putin during his official address to Russians on TV and condolence offering mentioned that he had known Prigozhin since much earlier times – the beginning of the 1990s.

Besides, versions of Prigozhin staying alive also emerged in some of the Western media – The Daily Mail, The Economic Times, The Sun, and several others.

Still, many in Prigozhin's close circle thought he was a "dead man walking" after his mutiny. Many high-ranking commanders, when interviewed, said they were sure that his liquidation was a question of time when it would happen rather than of probability of it taking place.

The thing is that four years earlier, in 2019, a plane with Prigozhin on board was hit by a rocket near Congo in Africa and he was believed to be dead. Three days later, though, he emerged safe and sound. The aforementioned Western newspapers also mentioned that it could have been a double of Prigozhin who actually got killed on that jet.

There are real grounds for believing that actually and I have mentioned them before – when during the mutiny the police and FSB were searching his mansion, they found wigs, sets of fake beards and moustaches, and forged passports for several countries with Prigozhin under different names in them. In those passport photos, his appearance changed, depending on the country. The photos below emerged on the Internet after the search in his mansion. And not only the passport photos.

Still, after two weeks after the crash of the plane Prigozhin did not appear alive and did not give any interviews. He was buried in St. Petersburg. Some of those who went to the funeral told journalists that it was a regular VIP funeral with just 20-30 close people attending.

If you think retrospectively here, Putin does not let his critics walk out alive or stay free. The only political opponent of his who is still alive (but imprisoned in deliberately very poor conditions) is Alexei Navalny, who has survived being poisoned with the Novichok nerve agent.

Boris Nemtsov, an opposition politician, who investigated Putin's corruption schemes, was assassinated in 2015. Many believe that the suicide of oligarch Boris Berezovsky, who opposed Putin, in his mansion in London in 2013 was "performed" on the Russian president's orders too.

After Prigozhin's death, Putin demanded that all Wagner mercenaries swore an oath to the Ministry of Defence and went fighting under their command (not only in Ukraine but

Africa too and other parts of the world if necessary), basically becoming part of the regular Russian army.

Even Ukrainian soldiers admitted that Wagner troops, when they were led by Prigozhin, were a lot more efficient on the battleground than regular Russian soldiers.

RUSSIA KEEPS BOMBING UKRAINIAN CIVILIANS

In the meantime, Russian missiles keep hitting civilian buildings – apartment blocks, hospitals, shopping malls, and even regular supermarkets in Ukraine.

The autumn 2022 and the winter 2023 that was especially a hard time, since rockets and drones were aimed at the infrastructure that produces energy for central heating. Ukrainians were desperate for generators to keep their flats and houses warm. Besides, they often had power cuts that lasted for many hours.

Can you imagine the fear and despair they felt when sitting in a freezing cold flat in winter with no electricity, when they hear an air-raid alarm and have to grab their children and rush to the basement or anti-bomb shelter to stay there for an hour or even more? I bet by now Ukrainians have got used to the bombing (in the summer it became not so frequent) and are not in a rush to dash to a shelter. It depends on the region, of course. In those towns and villages which are near the firing line, the threat is more real, while in towns like Olexandriia where we used to live, there were only a couple of rocket attacks last year, luckily, and all the rockets were hit in the air.

Russians now have again started shelling Kyiv, fortunately, defensive rockets have been hitting nearly all the shells and drones. Ukraine has begun striking back too – several times Russian regions near the border have been hit, Belgorod was one of them.

A few times, drones hit sky-scrapers in the Moscow-City district, the large business area in the centre of the Russian capital with immensely tall buildings, futuristically designed and (called "Towers") made of concrete and blue glass was hit.

Guess what, Putin forbade the official state media, both TV channels and printed/online editions, to cover those attacks, as if nothing has happened and the war has not come to the Russian capital. So now Telegram channels have become the only source where you can read about those revenge air strikes.

Average people are getting afraid, Russian propagandists on TV and Z-bloggers are shocked. Hang on guys, did you expect to hit Ukrainian cities, killing civilians and destroying their homes, killing women with their children in their beds, and to get no response after that? You are so naive...

At least Ukrainian drones so far have only been hitting business centres and military objects, unlike Russian rockets, though Putin and his surroundings are still lying that they are targeting only objects of military importance and all the destructions of civilian builds have, per them, been the results of "badly working air defense rockets" – they "simply ricocheted".

PUTIN'S "NINE RINGS" OF POWER

In December 2022, a funny and strange thing happened. It occurred during the summit of leaders of nine of the former USSR republics – they are now part of the CIS (the Commonwealth of Independent States). The summit took place in St. Petersburg.

When the event started, Vladimir Putin gave each of the nine country leaders a ring as a New Year present. According to media reports, those rings looked like they were made of white gold. Each of them bore an inscription – "Happy New Year 2023" and "Russia" – the country that acted as the platform for the summit. Putin gave a ring to the presidents of Armenia, Azerbaijan, Belarus, Kazakhstan, Kyrgyzstan, Tajikistan, Turkmenistan and Uzbekistan. Belarusian president Lukashenko put his ring on right away.

One ring Putin kept for himself. After this news spread around the Internet, and many people on Telegram channels began jokingly likening those rings to the Nine Rings from The Lord of the Rings, which Sauron gave to the nine kings to enslave them – later on they turned into the Nazgul. Putin's ring, therefore, was likened to the Ruling Ring. "One Ring to rule them all," you know.

Putin's press secretary told journalists that the Russian president was not going to wear his ring since it was just a New Year souvenir. Still, Putin's critics and those who oppose the Ukrainian war keep wondering whether that was a masterful trolling or if Putin is an idiot since he most certainly read The Lord of the Rings or at least watched Peter Jackson's movie.

Literary critics believe that when Tolkien wrote his famous book, he placed Mordor in the East because he kept the USSR in mind with Sauron being a metaphor for Stalin. Putin's supporters, even before the 2022 war started, but after the military conflict in the Donbas began in 2014, started jokingly calling Putin "The Dark Lord". A joke that is funny and sad at the same time.

“BABUSHKA Z” WITH USSR FLAG

For a long time, Putin and his first circle desperately looked for something or somebody that could symbolize his “righteous war” against Ukraine. And soon after Russia began its invasion, such an opportunity presented itself.

This old woman (“babushka” in Russian) became known as “Babushka Z” or “the old woman with a Soviet flag”. Her real name is Anna Ivanova, born in 1952 in Ukraine. In 2022, when the Russian army attacked the Kharkiv region in the east close to the Russian border, this elderly lady lived in a village near Kharkiv. Her old house had been damaged by Russian rockets. When Ukrainian soldiers came to that village to bring food to the locals, Ivanova came out of her house to meet them, carrying a red Soviet Union flag.

It happened after the Ukrainian army freed her village from the Russians during the first week of May 2022. A curious coincidence it was – on May 9 Russia celebrates Victory Day over Nazi Germany in WW2. Ukraine officially celebrates the Day of Victory over Nazism on May 8. So as not to have this celebration on the same day as Russia does, since WW2 has become a tool of state propaganda for the latter.

A Ukrainian soldier took the flag from Ivanova and gave her a plastic bag with food products instead. He threw the flag on the ground and stamped right on it. Ivanova then refused to take the food and asked to give her the Soviet flag back. Later on, Ivanova told the Ukrainian military that she had mistaken them for Russians. She wanted to ask them (Russians) to stop the war and to remind them that Ukraine also used to be part of the USSR and they together fought against Nazis during WW2. She took the bag of food after the Ukrainian soldiers explained to her who they were and why they threw that flag down.

A while later, a Russian bomb hit Ivanova's house and she was taken to a hospital in Kharkiv, where she gave several interviews to the Ukrainian and Western media, including BBC. Russian propagandists immediately decided to turn this old woman into the symbol of their invasion of Ukraine. They began talking about her on TV shows, calling her a brave woman, who remained loyal to the values of the Soviet Union and showed that she was against "Ukrainian Neo-Nazism" and that she was bold enough to show it.

Very soon, a monument to Ivanova (a sculpture made of plastic) holding a USSR flag was installed in the Ukrainian city of Mariupol, which was 90% destroyed by Russians after harsh battles inside the city (based on the bank of the Black Sea, therefore strategically important to Russia as part of the "land corridor" to Crimea) and fighting for the "Azovstal" factory, where Ukrainian battalion Azov stayed surrendered for weeks fighting back until they were forced to surrender. The city remains annexed by Russia with the lands surrounding it.

Another statue of "Babushka Z" was erected in the central square of Voronezh. People waited in long lines to get their pictures taken against this monument. But then it was quickly moved to a local WW2 museum. The third statue was created in Belgorod, close to the border with Ukraine. Below, there is a photo of the monument my friends took in Voronezh on my request.

Murals and other types of street art with Ivanova holding a Soviet flag also started emerging, and in a much bigger quantity than those statues. Merch depicting this elderly lady appeared in online shops for sale. However, when she clarified her position on the war and told the media about the mistake she had made, Russian propagandists stopped talking about her and no longer promoted the image of "Babushka Z". However, they began promoting a story that she had been taken as a hostage by Ukrainian soldiers.

They picked up a new figure as a symbol of this war – a six-year-old Russian boy from Belgorod named Alyosha, who greeted the Russian army there when it was heading to fight in Ukraine. Frequently he came to the road to wave greetings at Russian soldiers who were going past on military vehicles to kill Ukrainians, including boys like Alyosha. The boy did not understand what was happening and did not realize what role the propagandists gave him.

He is being filmed by news channels, and the media often writes about him. Children were often made main figures in stories about WW2 in the USSR, same as old people, all of them were presented as heroes. Children, old women and now cats and dogs usually raise compassion, and other deep emotions within people. This is so convenient for Putin's propaganda machine now.

Besides, the image of an old woman ("Babushka Z") is very similar to the symbol of the "Motherland" in Russia. Since pagan times, Russians have been calling their native lands "Mother", thus worshipping the local versions of the Great Mother Goddess and the Goddess of Earth joined into a single figure.

There were many statues of "The Motherland" built in the USSR after WW2. The two biggest and most famous ones are located in Volgograd – "The Motherland Calls" (known as Stalingrad during WW2 (85 metres high), a big and important tank battle took place there where the Nazis were defeated) and the second one is based in Kyiv (102 metres high).

Both statues hold a sword and the one in Ukraine also has a shield. The USSR coat of arms from the shield was recently replaced with the coat of arms of Ukraine. Z-patriots in Russia were beside themselves with fury.

PART 7

UKRAINIAN FAMILIES FALLING APART

Another sad thing I wanted to tell you about is the huge number of divorces that emerged among Ukrainians after the war began. However, this is just one side of the coin – now in Ukraine, it is not only the time of the biggest number of divorces but new marriages as well. It has hit both Ukrainians who remain in the war-struck country and who have fled to seek refuge abroad.

All of a sudden, marriages started to fall apart at an alarming rate. Women with children began to leave Ukraine to get over to safe countries – apart from Germany, they went off to Romania, Poland, Slovakia, Norway, Canada, the US, Ireland, etc – and their husbands either just stayed in Ukraine as civilians or went to fight to the front line or joined the terrestrial defense forces. It was mostly women who decided their marriages were now over. Men also did but, as usual, they are leaving if they meet somebody else. These days they mostly meet other women in the army, the ones who are near them as they have to fight for their country and cope with various hardships while doing that.

Let's start with divorces initiated by women. As they find themselves in a safe place, they suddenly realize that there has been something wrong with their marriages. As I read a lot of messages in chats of Ukrainian people on Telegram, where they help each other deal with various practical issues in particular countries, I saw them talk about their divorces quite a bit. I also asked psychotherapists who are treating a lot of women who have left their husbands and men dumped by their wives.

A lot of women are leaving their men because of the domestic violence they faced before the war. Once those women started to break free from their husbands who used to beat both them and their children, they began filing applications for a divorce. Aside from that, for many the war became a spotlight that made them see that their marriages had already been going wrong for years but they either had been unable to see it before or unable to put a full stop to their relationships/marriages before the war broke out.

Many Ukrainian women, in Germany, for example, saw their departure from Ukraine as a great chance to start a new life. Those who were dependent on their husbands financially began to receive a social dole here, got a chance to learn German, and could acquire a new profession free of charge. Many are taking that chance, striving to settle in Germany with no intention to go back to Ukraine even once the war is over. But many are also just waiting for the war to end to head back and help raise Ukraine from the ashes.

Some women are also ending their marriages because they are unexpectedly meeting new men here in Germany – somebody who also fled and is sharing their current position of a refugee with all its hardships. Alternatively, they are meeting somebody already well-established here with property and high income.

A psychotherapist I know told me about one of her clients, a man in his fifties, who is a doctor and he is fighting in Ukraine at the moment. His wife left for Germany and met another guy here, so she filed for a divorce.

Another woman I briefly corresponded with here has three children and she dumped her husband, who is currently in Ukraine, because he used to give her and the children a hard beating regularly.

As for the marriages that are now beginning to form in the Ukrainian army, the psychotherapist, let's call her Natasha, said that a similar phenomenon was observed in 2014, when the war in the East of Ukraine started after the Crimea annexation. Those military men and women in the army became really close to each other, helping one another with everyday hardships in the front line and fighting side by side.

However, these marriages, according to Natasha and the statistics she shared with me, did not last long. Nor, she believes, the similar currently quickly made army marriages will. The majority of them are doomed to fall apart as soon as the war is over.

This situation is similar to that of men's health when they get to the army – due to hard physical activity and also a lot of other things to worry about, the body gets into the best health shape ever. Even the slightest illnesses are forgotten. However, once these men go back to normal life and leave the army, old diseases begin to return, sometimes worse than before. The same is true with these marriages – a lot of them were short-lived in the past and are likely to be over as soon as the intimacy that fighting together against the mutual enemy is giving these people is gone.

Did you know that in Russian the word "wedlock" and "flaw", "foozle", "flop", etc, are called the same word? My native language sometimes indeed shows a dark irony when describing the reality the world makes people face.

TIME FOR CONCLUSIONS

Let's sum it up now, shall we? I will say things that are perhaps unpopular now but anyway. Russia is attacking Ukraine because the latter wants to break free from its political influence and get as far away from the post-Soviet world as it can, believing that its people's lives will substantially improve if it gets accepted into the European Union and NATO.

Putin is doing his best to make a new version of the Soviet Union and the Russian Empire at the same time, to write his name into history. Therefore, he wants to grab the South of Ukraine along with all the fertile lands, natural resources that lie within and the way to maintain a constant presence at the Black Sea and ensure a land corridor to Crimea.

He in fact does not give a damn about the ethnic Russians living in the East of Ukraine. Many experts in Ukraine and in the West believe that it is all the country that he wants and even if the war gets frozen now, there are no guarantees that Russia will not attack Ukraine again after gathering fresh forces in the future.

The US is supporting Ukraine, but also this country is continuing the confrontation that has been going on since

Franklin Roosevelt left the post of the US president and the "cold war" began. Actually, it started even earlier, when in the early Middle Ages knightly orders moved to Russia blessed by their church leaders to bring "the light of true God" (read – Catholicism), invade ancient Russia to take over its lands and people. The Battle on the Ice (the Battle of Lake Peipus) in April of 1242 led by Prince Alexander Nevsky put an end to that.

There, Russian troops beat the shit out of the Livonian Order and Bishopric of Dorpat making their knights sink under the ice because they were packed in heavy iron armour and the thin ice just broke under their feet.

Also, think of the Vietnam War. Back then, the USSR and China supported the Northern part of the country, whereas American soldiers actually attacked it to support South Vietnam. The USSR and China were lavishly providing weapons, military vehicles, and instructors to their Vietnamese proteges.

John Kennedy wanted to withdraw the US from that war, where millions of Vietnamese and tens of thousands of American soldiers died for nothing (with these official figures for the US likely diminished), not even for the sake of the local oil as it was in Iraq. I'm not a supporter of conspiracy theories but look how JFK ended up.

That war lasted for twenty years. Just think about that. For twenty years, US soldiers were sent to die (many also came back as invalids) in the country just in an attempt to prevent the expansion of the geopolitical influence of China and the USSR. The US military-industrial complex leaders were happy as they were making billions and trillions of dollars on that. So was the Soviet government, selling weapons and expanding its political influence. Now, try to see if these "clothes" can be put on the current war in Ukraine and you will see that this seems like a perfect fit.

The Cold War has never stopped, it seems, it just took a smoking break when the USSR collapsed. And now as China is getting stronger (with the US considering it a major geopolitical rival), and yuan is becoming one of the leading currencies after the US dollar.

Another example is the Korean War, where the USSR and China supported North Korea's attack against South Korea and the US sent its troops to defend the latter.

The US has taken on itself the role of the world's leader, the globe's gendarme, and so it is trying to keep the dangerous regimes down. However, take the USA away, and somebody else will immediately pop up to take its place – Russia or China come to mind first of all. North Korea has always seemed like a yob with its nuclear weapons (so does Russia now; North Korea has not yet started another war against South Korea, luckily). I think I would prefer the US in this role, since it does not have communism as the dominant ideology and this is only partly an authoritarian state, unlike China and Russia. Besides, the US is the most highly developed country both in terms of economy and science. All China can do is copy what Americans come up with.

Still, I think it would be naive to think that all the US wants is to protect weak countries in wars against their strong and aggressive neighbours. America has its own interests to take care of.

Perhaps it is good that Elon Musk is building rockets with SpaceX to set up a colony on Mars. If these idiots eventually push the world to a nuke war and destroy everyone, themselves included, or roll mankind back to caves, metaphorically speaking, at least the colony on Mars will perhaps survive. Until the moment when the number of humans inhabiting Mars grows to the point when they begin to fight each other again.

Rather than join forces to deal with the challenges that the future brings to humanity, every nation here on Earth seems to be locking up within itself, trying to benefit from their neighbours' troubles and pushing them deeper into those troubles.

Religions have been trying to solve these issues, or at least they pretended to be doing that. But in the end, Christianity and Islam showed their true faces – official Christianity became a global financial institution – probably, there's nothing wrong with that but it depends on how you look at it.

First, Christian leaders granted political power (what the Popes did to kings in Medieval Europe) and now this religion is being used as a political tool. In Russia, in particular – the Russian patriarch Kirill is a loyal supporter of Putin and the war.

Russian priests are blessing soldiers to go and join the war, saying that Ukraine is being led by Satan and by killing them you are protecting your Motherland and the faith in Christ. They also consecrate missiles and other weapons, there are many "staff priests" in the Russian army. Radical Islam has become an inspiration centre for global and local terrorism. Curiously, the Russian army has missiles called "Satan" in its arsenal and priests also consecrate them. They *bless Satan*, so to say.

Ukraine now seems to be a bargaining chip between Russia and the US. Only Russia is now led by an old man who wants to make history as a great reformer and the "collector of Russian lands", similar to Peter the Great, as Putin told the public a few times.

Also, he wants to stay in the presidential chair for as long as he can and ensure his further rule by grabbing lands from Ukraine. Guess who is going to be the winner of the upcoming elections in 2024. Besides, being too proud of beating German fascism in WW2 has played a bad joke on Russians. They seem to have become a new easy victim of this "demon".

As Carl Gustav Yung once wrote:

"No, the demons are not banished; that is a difficult task that still lies ahead. Now that the angel of history has abandoned the Germans, the demons will seek a new victim. And that won't be difficult. Every man who loses his shadow, every nation that falls into self-righteousness, is their prey.... We should not forget that exactly the same fatal tendency to collectivization is present in the victorious nations as in the Germans, that they can just as suddenly become a victim of the demonic powers."[1]

Putin's Russia is a hell of an angry beast now that it is grabbing all it can reach in the post-Soviet space. After Ukraine, he is likely eyeing Transnistria, part of Moldova; he has been for many years already. Poland also had a butt clench when Warger mercenaries began to gather close to its border in Belarus, I bet the Polish were particularly happy when Prigozhin got killed and the Wagner Group is being dismissed now. Half of Poland used to belong to the Russian Empire after Napoleon lost the war with Russia.

Later, under Stalin's rule, a large piece of this country was part of the USSR again as I mentioned earlier. Now, Russia keeps threatening to reclaim its former Polish territories with another military operation after the war with Ukraine. Those are likely empty threats but you never know how far crazy old man Putin can go to hold on to his throne.

But if we are having an honest talk, the USA is not cute and cuddly either. Remember the war in Iraq against Saddam, where they first claimed to have spotted weapons of mass destruction, and in the end, none of those were found. Instead, they found a lot of oil deposits.

The US is now providing a land lease to Ukraine but once the war is over Ukraine will either have to return all the weapons and military vehicles or pay for them – in funds or by allowing

US contractors to rebuild the country with all the profits going into their pockets (and do not forget about big tax deductions that they will likely get from Ukraine).

In terms of the cold war, the US is winning, because it is thousands of Russian soldiers who are dying, not American ones. And Joe Biden hardly gives a damn about Ukrainians getting killed in the battleground or Ukrainian civilians perishing from Russian missiles and drones.

The US seems to be definitely profiting from this conflict. For example, look at this: the US dollar has strengthened greatly since the war started after a major drop in 2020 during the Covid pandemic. What a coincidence.

Here are a few facts:

"The DXY index, a weighted average of the dollar's value against six major currencies, reached a 20 year high in mid-May, having appreciated by 9 percent since February 24th. Many economists are predicting the dollar will reach parity with the euro by the end of the year, a value not seen since 2002," according to the data provided by econofact.org in 2022.[2]

"The US dollar is at a value more than 10 percent higher than at the start of the Ukraine war in February 2022 and 30 percent higher than a decade ago. At one point in October, the dollar was at its highest mark since 2000."[3]

When the world is being shaken by wars and gets hit by instability, retail investors, companies, hedge funds and governments rush to buy US Treasuries and US dollars, getting themselves safe haven assets, and thus also providing financial support for the USA as a side effect.

And while the sanctions are imposed on Russia, they are rather hitting average Russians (both those brainwashed into supporting the war and those who are against it) and their welfare, while Putin and his friends oligarchs are not even starting to order cheaper prostitutes to cut down expenses.

Russia is strengthening its friendly relations with North Korea and – surprise, surprise – with the Taliban. The goal of the upcoming meeting of Russia with Taliban representatives on September 29 in the Russian city of Kazan sounds like a joke – "fighting terrorism". Ah-huh, just the right subject to discuss with the Talibs.

This is called an oxymoron – "alone together", "awfully good", "exact estimate", "a holiday with toddlers", "love to your mother-in-law", "rock-n-roll against drugs", "the Taliban against terrorism". "Winnie the Pooh against honey". "Harry Potter against Hermione".

As I'm finishing this book, Kim Jong Un arrived in Russia in his armoured train. While Putin wants to ask the North Korean dictator for ammunition supplies, Un has already stated that he is willing to collaborate with Putin to defend "international justice". What a disgrace for Putin to turn to this absolutely totalitarian and inhuman regime for cooperation. Well, birds of a feather flock together, don't they.

SOULS AND INFRASTRUCTURE TO REBUILD AFTER WAR

As for the consequences of the war, the destruction of the infrastructure, civilian buildings, and apartment blocks in Ukraine are already estimated to be worth several hundred billion US dollars. Still, homes and infrastructure can be rebuilt but you cannot "rebuild" families where the husbands were killed in the front line or the wives with the children killed in their beds by rockets fired by Russians.

The psyche of men who fought and of civilians who had to live in occupation for months or hid in bomb shelters waiting for the air raid alert to shut off and for rockets to be struck down by air defense forces will never be the same.

Already now psychologists and psychiatrists are working hard to help Ukrainian refugees or those who chose to stay on the Ukrainian ground. They help them not to lose their minds from stress and to soften the adaptation in new countries if they had immigrated. After the war, soldiers who survived it (while hundreds of thousands have perished there already), with limbs missing will start coming home. Men will be completely stressed out and "burnt" psychologically, including a lot of young men. They will have a hell of a time adapting to a new life in peace.

You get used to adrenaline easily, you get used to new situations and circumstances finding you every day and start enjoying them in a way, and you get used to risking your life in the battleground. No wonder there are a lot of adrenaline junkies who seek situations to get this feeling of huge excitement mixed with real danger.

Psychological assistance to those soldiers and their families will be certainly provided to help them deal with post-traumatic stress syndrome. Ukraine has even been working to officially approve the use of cannabis for medical purposes. But these people will come back with arms and legs missing, the state will be unable to provide them with a monthly compensation big enough to live off it.

They will start begging in the streets and in underground trains, maybe will start singing songs in the streets, as did Russian soldiers who came back from the Chechen wars – they composed war songs, rented music equipment, sang them in the street to raise money for themselves and their badly wounded mates in hospitals or families of those killed in Chechnya. I already saw soldiers singing songs to raise money in Kyiv several times after the Donbas war began in 2014.

There is a very old British song that describes an Irish soldier coming back home from the war in Ceylon in the 19th century – “Johnny, I hardly knew ye”. I’m not sure I can quote it here without getting in trouble with the copyright, so I suggest you google it unless you have heard it before. Personally I like it best when it is performed by Dropkick Murphys, who made it sound like a rock song, a satisfactorily heavy-ish one, but The Irish Rovers' folk-style acoustic version is also fine.

Anyway, this is what awaits both Russia and Ukraine in the near future. For Ukraine in particular, as an old Eastern saying goes "every victory will be met with a funeral cortège". Russia will not have to rebuild any of its infrastructure but Russian civilians will have to deal with aggression that many soldiers coming back will definitely demonstrate.

And those injured and traumatized military will face lack of support and understanding from civilians as well. Rewatch "Rambo. The First Blood" to get a rough picture (or even better, read the book "First Blood" by David Morrell, which the movie is based on); it was perhaps slightly exaggerated but basically describes what many of those guys face coming back to the world of civvies.

In particular, this will be true for Russia, which is already facing this – drunken soldiers, especially those from Wagner, who are convicts released way before they had finished doing their time in prison. They are picking fights with other people, threatening their families and neighbours, often with a lethal outcome. A lot of videos on Telegram public channels show aggressively behaving soldiers in public.

Many Ukrainians believe that Russia will be struck by a severe economic crisis soon or after the war, that people will begin dying from hunger there. I find it highly unlikely. Let's be realistic, we are not living in the 30s, when hunger was a frequent thing. Russia has China as a major ally and Putin continues to sell oil and natural gas to the East (India), even though it is doing that at big discounts. Russia is collaborating with Iran (a country sanctioned by the US). Even some Western countries are rumoured to still be buying Russian oil secretly.

So, yes, they may rest assured that hunger will not be a threat.

I have already written above what my countrymen should be afraid of. Perhaps keeping a gun at home to protect their families would be a good idea. Just in case, you know. However, using a gun against a "war hero" – anyone fighting in that war is now being patriotically called so, including Wagner's former convicts – will likely result in an arrest and a prison sentence even in the case of self-defense.

Since we are talking about keeping a gun at home, here's a little story for you. When I was a teenager, my father had two gas pistols at home. He ran a profitable educational business in the 90s and often carried a lot of cash on him. One of those guns was a revolver, the other was an automatic pistol, smaller in size. But he also bought them for fun – 30 years ago, when dad was still young and manly, he enjoyed that kind of stuff.

Fortunately, the only time he used it was when he decided to shoot out of the window to see how it would work eventually. The wind blew against him, bringing the gas inside our flat. I was a teenager and I remember that very well – for a whole day we all were coughing our guts out, our eyes dripping hard with tears. It was worst of all for my mum and paternal grandma, who was in her 80s.

UKRAINIANS BLINDLY HATE ALL RUSSIANS NOW

A few words should be said about those Ukrainians who began hating all Russian people, promoting the idea of Russia's "collective responsibility" for this war. There are no "good" Russians ("Ruzzki") they say. These Ukrainian people believe that if people in Russia indeed were "good" and worth any respect, they would have stopped the war. How? That's elementary, Watson – Ukrainians believe that Russians must all pour out to the streets of their cities and demand Putin to give up his presidential post. Yeah, right, you wish...

Unlike all those presidents who ruled in Ukraine after it became independent starting at the time of the USSR crash (there have been eight presidents in Ukraine, including Zelensky). Bloody eight of them, which means Ukrainians enjoyed more or less fair elections. Compare that to the number of presidents Russia has seen since 1990: yes – just two. And Putin, who was basically a successor appointed by Yeltsin in the first place, "glued" himself to that seat in the Kremlin and has been in it for 23 years now. He is a former

KGB officer and he will go out of his way not to lose power. As a former intelligence officer, he knows how to manipulate people and how to falsify election results.

Until 2011, he pretended to be a cute and cuddly president (except Anna Politkovsakaya's assassination in 2006 and the very strange death of his potential strong opponent in the presidential campaign of 2004 - General Lebed. By the way, Lebed died in a bizarre helicopter crash, just like Prigozhin did). In 2011, the first protest meetings started which Putin began to handle harshly.

Now, do those Ukrainians, who demonstratively despise Russians, know what it costs now to come out to the street holding an anti-war or even an anti-Putin poster? A big fine is the least harmful outcome. Imprisonment comes next. Fifteen years for "discrediting the Russian army" and or for "justifying terrorism/Nazism propaganda".

When you are in prison you may be tortured, left without medical assistance, and again tortured by regular hard beatings. People who come out on protest marches get wound down and put into "avtozaks" – prison trucks and transported to the police stations. Men often get worse treatment than women – men may be raped with a police baton or an empty champagne bottle.

In 2020, Russia-controlled Belarus was shaken with multiple waves of protests, and Lukashenko, who has also been in power since the 1990s, began doing the same thing. The police and security organs' officials were given limitless power to arrest anyone in the street, and to break into anyone's house should the slightest suspicion arise that the person living there could be dangerous for the regime.

The Belarusian police gave up wearing uniforms and were free from the obligation to demonstrate their IDs when arresting people or when breaking into the apartments of those who opposed the regime.

Recently Putin's opponent Alexei Navalny, who was first just a blogger talking about corruption in the Russian government on YouTube and then turned into the biggest activist and a protest figure in politics, has been given a new prison term of 19 years for "justifying terrorism", i.e. speaking against the war and calling for Putin's removal. Before that, Navalny was poisoned with a Novichok nerve agent in 2020 and almost died, but he was allowed to go to Germany for treatment. He was arrested upon his return and just a few days ago he got the aforementioned 19-year sentence after he had spent several years locked in prison on other faked charges.

All anti-war meetings are facing this – people end up in "avtozaks" beaten with truncheons, and taken to police stations. So-called "single protest meetings" are punished in the same way. When arrested for the first time, the punishment is only a fine. When arrested again – you go to jail with all the consequences which are certainly "bad for your health".

The father of a 12-year-old girl Masha Moskalyova, the girl who made an anti-Ukrainian war drawing at a school lesson in April 2022, was sent to prison for three years for "discrediting the Russian army" as he refused to plead guilty to teaching the "anti-Russian ideas" to his daughter. He had been bringing up Masha by himself, so she is now facing being sent to an orphanage.

Unlike Ukraine, Russia has been under the authoritarian leader for more than two decades, who turned into a totalitarian one. Putin will openly crash anyone who tries to speak or act against him – now criticizing the president in Russia is almost equal to terrorism. His political opponent, a popular liberal politician Boris Nemtsov was assassinated in 2015 a few hundred meters from the Kremlin on Bolshoy Moskvoretsky Bridge when walking across it with a female top model friend after a dinner in a restaurant in the Red Square.

He got several shots in the back from a car that was going past. The assassins were arrested, but the person who ordered that assassination was never found. Look at what happened to Prigozhin – the most recent example – and you will see what I'm trying to say here.

A lot of Russian people prefer not to criticise Putin's invasion of Ukraine since they are afraid of repressions – those who have been publishing anti-war posts on social media, or even liked anti-war (anti-government) posts of others get fined, sometimes fired, depending on their persistence in expressing their opinion.

Teachers are being fired, fined and sometimes also arrested if they decide to express their anti-war position during classes in schools openly – they get reported on by their own pupils. A few cases like that were covered by the Russian opposition media in 2022.

The same happens to popular actors who are openly opposing the war – once famous for their roles in popular films and serials they get fired from theatres on pretexts not even connected with their anti-war stance. Many choose to immigrate and then start acting in the Russian language plays abroad, give interviews and speak from stages about the situation in Russia now, criticising the war and Putin's regime.

If this example with Putin is not enough, you can also recall the Tiananmen Massacre in China in 1989, when a protest movement of students was suppressed by soldiers shooting them and military vehicles driving over them as if they were mud. Several hundred to several thousand dead by various estimates. What would you say to that, Elon Musk? (a Russian saying used in multiple contexts – from jokes to gloomy sarcasm, usually when you are presenting something that either makes you laugh or makes you want to beat your head against the wall from despair).

None of the Ukrainian uprisings in The Maidan Square have seen such harsh and ruthless responses from the government apart perhaps from seeing 100 people shot to death during the latest one.

Even despite that, many Russians risk donating money to Ukraine in Russia, and some volunteers help Ukrainian citizens forcefully transported to Russia from the annexed regions. An organization has been set up in Germany called "Free Russians" with the slogan "Peace to Ukraine, freedom to Russia and Belarus".

The most recent invention of the Russian government is to confiscate the property of those who make "fake statements" about the Russian army (read who criticises the war in Ukraine), of those who criticise the actions of the Russian government and for other similar things. The same will be applied to their relatives, even if they carry a different surname or are in divorce. The law was passed in 2024.

So now if you are openly making anti-war statements, you can get your bank account closed, the money and your flat confiscated. Or if you live abroad, for example, and do the same thing, your relatives may lose their property and will become bankrupt and/or homeless. As you can see, Putin and his close circle are trying hard to crush any anti-war sentiments completely.

* * *

However, the majority of Ukrainians not only despise all Russians on a national basis but also refuse to speak Russian, this includes not speaking it to Russians who support Ukraine.

Let me give you an example. When I started work in Kyiv in 2012, on my first day I met a nice ginger-haired girl who began working in the company on the same day as me. We were on good terms while we worked together for a few years and stayed on fairly good terms after she left to start her own business. Over the past few years, she has been living in the US and recently stated in a social media post that she will not speak Russian to anyone now – only Ukrainian or English. Before that, she spoke Russian to everybody, including myself.

When I see people like that, it always makes me think: if you like Ukraine so much, why the hell have you been living not there for the past five years but moved to the secure and "well-fed" US? All of a sudden all immigrants are seeing their feeling of national identity awakening. This is happening to Ukrainians abroad and to many Russians as well, who, for example, live in Germany. They watch Russian TV and support Putin and the war.

Go back to Russia, hide from the police and the conscription agents, or allow them to send you to war at your own cost, I always want to tell these Z-patriots who live in the US or Europe.

I am a member of a couple of chats on Telegram where Ukrainians in Germany discuss their lives here, the problems they face and help each other with practical advice. 99% of the time here the conversations are in Russian. 99% of the Ukrainians in them are communicating in Russian – 15,000+ members in one and 17,000+ people in the other. What can I say, there are still sensible Ukrainians who realize that not all Russians are to blame for this war and the language has certainly little to do with it. It has not got Putin's copyright on it, has it?

I do understand the hard and negative emotions of Ukrainians about Russia now. But you have to remain sensible under any circumstances. Otherwise, it is indeed to be called Nazism – hating somebody on a national basis. This is what Putin's propaganda is trying to make others think (that everyone hates Russia and there is only Russophobia everywhere in the world) and such people as my former friend are just contributing to that idea.

The same goes for Pushkin, Leo Tolstoy, Dostoevsky, and other Russian writers, who died long before Putin was even born, the Russian culture overall. Were Goethe, Schiller, Herman Hesse, and their cultural heritage responsible for Hitler's horrible actions? Should all their books and poems have been rejected by the world after WW2? That would have been shooting yourself in the foot. Was Italian culture with Michaelangelo, Da Vinci, and other great artists, cancelled (and all Italians around the world bullied?) because of the fascism "founder" Mussolini, who inspired Hitler?

Were classic Russian poets Osip Mandelshtam and Marina Tsvetaeva responsible for Stalin killing millions of people in the early USSR? Mandelshtam died in a transit prison camp in 1938 in Russia thrown there by NKVD. Tsvetaeva also faced a nasty fate when she, feeling homesick, returned to Stalin's Soviet Union after leaving for Europe as she had not accepted the 1917 revolution.

With her husband, sister and daughter arrested, the official Soviet community of writers and poets rejected her totally. She could not get published or even have a job as a dishwasher, so she got to the point when she began starving and eventually, she hung herself.

My Ukrainian yoga teacher, who gives me online sessions, writes her Instagram posts in Ukrainian, but she still speaks Russian to me, for which I am grateful. Not only because our lessons would be impossible otherwise but because she realizes that I am not to blame for the war. My friends from Kyiv also still speak Russian to me, they have not been infected by the "I-hate- everyone-who-comes-from-Russia" virus. I send them my hearty gratitude.

I would like to give you a small note about the title of the book. Being betrayed is one of the worst things that can happen to you. Most often you are betrayed by those you love or trust entirely.

Mostly that is related to people but sometimes it is about your homeland. As it is in my particular case. That is not even so much about the homeland but rather particular government. Putin and his government have betrayed all Russian people – both those who have stayed in Russia and are against the war and those who chose to leave.

It will be a pure miracle if Ukraine can defeat Russia, I reckon. Support of the US, the major ally and weapon provider now, will not last forever, unfortunately, especially with the presidential elections in the US coming up.

Besides, Ukraine has already lost too many people. Those who have stayed to fight or are just reluctant to leave Ukraine are growing tired and desperate. Too many Ukrainian people already need psychological help, both in Ukraine and abroad.

You have to wait for weeks and months to see a psychiatrist (in Germany in particular, getting to see a profile doctor here takes ages of waiting). A lot of people are on sedatives, including strong ones, such as barbiturates. As for Russia, the demand for strong sedatives has also soared several times after the war started, according to local statistics. People are just grabbing tonnes of them from chemist stores.

Ukraine, unfortunately, cannot afford to fight for years, unlike Russia. The Soviet Union already proved it can waste people as easily as one burns oil – this is what happened during WW2 and was one of the reasons why the USSR defeated Hitler (among the other reasons, including the help from Western allies). As for Ukraine – there are not so many people and not enough local resources. I would be happy to prove wrong in the end, though. Now (in 2024), Zelensky wants to summon

Ukrainian men from abroad since the army needs new soldiers badly.

Multiple videos on social media show men being caught in streets in Ukrainian cities by men in camouflage uniforms and forced into cars; their wives are trying to save them and calling for help to the passers-by but those women just get pushed away and threatened.

Those caught men are driven to Voenkomats and then sent directly to the firing line. These are signs of despair already. The same happened in Russia in 2022 during the mobilization but Russia has a lot more people than Ukraine.

And by the way, I have not yet heard of children of Ukrainian/ Russian politicians fighting in the war to set an example to the rest of Ukrainians/Russians. Wars are always fought by common people while the government and the "elites" prefer to send them to die.

ZELENSKY AND ELON MUSK; UKRAINIANS GETTING TIRED OF WAR

In November 2023, Elon Musk talked to Lex Fridman, recording a podcast. When asked about the war in Ukraine, Musk suggested that Zelensky should not send "the flower of Ukrainian youth to die in trenches."

That was the time when the Ukrainian counterattack was taking place intending to push Russians out of the occupied territories. Whoever starts attacking – Russia or Ukraine, Musk stressed, will lose a tremendous number of people, since those who attack always have a lot more dead ("Cargo 200") rather than those who defend their positions.

The Ukrainian counter-offensive did not bring as good results as Zelensky hoped it would. He said it was because of a lack of weapons from the "Western partners".

While many Ukrainians are still eager to fight until the end, many of their countrymen are already getting sick and tired of this, even if they do not dare to say it out loud (for fear of being arrested for treason). They hate to see their sons and husbands dying on battlefields and hate to see civilians (including children and teenagers) getting killed during missile/drone strikes that are hitting cities and towns.

Many are beginning to say in private talks and on social media that if Zelensky had agreed to Russia's terms not to join NATO and keep neutrality at the very beginning, the war would have ended in April-May 2022 with little bloodshed. And all those people who have died fighting (many were thrown to the firing line with zero army experience, like gun fodder, basically), would have been alive now.

Changes in negotiations like this, most often touch the government rather than the average population. And it is the ordinary population of Ukraine that is suffering now, rather than Zelensky and his team. It is average Ukrainians who are getting killed in trenches, rather than government officials and their children.

Perhaps Zelensky was misinformed and convinced that Russia was not ready for a big and lengthy war. Perhaps and he thought he would be able to win supported by the US and the EU. Well, hopefully, he sees now that he was wrong. NATO is unlikely to send in their troops since it would likely mean the start of WW3. He is ready to fight until the end and Putin is ready to fight until the end. However, as I said before, Russia has a lot more people (it has lots of expendables from the poor regions), weapons, and money than Ukraine as it keeps selling oil and gas.

Is Zelensky going to see the very last Ukrainian die fighting in this war? Is he going to start conscripting women and let them die too, leaving children not only without fathers but without mothers as well? What will be his next strategic move? High school boys armed with AK-47s? Is he eager to fight for the Ukrainian lands or the Ukrainian people? If he wants to preserve the people, he should not waste their lives at war – the line when it was heroic has long been crossed and left behind, and now it is nothing but manslaughter.

An outcome that seems to be more and more likely (and not a pleasant one), which is being discussed by some Western experts in the media, is that at some point the USA just stops providing weapons and will leave no choice to Zelensky but to start negotiating with Putin or his successor. Putin will hardly give back the territories he has annexed. And I have already mentioned earlier the West will likely make Ukraine repay all these debts from the war in the coming years. It is worth repeating it. **There is no such thing as a free lunch.**

You know, on the one hand, you keep believing that Ukraine will finally be able to win and the victory will take place very soon, and you need to cope just a little longer. But then you realise that the war has been going for nearly two years already and Putin is unlikely to stop it since he has got the elections coming in 2024; he will just press on with attacks both on the battlefield and on the civilian infrastructure.

Overall, I reckon Zelensky was a naive idealist when he became president in 2019 with zero experience in politics. He thought that he would easily break down the corrupted system of the Ukrainian government, drastically improve the lives of Ukrainian people, and take the country into a better tomorrow by letting it join the EU and get away from Russia's influence.

However, he probably did not realize that once he started talking about joining NATO and restoring Ukraine's nuclear arsenal, he began waving a red cloth in front of the bull called Putin. They say that it is the worst scenario when a naive idealist, who "knows what is right" emerges because then seas of blood are spilt either by themselves or at their fault. Lenin also had a "foolproof plan" how to make all Russia happy. But at least he knew that seas of blood will be spilled and warned everyone in advance.

You know, there is an old semi-scientific theory of how the asteroid belt came to exist in the Solar System between Mars and Jupiter. Some astronomers believe that in ancient times there used to be a small planet (much smaller than the Moon) which they named Phaeton. At some point, Mars and Jupiter began pulling the poor thing towards themselves at the same time.

The gravitation pull of Jupiter was gigantic and Mars did not let go either. The planet exploded; there is a beautiful Greek myth about this. This theory was rejected by scientists later but that is not my point. I sincerely do not want the small and cosy "planet" called Ukraine to turn into a zone of huge lifeless stones moving through space, metaphorically speaking.

WOULD WAR STOP IF PUTIN DIED NOW?

The best case scenario would be for someone within Putin's close circle to overthrow him to stop this war and give Ukraine back all its lands to bring it back to how it was in 1991. Alas, the current state of things has been going for almost two years now and Putin is still alive and remains the country's official leader – everyone in his close circle is either too scared of him or happy with what is going on.

Now rumours are spreading that Putin's health is in a very poor state and he is about to die from cancer any week now. A message on one of Telegram channels recently said that Putin had a heart attack in his Valdai residence.

Look, even if this happens indeed, many Russian experts name Nikolai Patrushev as Putin's most likely successor – Secretary of the Security Council of the Russian Federation since 2008. Before that, he was also the director of FSB, like Putin before he became president. The mainstream media in the West claims that it was Patrushev who persuaded Putin to begin the war with Ukraine. His report was allegedly the final straw that drove Putin to command an attack.

So if it was really Patrushev who provoked the war, do you

think he will stop it should he replace Putin on the throne? There may be two options, of course, but for some reason, I'm inclined to think that he will not.

Why, while Putin is playing with himself (metaphorically speaking) as "the one who collects back together historic Russian lands" and the one "who leads Russia to beat Nazism in Europe again", Patrushev and others in Putin's close circle are stealing billions from the funds that are supposed to be going to war; they are winning tenders for supplying the army, like Prigozhin did, to steal part of the money that will be sent to reconstruct the newly annexed lands of Ukraine, such as Mariupol, the Donbas, etc.

That's the way it works in Russia. People go into the government not to change the lives of average people for the better. They go there to steal astounding sums of money, take tremendous bribes, and stay untouchable while doing it.

What is more, there is a conspiracy theory saying that Putin is already dead (the body being kept in a freezer in his Valdai residence) and the country is run by Patrushev who uses a double of Putin.

BEING A RUSSIAN FLEEING/OPPOSING THIS WAR

Now, I do not want you to misunderstand this, thinking that I'm complaining or that I mean to diminish the suffering of Ukrainians in this war. Still, the situation is pretty simple and clear for people from Ukraine – their country, their homes are under constant rigorous attacks. They are dying in those attacks, even women and children. Thousands of lives (both of soldiers and civilians) are lost. That's a fact. An absolutely horrid and awful one.

But they have a clear enemy – Russia; they are free to call Russians anything – "orcs", "Ruscissts", "Ruzzki", etc. A lot of them believe that "a good Russian is a dead Russian". They have a clear goal – to see Russia defeated and Russian soldiers who came to invade them – killed.

It's quite different, though, if you are a Russian who lived in Ukraine and now you have to flee abroad. Let's set aside the fact of personal safety. Since, as I said above, a lot of Ukrainians now merely hate all Russians, you cannot join them to share your feelings, since you just hate this war and Putin but not Russia and its culture.

On the other hand, you hate being associated with Z-Russians who support the war and you want to steer clear of them – a lot of Russians abroad, in Germany in particular, are Z-patriots, strange as it may seem. The Russian community here is one of the biggest in the world. Therefore, you feel like you get into a sort of social vacuum. Besides, you constantly feel betrayed by your homeland. With every missile/drone attack on civilian buildings, supermarkets, shopping malls, theatres in Ukraine. Especially those you know very well in the cities you have often visited and where you had a great time many years ago. There are a couple of particular cities where my life in Ukraine started and I have a lot of good memories about them. A lot of them were hit with missiles and particular public places that I remember very well turned into ruins.

Putin then seemed to me like a demon whom the whole country of Russia is now possessed with. Like in the Evil Dead movie trilogy, where ancient demons, awakened by reciting the Necronomicon book, took possession of Ash Williams and his friends.

Fuck this war...Fuck Putin. As for Zelensky, he just bit off more than he can chew - he is a "national hero" now but Ukraine is drowning in its own blood and choking on it.

* * *

Despite all what is happening, your national identity doesn't go away, you still feel Russian, and you still feel deeply connected with your home country – mentally, linguistically, culturally, etc. You still like Russian films that were made before the war, Russian music, Russian books. You keep listening to those rock singers who now support Putin because you adored listening to them when you were a teenager. I love my friends in Ukraine and feel for them but I cannot give up being a Russian and everything to do with my country.

Another awful thing here is you constantly remember that a lot of your relatives (including your immediate family) and friends are pro-war now. So you either avoid discussing this subject with them (otherwise you will start cursing each other) or stop talking to them completely. And if you do, you then often feel like texting them anyway, since they are still your family, so you still try to keep some sort of contact with them.

You feel torn between the two poles and while you are fully supporting Ukraine in this particular situation, you cannot cut Russia, your childhood and the decades of your life spent there from your heart either. I'm sure the situation is pretty much the same for those who chose to leave Russia so as not to support the war and not to see all those Z-brainwashed people around. It is not always easy to find an anti-war Russian community abroad to stick with.

While Ukrainians are suffering a lot more in many respects, it is still a clearly "black and white" situation for them. They do not feel any doubts or regrets about this. For Russians who support Ukraine, it is rather like "50 shades of grey". And if these people continue to live in Russia (cannot afford to leave, have disabled relatives to look after, just incapable of psychological adaptation abroad, etc.), it is a lot worse for them – having to face the ideology, Z-signs everywhere around them in streets, hear Z-patriots talking every day on public transport, in offices; reading about this on the news and unable to speak their mind openly or even put a "like" under an anti-war post on social media for fear that the police will break the door of your house and arrest you.

They have to watch their every word not only when discussing the war in a public place, but also when talking about Putin, his government and their actions, or the army, even when speaking in general.

Somebody can easily report on you if they overhear you in a restaurant, in the office, or school – there has been a case like that covered by the Russian media when a young couple – husband and a wife – were arrested for such an anti-war chat in a cafe. The wife was fined and released, but they held the husband for three days at the police station.

Pupils are already reporting on their teachers who are sharing their anti-war positions during classes. Students are reporting on their classmates at universities for their ant-war opinions and social media posts.

Russia in this respect has gone back to the times of Stalin's rule basically. Those two decades of Putin's reign just went down the drain for the whole country.

While Ukrainians can hate Putin and criticize him openly, people in Russia have to explain the real state of things to their children, teach them how to stay invulnerable to all the propaganda in schools, and how not to get in trouble at the same time. They have to teach them what to say at exams in order not to get in trouble – the war with Ukraine is now part of the school and college curriculum. If children or teenagers begin to criticize the war openly, it will be their parents whom the social service workers or the police will ultimately visit.

I'm not justifying Russian people here. All I'm trying to say is that it is not that simple for us these days either. To those of us who do not agree with this war and want Russia and Ukraine to be friendly neighbours who cooperate and trade with each other as it was before.

But that is certainly a poor consolation for Ukrainians who are dying in trenches or under missile strikes; women, children and elderly people who have to constantly stay in bomb shelters or spend winter-time with no heating and electricity because Russia is destroying the power plants around them.

TWO STORIES FROM UKRAINE

I could write a lot more about this war, about the damage and suffering brought to Ukraine by Putin's Russia, about the Putin-Soviet ideology that is being forced onto Russians now to justify the war and make them share the responsibility for it. But I do not want to bore you with "the details of details", you know. I've already given you the main picture of what is happening.

To finish off, I would like to show you a social media post from a person called Natalia. She is a psychotherapist in Kyiv, 49, and currently remains there after spending the first several months of the war in the West of the country. Her husband, a coach by profession, was in the firing line, where he volunteered to fight the Russian army. He has recently returned home safe and sound.

That's what she wrote about the very first day of the war on Facebook exactly one year later – on February 24, 2023.

"On the morning of February 24, 2022, I felt very tense. I hardly remember how I had felt the days before it. But I remember very well the morning of the 24th.

I woke up from light of an incredible intensity. Ten minutes later,

I heard a horrible loud sound and I realised it was an explosion. Feeling nervous and terrified, I jumped to the window, trying to see what could be the source of this awful sound.

The only thought buzzing in my head was: "It has begun!" My brain still was trying to find another explanation for this roar, but it could not. A voice inside was telling me that this is all for real – I had just heard an explosion.

I rush to turn the TV on and begin to switch channels, hoping to get an answer, but all it is showing is nothing but movies, talk shows and other regular stuff... I start scrolling through my Facebook feed and see that it is flooded with reports of explosions happening.

Meanwhile, my husband keeps sleeping soundly. "Sasha, we're being bombed!" I tell him loudly, hoping to wake him up. Without opening his eyes, he answers that I probably saw a nightmare, he suggests I should lie down and sleep a little more. Still, it was definitely the sound of an explosion.

Down in the street, the number of cars increases with every passing minute, there is already a long queue at the petrol station – I can it see from my window... People are starting to realize what is happening.

Then a "marathon" with the first news about the beginning of the invasion starts on TV.

Our daughter Nastya calls me on the mobile: "Mum it has started, what shall we do?!"
I begin calling my sister, then dial my parents' number. My consciousness still refuses to accept the new reality.

I grab my phone and start texting clients cancelling their consultations today. It hardly makes any sense now but it was important to me then. With the edge of my eye, I see that Sasha is doing the same, texting and calling his cadets.
6 am: outside the window, there is already a huge traffic jam – those are cars heading out of Kyiv.

My husband is trying to get me to eat breakfast. And I'm seeking more information online.

The realization of the apocalypse is slowly descending on me and growing. I find myself thinking that I had my teeth fixed timely, thank God – I had crowns put on them just four days ago.

I feel totally lost... My phone won't shut up from incoming text messages.... My husband and I are heading to find a bomb shelter. ... Nastya is waiting to join us downstairs."

* * *

I would also like to tell you about Ukrainian woman called Tanya. She is Mary's friend and was her first teacher of psychotherapy in Kyiv. I know her in person too.

Tanya is in her late 40s. She lives in a town in the South of Ukraine, in the part of the Zaporizhzha region occupied by Russia (part of the Russian Federation officially now after the "referendums").

Tanya refused to leave when the war began, since she had elderly parents (they would not leave either) to look after and a sick sister who needs constant care. She also has a teenage son who refused to go without her.

After the town was occupied, Tanya went to work first into the social service to provide psychological support to the local people. She survived all the horrors of the Russian occupation - lack of drinking water, regular and long power cuts, having to hide in basements; shooting in the streets, rockets hitting apartment blocks, constant ID checks and Russian soldiers checking people's phones - correspondence in messaging apps, social media accounts to see if they have any connection to the Ukranian army or if they made anti-Russia posts.

Later they offered her to work in the town administration

controlled by Russia. To survive and provide for her family, she had to take that responsible job. Tanya had no choice but receive a Russian passport, citizenship and give up her Ukrainian one, even though she loves Ukraine and wants to be part of it, just like she wants Russia to lose.

In January 2024, the town administration building where she worked was hit by a Ukrainian missile during the day, when she and the other workers were inside.

She survived, she had a heart attack and survived it on her feet. She told Mary on Telegram that it was her second heart attack already, the first one also happened after the town got occupied.

By the way, Zelensky announced that anyone who cooperates with the Russian administration in the occupied territories and receives a Russian passport, will be automatically considered a traitor and a collaborant.

Some Ukrainians, especially politicians and policemen, began collaborating for their benefit, picking anti-Ukrainian political rhetoric.

But there are a lot of average people like Tanya, who just have to survive and protect their families, who have no other choice but to cooperate. I do not know what Zelensky will do when/if those territories are freed from Russians. I hope he will have the sense not to set up a trial but will just leave them alone and accept them back to Ukraine without bad consequences.

EPILOGUE

Wars are like hurricanes. They come all of a sudden or can be predicted, they happen seemingly on their own accord but in fact, they result from human activities towards the environment, which are often hard to notice. They tear apart your house, crash your car, turning it into a piece of junk.
They kill everyone who gets caught in them, laying waste to entire cities and regions. If you manage to get out of their way and survive, you are lucky. Wars are like natural disasters – you know why they may happen but you can hardly prevent them.

You may curse hurricanes, blame them for destroying your life but they don't care. Some people begin to worship hurricanes... and wars. They praise them and offer them sacrifices.

The important thing is what you do and how you behave after the hurricane goes away. Some people rebuild what was destroyed and learn their lessons. They come back to their lives, helping the injured and remembering their dead. Others begin boasting they have witnessed a hurricane since they have got nothing else to show for in their boring lives.

They begin worshiping those killed by hurricanes without letting those dead souls go. And they wish a hurricane would come back once again, so they can again become part of it by standing close and watching it kill others.

A hurricane would again bring a difference to their meaningless lives. Those people are even willing to give themselves to that insatiable monster and take an honourable death, becoming "heroes" in the eyes of those similar to themselves who will worship their deaths when the hurricane is gone.

* * *

P.S. My family and I continue to live near Dachau. Mary keeps working as a psychotherapist to help Ukrainians, Dasha attends the same school. She is picking up more German and has made a lot of friends in her class. The classmates are fond of her. By now (February 2024) it's been almost two years since we came to Germany.

P.S. In June 2024, a draft notice arrived for me in Russia. The curtain drops.

---

[1] "The Postwar Psychic Problems of the Germans", Carl Yung (1945)

[2] https://econofact.org/the-strong- dollar-and-the-war-in-ukraine

[3] https://www.aljazeera.com/features/2023/3/7/will-russia-sanctions- dethrone-king-dollar#:~:text=The%20US %20dollar%20is%20at,its%20highest%20mark%20since %202000

Please, see reviews of

this book: amazon.co.uk/

BOCSXJJBSW

zero

Please, leave a

review:

amazon.de/BOCXJJBSW

zero

Thanks

Danke

The author

Printed by Amazon Italia Logistica S.r.l.
Torrazza Piemonte (TO), Italy

68567261R00218